Dr Joseph

Dr Joseph Goebbels

A Bender of Minds – A Study of a Propaganda Expert

Andrew Sangster

Pen & Sword
MILITARY

First published in Great Britain in 2026 by
Pen & Sword Military
An imprint of Pen & Sword Books Limited
Yorkshire – Philadelphia

ISBN 978 1 03619 739 1

A CIP catalogue record for this book is available from the British Library.

Typeset by Mac Style
Printed in the UK by CPI Group (UK) Ltd, Croydon, CR0 4YY.

MIX
Paper | Supporting responsible forestry
FSC® C013604

The Publisher's authorised representative in the EU for product safety is Authorised Rep Compliance Ltd., Ground Floor, 71 Lower Baggot Street, Dublin D02 P593, Ireland.
www.arccompliance.com

For a complete list of Pen & Sword titles please contact:

PEN & SWORD BOOKS LIMITED
47 Church Street, Barnsley, South Yorkshire, S70 2AS, England
E-mail: enquiries@pen-and-sword.co.uk
Website: www.pen-and-sword.co.uk
or
PEN AND SWORD BOOKS
1950 Lawrence Road, Havertown, PA 19083, USA
E-mail: uspen-and-sword@casematepublishers.com
Website: www.penandswordbooks.com

Contents

Acknowledgements

Many thanks to my Italian historian colleague and friend Pier Paolo Battistelli for sending me various texts and photographs relating to Goebbels. It has been like having a fellow researcher tucked away in Italy. I am also grateful to my wife Carol, my sons and their families, as well as my closest friends (Simon, Peter, Chris to name the few) who know I disappear into my study for months on end thinking understandably that I am a social isolate. I am driven by my study of history because I fear that today we do not heed its warning signs.

Preface

All autocrats surround themselves with trusted people whom they can trust and assist in their domination of the country they rule. Adolf Hitler had such people, but it is recognised that his three major stalwarts or henchmen were Hermann Göring, Heinrich Himmler and Joseph Goebbels. Of these three Goebbels was the most intelligent, the most loyal, and was driven by a personal ambition second only to his demi-god Hitler. As today when autocrats still emerge on the political scene political analysts, journalists and critics of the system view and study with interest the type of person in close support, to try and gain information of the direction the regime may be moving towards, be it war, isolationism, or simply using power for egotistical and financial reasons. In the current climate of today (2025) it would have been as complex as it was in 1933 when Hitler assumed total power, but historians have the benefit of hindsight as the past is opened for their review and analysis.

Goebbels was a fanatical diary keeper, and although they are useful works to study, they were not personal diaries used for his inner personal thinking, as he saw them as would-be literary works for posterity. However, many of his speeches and other material are accessible and over the years much material has become available. It is known that he was obsessed with being important, first ambitions in the Church, the literary world, and then in politics. He was a man who had all the weaknesses of many humans, he enjoyed wealth, power, and had a sexual lust to such an extent he could be described as a sex-addict.

More importantly he developed a propaganda system which in many ways was more effective than those deployed in other countries, and he reflected a major problem of propaganda as it was enhancing a warped and criminal regime. He was representing what is now known and accepted to be a corrupt system, which was soon representing many of the immoral forces which drove the Nazi state between 1933 and 1945. He was determined to ensure that he not only controlled the German public mind, but that they would obey their leader.

At first his propaganda machine assisted Hitler to power, making it a more powerful tool than those systems used elsewhere by overturning the Weimar democratic system. He attacked (albeit reluctantly at first) Bolshevists (communism), then the Jews, and tried to undermine the Church. He was a perceptive person and did not want war, as he could tell it would lead to death and destruction, but he always obeyed Hitler without question.

When war started at first it was a matter of rejoicing in the leadership of their warrior demi-god, but as the international conflict turned against the Nazi regime his style of propaganda became more coercive, condemning the 'moaners and groaners' and anyone else who did not believe in a final victory, then demanded every German should fight to the bitter end, even though everyone knew it was a lost cause. His obsession for power and his need to be recognised as important had caused him to worship Hitler, which meant that he followed Hitler's suicide not just by killing himself but taking with him his wife and all his young children.

His role in the Third Reich was important, which is why this biography of Goebbels tries to explain the nature of the man and what he was like, tracing him from an early boyhood worshipping in Church to the horrors of the Bunker. This study also includes many pages on the nature of propaganda from his perspective, and acts as a warning to this day, to be wary of those major servants of autocrats who project themselves as saviours of their nation claiming their country will always be the greatest in the world. Autocrats keep appearing, so does Goebbels, the dangerous and astute supporter of power at any cost.

Foreword

This book is about Joseph Goebbels who will always be known for his role in propaganda for the Nazi regime, as it was a major factor in their rise to power in Germany. The word propaganda comes from the Latin to propagate and was originally associated with the Roman Catholic Church spreading its defence against the Reformation in various countries. By the end of the 1700s in English terms it was more associated with the secular world and had taken on a more negative connotation as it related more to political activity. It was beginning to be recognised as an emotional means of persuading and manipulating people to a particular viewpoint. Propaganda has similar leanings or methods as advertising, but it is more associated with selling ideas, policies, ideologies, and concepts rather than a product for sale.

The word propaganda has always been treated with a degree of suspicion, as critics have seen it as a clever form of soft power to change people's minds by persuading them down a particular road of thinking. It often leads to the accusation that it is a form of manipulation, and in this sense has been deployed for centuries, long before it was given a specific name for its activities. Whether this is a fair assessment or not is open to debate. It may be speculated that tribes bolstered their own people by making claims they were strong and the enemy weak and may well have let their potential enemies think the same way. It has been claimed that the Holy Roman Emperor Maximilian I was the first to use the printing press for these means of propaganda.

The phenomenon of propaganda has been a feature of human history, but only in the last few centuries has the word propaganda come to be commonly used, and over the last 100 years has tended to develop negative connotations. In the modern era propaganda has found multitudinous ways of being used, not just pamphlets, speeches and the spreading of rumours, but other means such as radio, television, films, newspapers, magazines, often news programmes have been used in a less than subtle way. Films are amongst the best means for popular propaganda as they have often been used to produce a patriotic mindset, or portray the enemy as a threat and evil, which were frequently used during the twentieth century during the two World Wars followed by the Cold War. It was used to change the corporate mind of a population or as a military strategy, and because of this experience propaganda developed a negative feeling, as the word itself started for many people to imply that intentionally false information was being spread, and at times the word has become an epithet of contempt and hate.

If the propaganda were spread that loving and helping our neighbours was the right thing to do, and that racism and war was wrong and peace right, then in this writer's thinking it would be excellent. What makes propaganda an obnoxious word for many people is the type of message it often conveys, and because of the last century's pattern of behaviour spreading the message of love and peace is seen as preaching, while propaganda is more associated with national and international politics. It is a form of persuasion which sets out to influence the emotions of the wider public usually to persuade them than a particular political point of view or ideology is the only way forward. To achieve this, propaganda of a political nature often denigrates to one level or another the perceived enemy, evokes strong reactions, offering hope or its opposite fear, simplifies the problems, and is always based on the person or the system producing the messages. During the last century with its major wars, racism, varying forms of political ideologies, has made the word propaganda appear almost like a dirty word, suspected of using psychological means to fulfil its purposes, using insidious ways and giving disparaging disinformation about other groups or countries. What must never be forgotten is that propaganda was and is used by all nations, especially those in conflict. It was the clever propaganda of the British in the First World War which caught Hitler's eye, and he spent many pages on the value of the subject in his political autobiographical *Mein Kampf*.

Listening to the news both national and international (2025) propaganda is here to stay, and most people are confused by the various messages from Gaza, Israel, Iran, Ukraine, Russia, and many other conflict zones around the globe, unsure who or what to believe. Mention that a recent proclamation is propaganda promptly raises suspicion. It is now widely known and accepted that all countries and ideologies deploy propaganda for their own purposes to persuade others to their side, and in this sense, it could be seen as a suspicious form of psychological weapon.

The mere mention of the name Joseph Goebbels and most people will immediately think of propaganda, because he appears as the expert in what is often seen as the dark and sinister side of the subject. Many people have described propaganda as the 'soft power', but in Goebbels' hands it was more like heavy hammer blows, but unquestionably cleverly deployed. He used it to persuade many Germans to support Hitler and regarding him as a demi-god, he supported him to the very end of defeat and death. Driven by ambition he became a Nazi demagogue and one of Hitler's main henchmen. Goebbels was feared by most, despised by some, mocked in private groups, but he used propaganda to bolster and support the Nazi regime, lambasted the enemy, viciously attacked Jews, lampooned and ridiculed foreign leaders, and anyone who was not on his side. He never hesitated in his propaganda to exaggerate, concoct stories and sometimes outright lies or stretch the truth, and he did so successfully. This biography is an attempt to understand Goebbels, his way of thinking, his personality and the mindset which drove him. In the many books written on him he has had a variety of contemptuous names to describe him. He has been described as *Lucifer's agent*, *the spider*, *Judas*, *the liar*, and countless other insidious titles. Only a machine could write on this subject without exposing a writer's opinion, and although historians are always expected to be purely subjective, such was the impact of the Second World War this makes it a formidable if not impossible task.

In terms of history, it is important to know about Goebbels because he not only unfolds the way any dangerous autocrat can take such a grip on a once highly civilised country, but how important a clever propagandist could be in such a situation, not just a mere servant of an autocrat. On the 29 May 2025, when this Foreword was being sketched out, a new statue of Stalin appeared on the Russian Metro station looking strong and powerful, with one commentator noting that 'Russia is trying to reshape history to justify the present', whereas others might see it as a sign of past success against the enemy. The account of Goebbels' life reveals the dangers of not seeing the potential menace of misused propaganda to this day, though this aspect can still be seen in many countries, but Goebbels is of interest because he was a master of the subject, he was clever, an intellectual, but worked for a now acknowledged corrupt and criminal regime.

In any autocratic State it is all too easy to develop a dangerous or vicious propaganda to its most effective and dangerous, and it remains critical that democratic countries, which allow criticism and other opinions, do not give way to autocracy. The work of Goebbels, however clever and sophisticated is a major red-light warning. One of the curious historical questions is how in a traditional and strong country like Germany propaganda could result in a dictatorship under a man like Adolf Hitler. The question must be raised as to whether it completely managed to change the way people thought, or did it bring out already inherent beliefs based on the previous decades. In Germany there was a powerful sense of patriotism and nationalism, dented by defeat, the Treaty of Versailles with its guilt clause and economic disaster. Many social classes in Germany would have been all too aware of these issues, so it has been understandably argued that the Nazi propaganda carried some influence even amongst the traditionalists who believed that the current government of the Weimar Republic was not coping with the various problems of the post-First World War era.

According to one student of the subject, it was only a matter to forge a compelling weapon against what he termed the 'immorality of Weimar rationalism'.[1] It was a harsh criticism because it was a constant battle fighting the economic problems of the day, but to a certain extent justified. It was Goebbels who through his well-known propaganda expertise who helped bring Hitler to total power, and then later cleverly adjusted the propaganda in its many forms from radio, press, posters, to films and speeches to help booster the regime in war and even to its monumental defeat by distorting the truth and offering hope when there was none.

This study is about the man Goebbels, who he was, his reactions, his character or personality, and inevitably about the way he led the Nazi propaganda machine which has, albeit reluctantly, been recognised as clever and all too useful in placing Hitler on his throne. Chapter Five concentrates on propaganda as a subject and the way Goebbels developed it in Nazi Germany, first to boost the autocratic power of Hitler, then throughout this biographical text it often emerges, especially in the 'end days' of the regime, as Goebbels cleverly tried to find the necessary loopholes to avert the final disaster with his various solutions.

Introduction to Goebbels and Propaganda

Goebbels as a youth appeared to be an ardent Roman Catholic but within time the figure of Adolf Hitler became his new demi-god and his object of adoration. It was Goebbels who in a short time created the 'myth of Hitler, the man of destiny the new saviour'.[1] It was a dangerous concept which would prove disastrous for Germany, but in the meantime 'to Hitler went the praise and the glory, and Goebbels had the unimaginable satisfaction of his diabolical creation'.[2] History has outlined many times the way Hitler used or rather abused the democratic system to take complete control of Germany as a dictator. What is often neglected is the way that it was Goebbels who through his propaganda and electioneering, and with his outstanding ability at public speaking which helped place Hitler into the nation's mind as their leader. In creating the Führer myth, he turned the dictator for many people into their quasi-deity, he 'made the equation NSDAP equals Adolf Hitler', and it was Goebbels who introduced the title Führer and ensured it was made a compulsory way of addressing the new dictator. He made it more meaningful or significant than Mussolini's *Duce*, and the term Führer was agreed upon at the end of 1931, and alongside *Heil Hitler* could all be dedicated to the influence of Goebbels' propaganda efforts.[3] In an amusing side on a book about the history of France the writer Douglas Boyd quoted the time when Mussolini and Galeazzo Ciano (his foreign secretary) were listening to a speech about Nazi Germany's leaders. In this speech they were told that 'the heart is Goebbels, who guides the soul of the great German nation'.[4] This had always been Goebbels' ambition once he had his quasi-religious conversion to Hitler, to control the mind of the German public and from the beginning to manage to make them agree with what he was propagating, and this eventually developed into a time when the public had no choice but to believe him.

The major if not a critical factor in the rise of Nazi power was Goebbels' expertise in propaganda, regarding his work as an art. One historian wrote that 'possibly the most compelling vision of a developed totalitarian society was George Orwell's great minatory [issuing a warning or a threat] novel *Nineteen Eight-Four*...Big brother whose omnipresent features owes much to Stalin, while Rumpelstiltskin figure preaching hate with an outstretched fist is derived from the Nazi propagandist Joseph Goebbels'.[5] The nature of political propaganda expanded in the twentieth century, press, radio, film advertising, mass persuasion by any means, and Goebbels was soon a natural master of the subject, an intelligent man driven by ambition. As one of his earlier biographers wrote 'he had all the qualifications necessary for being a good propaganda and demagogue: he was articulate; he could write; he was inventive; he was courageous; he was unscrupulous', and he always insisted that he was called Dr Goebbels.[6]

At one time, a front-line German commander, the well-known Heinz Guderian, was having trouble communicating his thoughts to Hitler and asked Goebbels to help him. He wrote that in his opinion that Goebbels was 'undoubtedly one of the cleverest members of Hitler's intimate circle'.[7] However, Guderian was astute enough to note while Goebbels was clever, he was a 'dangerous demagogue'.[8] He was right on both counts, as there was no question about Goebbels' intellectual ability, but clever people are not necessarily moral and can be criminal as well. Many of the military men, who by their work were facing the realities of Hitler's often weak military plans, often and understandably became critical of Hitler's main henchmen, not least because they listened and read what Hitler was supposed to be proclaiming. During the Ardennes offensive (often known as the Battle of the Bulge) a mid-ranking officer heard Goebbels broadcasting, noting that 'we had heard about it marginally and had heard Goebbels' strident voice on the radio, that 'the Wehrmacht has launched its great offensive. "We will destroy the enemy". Our comment on this news had been unanimous, how did Hitler think he could ever succeed in getting through the snowed-in Ardennes', thus intimating a growing degree of cynicism amongst the fighting commanders and many officers.[9]

While in a British PoW camp for senior officers which was carefully bugged to hear their views, as it was done elsewhere, it was 'not surprisingly, in quantitative terms, the [German] PoWs talked about most often in their protocols was Hitler, followed by Göring, Himmler and Goebbels', mainly because they were regarded as the leaders in the German regime.[10] Yet the ordinary soldier often regarded these key personnel around Hitler as the same ridiculous characters as viewed from today. 'Himmler was perceived as a demonic figure...Göring, mostly referred to as Hermann...had lamentably little clout with Hitler...and Goebbels was alternatively the 'imaginative politician' or 'the cripple' with an impressive intellect'.[11] It was not surprising how far down the ranks these opinions flourished. It was well known as the war progressed and the Allied bombing killed civilians as well, that the Nazi leaders became the subject of jokes from the barracks to the civilian bomb-shelters, but only with those who could be trusted because they felt the same way. One of the popular ones was 'the true Aryan, is as blond as Hitler, as nimble as Goebbels, and as slim as Göring'.[12] These jokes could easily lead to the guillotine, a common form of execution in Germany for what was considered everyday criminals. The point of these observations is that most of the humour was aimed at people like Göring, Goebbels and Himmler, who were the ideal subjects for humour, but they were dangerous men to be mocked, especially Goebbels who arranged and organised for such popular gossip to be monitored.

As this short biography will indicate, Goebbels was bright and intelligent, a potential academic, or priest, but he was driven by a passionate ambition to be famous. Initially, he thought this could be achieved by being a famous writer, but this failed, and as he turned to the politics of his day, a new line of progress for his driving ambition to be renowned appeared for him. He made sure that the up-and-coming Hitler knew he was adored by this new disciple who would obey without question anything Hitler demanded. He was like Hitler's pet dog, sometimes a loving little Dachshund, other times an obedient wolf. From an impoverished student living off funds provided by the Roman Catholic Church, he came wealthy, owning several houses, boats, was showing signs of being a sex addict, but his ability at cruel propaganda was to fulfil his passion to be important and regarded as one of the regime's top leaders in the role of supporting Hitler.

It often crosses the mind of the history reader as to what it would be like to meet some of these long dead people from the past. Some of this dream for this writer was partially met when he read a book by an Australian Professor Stephen Roberts written in 1937 called *The House that Hitler Built*. This man purposely set out to tour Germany to see for himself what was going on in Nazi Germany and he met many of the leading figures, trying to be as objective as possible as would any true academic. Roberts wrote 'the outstanding feature about Goebbels is his searing contempt for humanity. One feels that he despises humanity and looks on people as so many ants to be managed or stamped on. His attitude may easily be explained by a mixture of tortured nerves and acute resentment-psychosis, due to his physical defects'.[13] This was an astute observation, and as this biography of Goebbels unfolds, he comes across as Roberts noted, as a man who looked down on everyone except Hitler and himself. He noted that Goebbels divided humanity into three categories: Germans, Jews and the third being the rest of mankind. Goebbels even then in the mid-1930s was seen as a man who wanted to crush every perceived enemy of Hitler, which included many Germans.

Roberts noted that as a man Goebbels was frustrated by his lack of Great War experience and the problem of his dysfunctional foot, making him less than a perfect man in his own sight. Roberts wrote that 'nobody is permitted to mention his extremely non-Aryan weakness of body', a charitable society for aiding cripples did exactly this by pointing out that the mind is better than the body and used Goebbels as a classical example; it was intended as an honour, but Roberts noted that 'Berlin still talks of the fate of the unfortunate sponsors of that book'.[14]

Roberts recognised Goebbels for what he was and explored his personality, writing that 'he should call Goebbels the most dangerous man in Europe, precisely because he is so diabolically clever and so frankly Machiavellian in his views of mankind and the methods he would employ'.[15] Roberts perceived Goebbels' function as a clever manipulator and propaganda genius backing his idol Hitler, writing that 'what made the demagogue might ruin the Chancellor were it not for Goebbels' astute control of the press. Even Hitler had found himself censored on many occasions, when his tongue ran away with him, and Goebbels' blue pencil came into play'.[16] Time and time again Roberts was able to perceive how potentially dangerous Goebbels could be noting that he is admittedly the brain behind Hitler. Goebbels once stated, 'the only instrument with which one can conduct foreign policy is the sword, the sword alone and exclusively'.[17] Roberts as early as 1935–6 realised how important Goebbels was in the ascendancy of Hitler and helping him maintain his position as Germany's only leader.

For many people the image of Goebbels is that of a control freak who spent most of his time uttering or writing sheer nonsense and telling lies. However, there were more aspects to him than this summary, and as Roberts tried, this study in the following chapters will try to demonstrate many of the critical factors. Goebbels was the man who helped Hitler come to the attention of the public, and not just with his electioneering techniques, when things became difficult for Hitler it was Goebbels who was able to come to the rescue. In addition to this he used the cruellest means, turning against German Jewish citizens, then against all Jews, and it was his vitriolic anti-Semitism resulted in one the greatest crimes in recorded history. As early as 1935–6 Professor Roberts had warned, as noted above, that Goebbels' attitudes 'may easily be explained by a mixture of tortured nerves and acute resentment-psychosis, due to his physical defects', and there was probably some truth in this brief analysis.[18] Whatever the cause of Goebbels' behaviour, his attitudes, his sense of self-importance and ambition, he was a major component in the rise and support of the Nazi regime, and as unpleasant as he was, this demands historical exploration, because those who as major figures support the rising tyrants, dictators and autocrats need to be understood as they did not die with Goebbels.

Chapter One

Early Life

Childhood

Joseph Goebbels was born with the first name of Paul, on 29 October 1897 in North Rhine Westphalia in a town called Rheydt (originally an independent city) from a working-class background. It was an area well known for Roman Catholicism and Goebbels attended one of their schools as a youngster. A person's early life tends to carry much significance during their lifetime. The area had been occupied by the French and Belgians in 1923 because of postwar economic problems, despite objections from Britain and America. Goebbels had a sister called Elizabeth who died as a child, later another sister was born called Maria with whom Goebbels always remained attached, and two brothers known as Hans and Konrad. He watched his father in one of the factories rise from a lowly status to the role of manager. There are no references to Goebbels ever mentioning it, but his mother Katherina was of Dutch, not German origin. Many tried to claim that Goebbels had a Jewish background, but these seem to be unfounded claims, and which it has been suggested stemmed from Otto Strasser, and another time it was 'put about' that his real name was the Jewish sounding Göbbeles which was entirely fictional.[1] The significance of one's youth did not seem to apply to Goebbels, and one of his early biographers noted that 'the home in which these children grew up showed no characteristic that would explain the qualities which would later appear in Joseph…they were honourable, upstanding people with a deep Catholic piety characteristic of the Lower Rhine region'.[2] These claims were probably made later when his forceful character became involved with politics.

One aspect of his youth which would have ongoing ramifications was discovered as a small boy, probably aged 4 to 5, when it was realised that he had infantile paralysis which following a medical operation left him clubfooted, giving him the unfortunate appearance of being disabled. His right foot was always turned inwards and was much shorter and bigger than his normal left foot. The biographer Reimann wrote that later this was frequently explained as an accident because a man 'born with a clubfoot would not have been acceptable to the NSDAP'.[3] He was not a presentably shaped boy, having stooping shoulders, and was very small in stature. It has been claimed that 'from his early childhood a seam of self-doubt was deposited deep in his nature', not that it lasted that long, because very quickly he was noted for his abundant assertiveness.[4] Another biographer noted that it was probably a difficult time for him as a youngster, and it may well have impacted on him when he became an adult. He had no choice but had to live with this physical defect, and he was 'a rather ugly child, with an enormous headset on a weedy little body'.[5] He could not play sport and become a team member as do most children, but he compensated for this loss by sitting and reading. He must have felt a degree of social isolation, may well have been a subject of sniggering from some and pity by others. He was undoubtedly aware of this element of his existence probably built up his sensitivity, which may well have imbued him with suspicion of what others might be saying about him. Many who knew him at school have spoken about him only as a child, but mainly after the war, which causes the reader to wonder whether they were factual or speculative, as many would have been gleaned in the postwar debris. The accounts of Goebbels being called by fellow school children 'Joe clubfoot' and 'Old limping louse' sounds possible given the nature of playground children and therefore Goebbels' 'first reaction was to run away...and he spent all his spare time reading', becoming something of a loner, which was understandable.[6]

Given these facts of his childhood the historian Heiber wrote that 'its emotional consequences can only have been negative. It is easy to imagine what the young boy had to endure: pitying glances from adults, no easier to bear because they were kindly, and ridicule from his peers'.[7] It is just feasible enough to suggest that he may have developed intellectually because of his physical difficulties, it remains an ongoing but only a speculative argument. The historian Longerich interestingly suggests it was probably as a child Goebbels developed some of the 'psychological problems associated with narcissism', a situation where a person develops a firm inclination to boost their own identity. There have been many suggestions that his well-known narcissism was because of his disability, and because of the nature of his difficult start in life this appears at least feasible. On the other hand, it has been suggested that his problems may have 'originated in his failure to develop independence at the ages of two and three; his dependence on his mother, the model for his future girlfriends and his wife lasted throughout his life'.[8] This need for recognition infused most of his life, he had always found it necessary to need his mother's support, as he would do later with his persistent dependency upon Hitler's support and friendship. Later in life he would hint that his clubfoot was an accident, and sometimes he would mention 'in an off-hand way, the name "Verdun" and automatically' people would assume he was wounded there, but he had never and would never fight in any war.[9]

It was because of his family's social status that his father arranged that his son should enter the Gymnasium, which was the equivalent of the English Grammar School, and lacking sport, he depended on his studies to herald himself as of value. As everyone knows most children have nicknames, often based on their known characteristics. Goebbels' nicknames have often been suggested with some differing explanations. According to the historians Manvell and Fraenkel he was given the nickname Ulex after Ulysses known as the *sly one.** Viktor Reimann is more specific and defines it as from Ulixes the wily hero of the Trojan wars.[10] The outstanding biography of Goebbels by Peter Longerich claimed that 'he adopted the name Ulex, after a character in a novel by Wilhelm Raabe, who was his favourite author… Goebbels recommended Raabe as a model to his fellow students as someone 'who fought for his ideals, fought for his worldview'.[11]

Early Youth

When he was nearly 17 years old, the First World War was just underway. Most of his generation were in haste to sign up with the military, but Goebbels, although he was just as keen, found his clubfoot and his physical size kept him out from serving with any branch of the military. He may

* He had another pet name sometimes used by a girlfriend Else and that was 'Stropp'.

well have been genuinely upset with himself, but later as a political person 'he was often to show exemplary physical courage', this episode of missing the Great War probably helped mark or scar his developing characteristics.[12]

It must be recalled that he was growing up and beginning to mature during the postwar depression following the 1918 defeat and the Treaty of Versailles, which with the guilt clause and economic ramifications producing a national sense of humiliation and physical hunger, which, under such circumstances, the Weimar Republic found governing the nation difficult and at times too fragile and difficult to resolve. As his youth unfolded with hopes in academia, especially the literary world, even the Catholic Church which he turned to at this stage of his life.

Goebbels was taking his Catholic faith seriously, and his father, thought he might become a priest. How far this crossed his own mind will never be known, though many observers and commentators enjoying pressing this feature home. However, a way of finding an important social position was important to him and he was to be always driven by this ambition. 'The Church's elaborate ceremonies and its astute display of power must have made a strong impression on the imagination of this ambitious boy'.[13] At school he was interested in drama and was regarded as a first-class speaker. In 1916, the government introduced civilian service where men and boys who were not involved in the fighting were ordered to work to assist in the war effort. He was nearly caught up in this demand during a university vacation, but he managed to avoid the task by attending at tertiary education level. In 1917, he had passed the *Abitur* (end of school examinations) and his headmaster was reported as saying 'you were my best scholar, Joseph, but you will never make a speaker', which sounds ironical given his later life.[14]

University cost money, which was a problem for the Goebbels' family, especially as he attended a variety of universities before writing a dissertation then thesis for his PhD. His first university was Bonn, and he was dependent for money on grants or from a Catholic charity. He was a member of the Catholic Student's Association, Unitas, which made grants easier to obtain. On reading this it causes the reader to wonder whether at this stage it was more the personal usefulness of the Church which engaged him, rather than a personal faith. He must have attended the Mass because 'members of this association undertook to go to church regularly and to advance Catholic thinking'.[15] These grants were immense, and he continued to ask for more, writing pleading and often grovelling letters for assistance. Paying the money back became a problem and was not resolved until 1930 when as a Reichstag member he had also become anti-Church.*

At Bonn University he studied literature and history, belonged to the Catholic Students Union and in 1918 transferred to Freiberg University, and the following year moved onto the University of Munich. It was during these years that attending many universities was not that unusual in Germany, and while wandering between these famous educational establishments he started to turn against his old adherence to the Catholic faith, which caused some tensions with his father who had constantly anticipated that he would be ordained a deacon then as a priest.

In 1920, he eventually transferred to the University of Heidelberg graduating in 1921. While in this university he was helped by the then well-known Jewish Professor of Literature a Friedrich Gundolf and under a Professor Max von Wladberg.** Gundolf died in 1931, and later the Nazi regime, under Goebbels' guidance, banned all his books. He was recognised as well above average by those who taught him and supervised his studies. It makes for ironical reading that given his later political future, that the Catholic Church which he tried to undermine had supported him financially, and he had been academically supported by the best Jewish intellectuals, whom he spent most of his later life encouraging their persecution and liquidation.

His academic success had helped him cope with his childhood problems of being seen as a small useless disabled boy. His PhD gave him a self-confidence but there was a long way to go. It has been noted by many writers that during this period of his life he was somewhat vain, and later he was described by Sir Nevile Henderson (an Ambassador in Berlin who hoped Hitler could be controlled through appeasement) as an 'Irish agitator with a Celtic manner'.[16] Goebbels had every intention of becoming a renowned writer and worked on a short novel called *Michael Voormann* which was a lightly disguised form of Goebbels' early autobiographical effort. He had written the book in a diary format based on his own background describing

---

* In 1929, the Court gave a judgment by default and led to the seizure of a radio and a phonograph from Goebbels.

** Friedrich Gundolf was a well-known national scholar whose Jewish name had been Gundelfinger.

the evolution of a typical young German. He revamped the work after his contact with Hitler who was promptly written into the text as the saviour, and as noted by an early biographer, it was full of dictums which 'are neither particularly original nor well formulated'.[17]

His literary efforts were nearly always rejected by the major publishing houses, as were his articles for the *Berliner Tageblatt* rejected by a Jewish editor which he never forgot. His lack of financial support meant he was obliged to return to Rheydt, arriving home as Dr Goebbels. He may have felt proud of himself, but he soon gathered the impression the family was disappointed in his change of direction, possibly because he was not going to train for the priesthood. He kept on trying as hard as he could to be recognised as a writer, and he managed to have some articles printed in the local newspaper, one of which implied an anti-Semitic attitude which for Goebbels was a novelty, but which was soon to be his main source for pent-up venom. His articles had 'dogmatic judgments and emotionally charged notions of world improvement' displaying with hindsight the better-known future Goebbels.[18] He was clearly showing signs of ambition which can be true of many young people, but it was not proving successful.

It was during the early postwar years that two features of Goebbels started to emerge. First, he had an almost unhealthy attitude in his private life in becoming what may be described as sex addiction, and secondly, he was driven by ambition and identifying politics as the necessary powerhouse for his future.

Throughout his life Goebbels had a series of love affairs or sexual liaisons, the first was an unhappy time with a girl called Anka Stahlern.* Goebbels was not physically attractive, weighing about 100 pounds and walking with a limp, but according to one historian he had the advantage of having long transparent hands, a baritone voice and deep brown eyes.[19] This lust for sex was the beginning of a life-long habit, an addiction which can come not just through pleasure but was probably also from the adrenalin rush provide by the feeling of adventure, risk and power. It was during the time when Goebbels was failing to find any publisher when this became a feature of his lifestyle. He started another liaison with Else who was a schoolteacher. The problem

* In some books and MSS it is spelt Stahlherm.

with Anka Stahlern had been that she had been the girlfriend of one of his close friends called Kölsch, and these features were typically like those of many immature teenagers. From his early diaries, which tend to be more personal, it is easy to gain the impression that Goebbels was in love with Anka. However, an old friend of Goebbels, called Prang, later claimed that the girlfriends were simply Goebbels' way of self-assertion, which may have been perceptive, as it was a habit which stayed with him. On one occasion because of girl problems, he contemplated suicide and wrote a melodramatic farewell note, but he did not attempt it on this occasion.*

Goebbels' friend Prang had joined the Nazi Party in 1922, but Goebbels was still immersed in hoping to become a well-known published author. In this he was always unsuccessful which he found deeply frustrating, but through his new girlfriend Else he found some employment working in the Dresdner Bank. Then Prang, encouraged by the girlfriend Else, found Goebbels a better position working in the Cologne Stock Exchange where his duty involved shouting out the rise and fall of shares. He eventually left this post (or, according to some rumours, was dismissed) which he hated so much that 'the plain facts are that at this juncture the almost twenty-seven-year-old Joseph Goebbels was just unsuccessful'.[20] He suffered during this time from fits of depression probably by his sense of self-perceived value was not being acknowledged, and possibly complicated by his growing female issues.

As a Young Man

The Weimar Republic was beginning to struggle with street violence during these years, clashes between communists and various right-wing groups of varying extremes, and they were becoming more and more violent. They were simply out of control and the wider public were all too aware of the problem and the seeming inability of the government to bring it under control. The political challenge of the extreme right and left wings had turned toxic, and most members of the public were all aware of this conflict, including Goebbels. From all available studies his youthful leanings were not in tune

* 'I am glad to depart from my life, which for me has been nothing but hell'. Quoted in Longerich, Peter, *Goebbels* (London: Penguin Vintage, 2016), p.20.

with those on the right-wing, as his early writings provided some evidence for his political left-wing views, and he probably had some sympathy for the communists. Goebbels later claimed that he joined the Nazi Party during this period of his life, but historically there is little evidence this was true, as he did not meet Hitler until 1925.[21] He later claimed that he wrote to Hitler when he was incarcerated in Landsberg prison, and gave an early date for finding his loyalty with the Nazi Party, but it is generally accepted that he was extending the truth to promote his importance with the kinds of exaggerations he deployed all his life, starting as a young man and increasing as he matured. Nevertheless, it seems only fair to note that an early biographer claimed that he did write, but Hitler and Hess decided not to reply, and Goebbels was supposed to have kept a copy of that letter which he published two years later.[22]

In 1918, it is known that Goebbels had voted for the *Bayerische Volkspartei*, the Bavarian People's Party which was decidedly right-wing and a Roman Catholic party.[23] He also went to a centre-left meeting of the German Democratic Party because he knew one of the speakers. It was clear that he was now beginning to take a keen interest in the politics of the day, and he was watching and looking at what was happening on the many sides of the political divisions, and probably early on hoping it could be vehicle for his inherent personal driving ambition.

During the postwar years, many in Germany had taken hold of the stab-in-the-back myth, known in German as *Dolchstoßlegende*, in which it was purported the Jews had caused Germany to lose the war. Many ignored this but others, especially on the more fanatical right wing and driven by the Nazi Party (NSDAP) made it popular, and hardly a meeting passed without it being raised and ranted about. During these early years there is little evidence that Goebbels was anti-Semitic, apart from noticing that his new girlfriend Else had a Jewish mother. The Goebbels' family lawyer and his favourite professor had been Jewish, but there were signs that in early 1923 Goebbels was beginning to turn anti-Jewish, maybe having its personal roots in his failure to publish his literary works which he started to blame on the Jewish publishing firms. Else remained with Goebbels for nearly five years and he was heavily dependent upon her for financial support, and her Jewish ancestry did not seem a major concern at that time.

Interest in the Political Scene

It was during the year 1923 Goebbels had started to attend political rallies with his friend Prang, and they even joined in some of the many violent street confrontations. In his hometown of Rheydt he had experienced a political confrontation between separatist groups demanding an independent Rhenish state, and the appearance of right-wing nationalists and communists. From his comments it appeared that Goebbels regarded all this with a degree of cynicism, but it is equally apparent that his developing political leanings was taking him towards the growing political battle scenes which would encapsulate his whole life to the very end. In his home area, as mentioned above, there had been some mild resistance to the French occupation of the Rhineland, and Goebbels later used this to exhibit his courage, purporting that he had been part of the more aggressive resistance. As one historian noted, this was extremely unlikely given his physical form and lack of military experience.[24] He was becoming cunning and claiming he had always taken an active role, but he used aliases which therefore no one could prove or disprove.[25] Had all this had any truth he would have undoubtedly spent more time on the subject, but like the vague inference that he had been at Verdun to explain his limp, in this matter it was mere asides and hints.

Goebbels was moving slowly but surely towards the right-wing nationalist and racial movements which were gaining popular support across the country, which was suffering from the effects of losing the war and the economic impositions of the Treaty of Versailles amongst the masses. Curiously, as one biographer noted, 'he was a radical, more or less; he was almost a Marxist, enamoured of the class struggle and repelled only by the internationalism of the Left', and he was always anti-bourgeoisie.[26]

However, he was deeply curious about the aftermath of the Munich putsch and especially the figure of Adolf Hitler, but he appeared to be vague about the values the National Socialists, and his diary entry for 13 March 1924 contained the following, 'away from paralyzing materialism. Back to devotion and God', all of which sounds odd given the man he became.[27] It was clear that it was not Hitler's intellect which attracted Goebbels, but that peculiar charisma Hitler seemed to wield on most people from all classes and walks of life he met. Goebbels was not at this stage seeking the Christian messiah, but a political equivalent which drew him towards Hitler.

Despite his interest in politics, he still needed work, first trying with the famous Jewish publishers Rudolf Mosse in Berlin, then a teaching post in Düsseldorf but both failed. These types of work were obviously driven by personal economic needs. On 4 April 1924, he and Prang founded the local National Socialist group, and this date can signify Goebbels' first serious interest into what would be the Nazi Party, the NSDAP. It was from this juncture in his life that he made a study of anti-Semitism, reading Henry Ford's *The International Jew* and *The Protocols of the Elders of Zion*. In the next election the Party only managed less than 7 per cent of the vote and the Rheydt results were even lower.

Nevertheless, for Goebbels this was a new way forward for his ambition, to help create a new Germany free of Jewish influence. Following a political conference in Elberfeld where he with a few others adopted the theory that Germany needed a new political leader, such as the re-emergence of a Bismarck or Frederick the Great, calling out for the end of democracy and looking for a gifted leader, namely an autocracy. All this political theorising and activity seemed to have given him a new focus in life, and he started studying political works including Karl Marx's *Das Kapital*. He was becoming immersed in politics at the national level, and with Prang attended a conference at Weimar in the August of 1924. Given his ambition with his egotistical leanings, this must have been boosted when he met some national figures including Ludendorff and Gregor Strasser. He and Prang founded a group of National Socialist Freedom Movement members in Mönchengladbach. It was here where he began his public speaking, which he knew was a gift he had, that his listeners also recognised it was good, and he rapidly became known for his public speaking and his ability to agitate and stir matters up with his contentious way of speaking.

It was through this ability in oratory that found his first political job as a secretary to a Franz von Wiegershaus an extreme right winger with similar views to the Nazi Party, but not of the NSDAP. Goebbels presented articles for the *Völkische Freiheit* (German Freedom Party) and wrote much of the content for that newspaper. On reading them, these were the first signs of Goebbels' characteristic acidic style and vitriol in these early submissions.

He always wrote what the right wingers wanted to hear, and he constantly projected his own image on whatever stage he happened to be standing to deliver his speeches. The small sad little boy with a clubbed foot had found a place on the stage and was attracting attention. In October he accepted the editorship of the *Völkische Freiheit* which was another boost for his ego. His growing public appearance attracted the Belgian occupying authority, and his house was searched, so he moved out of the occupied zone. Of importance to him was that his writing and speeches were beginning to attract attention, people were beginning to recognise the value of this intelligent young man.

Goebbels was hungry for power, almost obsessed with the need to be recognised. Although he worked for Wiegershaus and Kaufmann he saw Strasser as the stronger man. Goebbels seemed to like Kaufmann, using the familiar *du* with one another, but Kaufmann had noted Goebbels' jealousy if Kaufmann listened to someone else. This would be a later characteristic with his relationship with Hitler, as Goebbels always had a deep personal jealousy of his friendships. It was obviously clear to many that Goebbels was seeking a high profile for himself and consequently many kept away from him, or did not trust him. Strasser had heard Goebbels speaking and had offered him more money, as 'he was a realist'.[28] There is little question that Strasser chose Goebbels as editor because he had found 'a brilliant twenty-nine year-old who had replaced the methodical Himmler as Strasser's secretary...he was a facile writer and, despite an appearance of frailty, was a commanding figure on a platform with his magnetic baritone voice, expressive hands and appealing dark eyes'.[29]

It was not just his oratorical ability but his anti-Semitic vitriol which brought Goebbels into contact with other Nazis figures, and it was Gregor Strasser who engaged him as secretary for the Northern party organisation.* This was why Goebbels stepped into a post hitherto done by Heinrich Himmler, who according to many returned to his job of poultry keeping.** This claim was doubtful, because Himmler was building his embryonic SS.

* While in Landsberg prison Hitler had asked Rosenberg to lead the Party on the grounds that Rosenberg was weak. It had proved an error because that very weakness allowed Gregor Strasser in power.

** When Himmler married, he set up a small poultry farm for his wife to run, but he never left politics to keep chickens.

Having entered the employment of the Strasser brothers, Goebbels had found the means of establishing himself within the Nazi Party, and for him this was critical because he probably saw a road which might just lead him to the top. In many ways he felt closer to Strasser who demanded more social change in terms of making working people better off, and Goebbels knew the masses had to be onside. Strasser and Goebbels wanted a revolution for fundamental social change, whereas Hitler wanted a revolution to grasp total power, though he always promised a better future. There is no doubt that Gregor Strasser's brother Otto had a stronger social conscience. The Party at this time was divided with the Strasser brothers stronger in Berlin and Hitler in Munich. The tensions were both social and political, and they were well-known. Goebbels as secretary to Strasser had started to make his name known, especially his public speaking ability. During this period Goebbels had kept a personal diary intended for himself, which can be found in the Hoover Institution at Stanford University in California. It was written in his late twenties, but it reads like the romancing and rantings of a teenager. He stopped adding entries to this diary when he was made Gauleiter for Berlin on 26 October 1926. In this early personal diary, he revealed the problems and joys of his love life, his frustration at not being an acknowledged writer, and his feelings towards Strasser and later Hitler. Notably the diary also revealed that he was prone to moments of depression probably because of his sense of lack of achievement as he tried to climb the ladder of being recognised as important.

Goebbels the diary writer has left his diaries which are of great value to the historian, as they record not only his feelings but provide a detailed map of the growth of the NSDAP and all the various issues, including his own inner thoughts. He started the process of diary keeping from when he turned 26 years of age and kept them going until his death just over twenty years later. The first six or seven years of entries were every second or third day, but soon he was recording his current thinking daily. Until mid-1941 he tended to write them himself, but as life became more hectic and complex, he dictated to a secretary his notes and which were much longer than when he wrote them himself. Being Goebbels, he saw them as monumentally important for the history of Germany, writing in his diary on 30 March 1941 that 'I placed my diaries, 20 thick volumes, into the underground safes of the Reichsbank. They are too valuable to fall victim to a possible bombing raid. They describe my whole life and our time. If fate allows me a few more years, then I want to revise it for later generations. It will probably find a lot of interest outside'. He may well have at times have seen himself as a would-be historian of the Third Reich, but his diaries have been used by historians to gain insights into the Nazi regime, the early ones with his personal ups and downs are of less importance, though some entries reveal much of his personality issues.

He also edited a political magazine called the *Nationalsozialistische Briefe*, and his sense of self-importance was bolstered when his oratory and public speaking was applauded which he constantly referred to in his diary. He was always consistent in applauding himself in some of his entries. Later he was to claim that if he told his audience to jump from the fourth floor some may have done so, but most would have done it for Hitler.[30] Goebbels was an intellectual, and this was recognised early by most of his listeners and those he met, which helped to start his political career, but he always had that all too human element of feeling he was a cut above others. In a special edition of *Völkische Freiheit* Goebbels wrote several flattering articles on Hitler on following his release from Landsberg prison on 29 December 1924. As noted above Goebbels had tussled with his Christian faith which he was turning against, and it has frequently been suggested that he was turning his adulation and sense of devotion towards the figure of Hitler. One recent biographer noting that 'this transfer of the role of saviour to another person, somebody greater, and the desire for the most perfect symbiotic fusion with this idol played to Goebbels' narcissistic disorder. He himself could feel great only if he had constant confirmation from the idol he had chosen. Hitler was to be this idol'.[31] His one serious struggle at this stage was his agreement with the Strasser brothers, namely that it was feasible that the Party could win over the support of the communists, which would have been an anathema to Hitler as bad as suggesting Jewish people were a superior race.

However, Hitler was a free man again and ensuring he took the lead role within the Party structure. He emerged from prison seeing himself as a hero determined to take control and march on to victory. The public speaking bans were lifted, and Hitler was busy making sure that he would dominate the Party, and at a rally in Hamm everyone including Gregor Strasser swore their allegiance to Hitler. Goebbels was appointed as the man in charge of NSDAP affairs in the west and his Gauleiter was an Axel Ripke. Goebbels was now paid a moderate salary, and he started to realise his skill for producing propaganda posters which were becoming popular with party members as they were eye-catching. The swastika was always prominent on these posters and designed to hold the attention of those walking by. As early as 1924 he was always on the move displaying his skill at public speaking. He even turned against Gauleiter Axel Ripke accusing him of being a bourgeois, using his journalistic skills to attack Ripke, which proved to be useful. This turning against friends and colleagues was to become a feature of his life, especially if he saw them even as a minor threat against his growing status.

Chapter Two

The Ardent Disciple of Hitler

Meets Hitler

It was on 12 July1925 that Goebbels met Hitler for the first time at a meeting in Weimar, writing in his diary a year later that 'Hitler is coming. I venerate and love him'.[1] This virtually religious sentiment which had gripped Goebbels reflected his almost religious fervour he felt for what became his demi-god. Working with the Strasser brothers in Berlin, it was always a puzzle for Goebbels as to why Hitler tended to stay in Munich. 'As a Rhinelander, Goebbels did not understand the enthusiasm of his boss for the Bavarian city…the Nazi Party headquarters stayed put in the "Brown House" in Munich, where Hitler had an apartment'.[2]

Goebbels took to his new bible and studied with care Hitler's *Mein Kampf* with much enthusiasm, one of the very few who found this poorly expressed book full of his rantings interesting. He and Strasser worked together to form the NSDAP controls over the various *Gaus*, which were regions with a central town, but they caused some controversy when they and others attempted to overhaul the Party manifesto. It led to some noisy meetings in which some have suggested that Goebbels had tried to have Hitler sacked.[3] This was more likely to have been a malicious rumour spread by some Party members who had taken an instant distrust to Goebbels in his obvious personal efforts to elevate himself. As one historian put it, 'Goebbels had become an unconditional disciple of power'.[4]

During this early stage of Nazi development Goebbels and the Strasser brothers worked together having much in common with their politics with the need to change the social structures which tended to be at the top of their priority lists. Goebbels kept his role as business manager, but he was disappointed when Kaufmann was made Gauleiter which he had long wanted for himself. During these early years there was a high degree of ongoing controversy relating to the correct policy and political direction the Party should navigate. Goebbels was able to make his views widely known because he was writing for various papers including the *Völkischer Beobachter*, the *Deutsche Wochenschau* and his own paper *Nationalsozialistische.* In his section called 'Open Letters' in the *Völkischer Beobachter* they were often regarded as the most highly readable material.[5] Goebbels found himself at variance with some of Hitler's views in *Mein Kampf*, not least because at this stage they did not share the same views of their brand of socialism, and differing on their views of Russia, but he would soon swing into line with anything Hitler demanded.

Although Goebbels worked closely with Strasser this relationship became less important as Goebbels' came more under the influence of Hitler. The Strasser brothers tended to be seen as the developing northern branch of the party with Hitler and Munich in the south. There were two conferences held during 1926 between these northern and southern elements of the Nazi Party, and it appears that during these years Goebbels began his quasi-pilgrimage of worshiping Hitler. He was discovering that strange magnetic hold Hitler had over many people, which many people in their memoirs refer to when meeting him for the first time.

The major moment for Goebbels' change of direction towards Hitler was a Regional (Gau) meeting in Braunschweig where Hitler greeted him as his close friend. When they met again a few weeks later at Plauen they both spoke in public. Hitler could be shrewd in understanding people, and he probably saw in Goebbels a potential servant with political talent, sending Goebbels a present of a leather-bound copy of *Mein Kampf*. A major debate took place in Bamberg called for by Hitler in February 1926, during which he spoke for two hours. Goebbels was still aware that his own political way of thinking did not always work with that of his developing hero. There had been a rumour that Goebbels would challenge Hitler but he did not oppose him, 'but even his silence did not bode well for the future'.[6] Hitler had probably recognised that Goebbels, like him, needed to be needed, and to 'be loved and admired, a feminine trait in his nature which was so strongly pronounced that he only loved those who openly and emphatically loved him'.[7] There was undoubtedly more to Hitler's friendship than Goebbels was aware, as his 'behaviour would appear ridiculous if it did not testify to a state of pathological dependence, with all its implications'.[8] These were serious tensions in the party as there was an ongoing early danger of a split between the Strasser group and the men in Munich. Hitler invited the potential dissidents to Munich to resolve the problems, and he also travelled north to resolve the issues they had raised. Goebbels continued to ponder the anti-communist question which dominated Hitler's mind, but Hitler who lived on the habit of divide and rule was winning him over.

Goebbels had decided that communism rule in the east was the answer claiming, 'that is why we look to Russia, because it is the most likely to show us the way to socialism'.[9] He saw the West as in melt-down because it was too materialistic and decaying, preferring Bolshevism to the decaying capitalism. However, first and foremost Goebbels was always driven by personal ambition, and visitors had noticed in his office he had pictures of Hitler alongside Lenin, two revolutionary leaders, but he soon accepted Hitler's views of Russia.

It was not long before Goebbels, through his speeches, made it clear that he had taken onboard Hitler's political viewpoints and was duly criticised by others such as Kaufmann and Pfeffer for doing so. From the time Hitler had been freed from Landsberg prison, Goebbels had seen him as his political messiah and who was for him now glowing in the darkness. Hitler always saw himself as protected by Providence, for Goebbels he was amounting to a Divine revelation. Hitler who knew that propaganda was the way forward realised that Goebbels was potentially valuable for him, and by encouraging him knew this would weaken the Strasser camp. For his part Goebbels was seeing Hitler as the needed leader of the future. He was also amazed at the grandeur of Hitler' setting, observing the Munich leader had a chauffeur driven car and the huge authority he wielded. It has been noted that Goebbels had seen the 'Holy Grail', and the people in Munich 'had power, they had automobiles, they had money'.[10] At this stage it was Goebbels' public speaking ability which drew Hitler's attention, and in his diary, Goebbels was constantly writing entries of self-praise about his own skills on the public stage, indicating an egotism which could only be matched by Hitler and Göring. At the second Nazi conference, it did not take long for Strasser to realise that Goebbels was moving towards Hitler and losing sight of his usual socialist stand. For Goebbels it was when Hitler praised him for a speech that his key fitted the lock. From this point on Hitler could do nothing wrong, he had charisma, leadership, authority and for Goebbels was heaven sent. These two men even exchanged flowers, and Goebbels was hysterical with joy when Hitler sent him red roses. Goebbels wanted to go to Munich, but he was cleverly persuaded to become the Gauleiter and Gauführer of Berlin. These were grand posts that Goebbels could hardly resist in his driving passion to be elevated and regarded as important.

At a personal level these developments led to his girlfriend Else saying farewell to him. She as with Anka, had been an internal struggle for Goebbels' emotions. He had tried to dissociate himself from her, but he then missed her and her support, but by this stage he was more and more questioning and worrying about her so-called Jewish pedigree. The move to Berlin had, he hoped, settled the issue. His political progress was not as easy going as he had hoped, and he was disturbed when Strasser had been made Head of Party Propaganda. Goebbels was somewhat uncertain about going to Berlin, but he needed the extra money and was ambitious, but the decisive factor was that Hitler had personally asked him, and as Orlow, an historian of the NSDAP wrote, 'the true believer mentally clicked his heels, raised his right arm and went to Berlin'.[11]

He became promptly active in his new role and started to try and restructure the presence of the NSDAP in the capital city, always wanting things the way he thought they ought to be. He did not think the traditional system of pamphlets delivered to the door and small gatherings were sufficient, and he was constantly seeking ways to make a greater impact. He had noted the left-wing opposition were having for them a positive effect in advertising their hopes for the future, so he started to seek methods to do better than them. Throughout his life he knew with his instincts for propaganda that the visual picture had the best effect, and it was this viewpoint which encouraged him towards organised rallies and meetings, which he started to achieve with growing success, which began his rise to one of national standing, and this aspect had always been his ambition. He was perceptive in his thinking because as all modern professional advertisers work on the belief that what people see and hear is more persuasive than the written word, which is why today television advertising of products is a major industry.

Goebbels in Berlin

The mid- to late 1930s was a complex and confusing time for Germany, both for the government and the public, and the NSDAP was also struggling with its many issues. There was beginning to appear some tension between the SA and the political leadership with Goebbels finding himself caught between the factions. His popularity had lessened in Munich, but his survival or way to success depended on Hitler's support. Goebbels had proposed and supported different policies in both social and economic matters. His methods tended to be more aggressive and violent, whereas Hitler and the Munich followers were seeking a so-called legitimate rise to political power and trying not to be seen as overly revolutionary.

Goebbels was attacked in the courts, mainly because of his sharp-tongued language, and he suffered from a series of bans on public speaking and personal appearances, thereby restricting his ambitions. He tended to 'go over the top', not least by attacking highly respectable national figures with considerable vitriol and venom. As one historian noted, one Jewish policeman called Weiss 'was a heaven-sent scapegoat for Goebbels', whom Goebbels had frequently selected for constant attacks.[12] Despite the heat of the controversies which he stirred up, he survived not only the State's legal attacks, but some of the internal bickering within the Party. Hitler in Munich, knew he needed to maintain his leadership in Berlin and ensure his authority in the capital, a need which made Goebbels important as his trusted man. Hitler claimed he selected Goebbels as his trusted aide because he 'possesses two attributes without which no one could master the conditions in Berlin: intelligence and the gift of oratory'.[13] There were major differences between these two major cities of Munich and Berlin. In Berlin, the streets were more ruled by the communists than the right-wing street agitators. In the south Hitler had the Storm Troopers (Ernst Röhm was placed in charge in 1931) and the *Stahlhelm* (ex-service men), both were semi-military organisations and controlled many areas. However, even at this stage Hitler was already beginning to feel that the SA tended to be somewhat independent from his direct authority, and he was becoming concerned about their independence. Hitler's sole drive was that he was the leader and would only seek support from those who understood this factor. The SA appeared to live off street riots and brawls, always searching for a successful putsch, but for Hitler they seemed to lead their own independent existence.

How far Goebbels was alert to Hitler's concerns can only remain speculative, but he cleverly appointed a man Kurt Daluege as the head of the Berlin SA (Daluege later transferred to the SS and was executed after the war for war crimes) making him his deputy Gauleiter and thereby keeping him in his pocket, which eased any potential problems over the obsessive matter of power-holding. This apparent act of patronage helped to a small degree to resolve the type of SA problem developing, but only for a time as Hitler would have no form of even mild suspicion of others in his caged mind. Goebbels also copied the communist system of having cell groups situated in various key areas of Berlin, directing his work towards the proletariat and his 'rabid hatred of the bourgeoisie gave him the necessary tone', although he himself could also be described as petit-bourgeois and intellectual.[14] Goebbels was well aware that the Strasser brothers remained influential within their Party in Berlin, not least in having their own publishing house with their newspapers *Der Nationale Sozialist* and the Berlin paper the *Berliner Arbeiterzeitung*, and in the capital they held considerable influence. This was why Hitler used Goebbels to ensure that Berlin followed his line of leadership. The Strasser brothers worked well for a time with Goebbels, but policy conflict and his support of Hitler would later bring this relationship to an end.

Berlin was best described during these interbellum years, as one of the most open-minded capitals of Europe, but it was mainly dominated by the communists and the Social Democrats. The NSDAP was almost insignificant, once described as 'a mouse faced with two elephants'.[15] Faced with this dilemma the Nazi Party was having problems and the word Gauleiter in those days was virtually meaningless for the public, compared to the next decade. Goebbels tried to take a lead and held a meeting of major Party members, most of whom were uncertain about him, but by using Hitler's authority and techniques he carried out several purges of any dissidents and what he perceived as the weaker members. He cleverly held his rowdy meetings in the communist areas such as Spandau and at the Phärus-Sale in the Wedding district, which were deliberately violent and noisy, thereby making them known to the public. On these occasions Goebbels demonstrated his own personal courage, his usual duplicity, and he organised the proceedings start to finish. Not everyone was comfortable with Goebbels' appointment, but Hitler gave him his backing while ensuring he always remembered that Hitler was the top leader. Goebbels described these early days of trying to consolidate the Party in Berlin in his own book *Kampf um Berlin* (Struggle for Berlin) published in 1931. 'The unrevised version shows that, contrary to the stylised and self-serving propaganda account in *Kampf um Berlin*, Goebbels' beginnings in Berlin by no means represented a triumphal progress'.[16]

Nevertheless, the government managed to keep some restraint upon the activities of both the NSDAP and carefully watched Goebbels, already identified as a potential troublemaker. Despite its problems the Weimar Republic was beginning to make some economic advances and by 1929 unemployment was declining and the onetime Chancellor Stresemann was making some progress within the international community.* Stresemann always held a realistic approach even in these anxious and troubled days for Germany. He had finished the so-called 'Battle of the Ruhr, signed the Treaty of Locarno, looked to improved relationships with the French' and carried through the Young Plan.[17] After he died the financial depression started in 1930 which badly affected the German economy. Immediately after the Great War the extreme right-wing groupings were popular and remained so even as the economic situation showed some signs of recovery, but it was felt by some that they were losing momentum. However, on the return of the economic recession in 1930, the extreme political wings became once again more popular and attractive, with unemployment rising to an estimated six million. It has been claimed that the Nazi Party was never a political party but 'a conspiracy to gain power', and was constantly divided on how to achieve their desired supremacy.[18] Goebbels wanted to use the popular street riots and power, but Hitler was moving towards the policy of gaining power by constitutional means, he was beginning to find some backing from the rich industrialists and bankers and was assisted by Göring's contacts.

---

* Stresemann one time Chancellor (1923) and Weimar's Foreign Minister (1923–9) made peace with France signing the Kellog-Briand Pact in 1928 for which he received the Nobel Peace Prize; he died from a stroke in 1929.

For this reason, Hitler started to visit Berlin more often to establish his leadership and Goebbels revelled in this perceived friendship of Hitler. He was beginning, because of this allegiance to Hitler to have problems with the Strasser brothers, but for some considerable time he had always regarded Gregor as a reliable member, but he considered his brother Otto to be verging on being unstable. In many ways Gregor Strasser and Goebbels had been close friends, but this quickly evaporated as Goebbels rejected his original ideals for those held by Hitler. He was delighted when given by Hitler the second part of *Mein Kampf*, which he read, noticing Hitler's projected policy of *Lebensraum* in the Soviet Union which would have clashed with his original thinking.

In *Mein Kampf* Hitler had proposed that the masses were not influenced by what they read but what they heard, describing it as the *living presence*. Goebbels had readily fastened onto this fact, and he used it at every conceivable opportunity. For him, and many others, good public speaking or rabble-rousing for political agitation meetings was the best tool, supported by strong visual propaganda which should demonstrate the essential truths as seen by the party. Goebbels had worked on his skills on the soap box and used his voice and gesticulations well. Unlike Hitler, Goebbels rarely became too excited and was astute with his words, expressions and allusions, and ensuring that he could be understood by the dullest intellects in any audience. His oratory was clever and well presented, and as noted by one biographer he 'was able to create moods and emotions with the precision of a measuring instrument. He could foresee the reactions of the public' and his intelligence was well above the normal NSDAP member.[19] Again it should be noted that one thing in Goebbels' favour was his intelligence and intellect.

He was always known for his sense of efficiency, and when he established the Berlin administration office administration which had been disorganised, he developed it into a much better and efficient shape. He moved them to Lützowstrasse, making them effective and well-ordered. He was the only person allowed to use green ink so his comments would be immediately recognised and promptly followed if necessary. He acquired a car to fit his position, recalling the time he had been impressed with Hitler's private transport and chauffeur.

He organised a poster campaign to provoke the communists, and these posters were always coloured blood red and black with provocative titles, causing the passer-by to stop and read them. The biographer Heiber was at pains to point out that the 'red' was not Goebbels' idea nor did he produce the idea of banners and drums.[20] He developed a friendship with the graphic artist Hans Herbert Schweitzer who helped design the posters under the pseudonym of Mjölnir. Goebbels had always demanded the colour red on all posters because the party was revolutionary, and he made a point of studying this method of propaganda with assiduous care. For obvious reasons the posters were always about catching public attention and instructing the passing person how and what to think. He often argued the truth did not need explaining but simply had to be made obvious, which meant it had to be eye-catching and provocative. Goebbels always insisted that the poster headlines would become so well-known that they would eventually become slogans. It was intended to grip the attention of the masses and encourage them to understand the value of the Party's message. The American advertising world was already developing the psychology behind advertising, and it has been suggested that Goebbels had looked to the developments of this aspect of the commercial world.

In February 1927 he hired the Pharus Hall (Phärus-Sale) in the centre of Berlin's working-class district, deliberately chosen because of its well-known communist activity. In the anticipated street and hall battles which had become a feature of many German streets, he had the wounded street fighters sitting on the stage as he spoke in his form of dramatic way. Again, he had noted the value of the visual impact on spectators. He often deployed this dramatic gesture, indicating that he was effective in this work of propaganda. He imitated Hitler, making sure that before the meetings there were quasi-military parades and ceremonies. He would travel from his residence (in the Steiger's apartments who were friends of Strasser) always arriving with a sense of pomp and ceremony. He was quickly recognised as an outstanding orator and agitator which caused concern not just to the communist leadership, but the government of the day. On the other hand, it drew the attention of Hitler to his potential usefulness for the cause.

It was Goebbels' aggressive and eye-catching propaganda which often led to violence where meetings were held and, on the streets, making the Party a subject of growing interest and curiosity throughout Germany. As noted above Goebbels' selected sites, were frequently in well-known communist areas, ranging from the Seitz ballroom in the red district of Spandau, to a rally at Cottbus preceded by an SA march, then the Pharus Hall rooms in the Wedding district, a well-known hotspot for communists, and back to Spandau. In March 1927, Goebbels gave an aggressive speech in Trebbin where his growing characteristic of bitter anti-Semitism was vitriolic. There was so much social disturbance leading to mayhem on the public streets that the Berlin Police Chief Karl Zörgieble demanded the NSDAP should be dissolved. It was in May 1927 that Hitler made his first speech in Berlin since he had appointed Goebbels. Hitler had been banned from public speaking in the northern areas of Germany, but to avoid this prohibition the meeting had been cleverly advertised by Goebbels as a private member conference. The authorities were not fooled by this pretence and quickly listened to the Berlin Police Chief Karl Zörgieble, and the National Socialist Party was totally banned in Berlin and surrounding areas, and a prohibition was placed on all their meetings throughout Prussia, forbidding Goebbels any public speaking platform. Goebbels tried to avoid the ban by standing up in meetings to make a debating point, but the police were aware of his cunning ploys.

Goebbels claimed the police ban was a good thing because, he argued, it was indicative that the Party was being taken seriously, even if treated as a threat. Not every Party major figure agreed with his way of reasoning. He was harshly criticised in the Strasser brothers' paper the *Berliner Arbeiterzeitung* in which the Elberfeld district leader referred indirectly to Goebbels by using the hunchback image of King Richard III of England, and the limping court jester of King Francis of France. This attack infuriated Goebbels to such a degree, he promptly issued threats and warnings, calling for Hitler's help suggesting he might have to resign. The response tried to alleviate the issue with the paper suggesting or rather pretending they had not meant to make any allusion to Goebbels, but it did not calm Goebbels' fury as the original article was quite clear that it was Goebbels.

Arising from these attacks Goebbels, who rarely spoke about his physical deformity, started to publicly announce that his foot was not a problem of birth, but a result of an accident and later dropping hints he had been wounded in the recent war which was a deliberate lie. His problem of his foot and limp started a major affray when he was interrupted by the interjection 'you yourself don't look all that special'. There are a variety of accounts of what happened followed, but overall, the person who made this interruption was 'seriously mishandled' and it transpired to be an elderly clergyman called Stucke.* Those in the Party who were critical of the rising Goebbels would often refer or joke about his limp of which Goebbels was all too conscious. According to many sources he had more problems on this issue from members of the Party than his political enemies, which spoke volumes about the nature of many of the Party members. Even after Hitler demanded silence on the matter there were still whispered rumours about Mephisto Goebbels' clubfoot. Even Goebbels complained that his political opponents treated him more fairly than his Party colleagues.[21] It was not surprising that Alfred Rosenberg (the Nazi ideologue), who was to become Goebbels' lifelong enemy, enjoyed these personal attacks. When Goebbels published his book *Vom Kaiserhof zur Reichskanzlei* it was based on his diaries and on the surface appeared to adulate Hitler as the saviour and as his closest confidante. In this book he argued that public needed Hitler, but Alfred Rosenberg swiftly, and with symptomatic jealousy, a symptom he and Goebbels both shared, wrote with some justification, that Goebbels book should have had the title wrote '*I About Myself*'. All of Goebbels' life involved conflict with those who worked alongside him and those who opposed him and his politics. Goebbels revised his book many times between publications, smoothing out some passages, and later making sure the name Ernst Röhm (a cofounder of the SA) disappeared when he fell out of favour with Hitler.[22] One consistency in the book was the continuous attack on the Strasser brothers, with Gregor Strasser telling a friend that 'from now on, Germany is in the hands of a born liar from Austria, a perverted ex-officer, and a clubfoot. And believe me, the last is the worst of the three. He's Satan in human form', postwar many Germans would have seen the truth in this viewpoint.[23]

---

* See for details Reimann, Viktor, *Joseph Goebbels: The Man Who Created Hitler* (London: Sphere Books Ltd, 1979), pp.87–8. Another biography (Ebermayer and Meissner) suggests the clergyman had been sacked from the Church for drinking. The truth as in many incidents is evasive and not that important.

Apart from the insults and clashes with people like Rosenberg, Goebbels realised the government was strong enough to impose the restrictive ban on meetings from May 1927, but many Nazi members, especially the younger ones, took the violence onto the street, with special aggressive attention for those appearing to be Jewish. They were fined or even imprisoned, and Goebbels wrote protests about this in his many publications, arguing out that this was the fault of the police for banning the Party meetings. This failed to work, and the police continued to monitor and prohibit any meetings, trying to restrain the local Nazi thugs and many justifiable arrests ensued. There were many trials as a result, and Goebbels himself was threatened with fines and imprisonment, but he somehow managed to avoid most of such threats. Goebbels was more than happy, but 'within the Party his position was by no means unassailable. It seemed that the tactics he had introduced on arriving in Berlin at the end of 1926, especially the use of provocation to draw attention to the NSDAP at all costs, had led to a dead end' in the opinion of his critics.[24] There were those in the Party who believed that Goebbels with his rhetoric and rabble raising had taken the wrong direction.

It was not just the government forces which were a problem, it was apparent that the Strasser brothers were actively opposing the way that Goebbels had led the NSDAP as it had become a banned organisation. Their criticism was not without some justification. The atmosphere was so taunt that Goebbels decided to move from his lodgings and away from his landlord Steiger who tended to agree with his old friends the Strasser brothers. Hitler felt obliged to intervene and for a time there was a degree of peace, but it never lasted.

Even as this fraught struggle within the Party was heating up, Goebbels continued to pursue his love life, missing Else but having affairs with various women, one a Dora Hentschel and even a Russian émigré called Tamara Heede. The ban on his activities gave him more free time and he soon returned in trying to become a literary and intellectual star, by revamping his drama *The Wanderer* and rewriting his novel *Michael*, but naturally the reviews in Strasser's papers were not good. In the novel he redrafted his autobiographical figure in NSDAP style including anti-Semitism, political rebirth, and Michael's encounter with the heroic leader. It must have felt to him that he had created a hole in his political ambitions, but returning to his failures in the literary world would not and for him could not be the answer.

Undoubtedly because of the break with the Strasser brothers Goebbels had started (with Hitler's permission and to Goebbels' joy) his own publication known as *Der Angriff* (The Attack) which at first looked as if it might fail, as it was attacked even by Party members. Goebbels had to borrow some 2,000 marks from party friends to start the project, and although it first appeared to be an abject failure it eventually paid for itself.[25] The Strasser brothers (who had started their own paper in March 1926 called *Die Berliner Arbeiterzeitung*) were becoming more strident as the political and personal rift grew between them and their old friend. The paper *Der Angriff* was aggressive and unpleasant, but it was intelligent and adept, and much more literary than many others, it 'differed from Streicher's notorious sheet of hate *Der Stürmer* only by its superior German'.[26]

The major moment for the year 1927 for the Nazi leadership was the Party Congress held at Nuremberg at the end of August. Nuremberg with its old stonework of the Zeppelin field was designed by Albert Speer and organised by Goebbels and 'built for the adoration of the Führer'.[27] This rally was the forerunner of the later and over-dramatic and powerful scenes in which the Nazi Party tried to demonstrate their power to the German public and the international community, many of whom watched with amazement the show of power and dedication, and some with a sense of sympathetic awe. These rallies proved to a brilliant show case for the casual observer, especially for foreign visitors, even with visits from the British Fascist Party led by Oswald Mosley.

This demonstration of using pomp and ceremony of their political power became a critical part of the Nazi rise to power. Goebbels tried to ensure he was involved in these occasions, though Rosenberg, Rudolf Hess, and Martin Bormann continually interfered, Goebbels always tried to make sure it was seen as his creation.[28] Nevertheless, it was *Der Angriff* which occupied his mind, he was conscious that other party papers, especially those produced by the Strasser brothers were more widely read. Goebbels even encouraged the Storm Troopers to increase the sales of *Der Angriff* and demand blocking the sales of the Party's competitors. Otto Strasser decided this was going too far, and he also sought Hitler's help.

Chapter Three

Driven by Ambition

Reichstag Member

The following year 1928 was full of critical moments for the developing Nazi Party structure and especially for Goebbels. It was announced that there would be a Reichstag election in May of that year, and the ban on the Nazi Party was lifted. However, during the election they only polled some 800,000 votes winning them a mere twelve seats, three of them taken by Goebbels, Gregor Strasser and Göring. The NSDAP were disappointed with the results, not least because they had won less than 3 per cent of the vote, making them appear to the public as virtually insignificant. As noted above, by the late 1920s there had been an improvement in the German economy, but as the decade unfolded there was the global financial meltdown which affected Germany more than most countries. This downturn in economics helped the prospects for the NSDAP because they persistently offered a better if not ideal future. They worked on was called the 'protest vote', which with Goebbels' propaganda would change their situation, and within a few years making Hitler more a global political figure.

This thrusting activity by Goebbels indicated that he was rising fast and gaining more support from Hitler who then appointed him Head of Propaganda at the end of the year in place of Strasser, who was put in charge of the Party organisation. According to the biographer Heiber it remains a mystery as to the actual date of the appointment.[1] Goebbels totally immersed himself over the next few years in stirring the political scene with his oratory, demonstrations, and ceremonies. In September 1928, he booked the Sportpalast (a vast auditorium) for Hitler and this, along with Nuremberg, became significant rallying points for the Party, and Goebbels was succeeding in being seen as a critical component of the Nazi Party.

Being a member of the Reichstag undoubtedly gave Goebbels a greater sense of self-importance, making a diary entry that he was pleased that he was less likely to be noticed or spoken to by the police, and that it gave him a level of immunity and free travel. He used to declare himself *IdI*, standing for *Inhaber der Immununitat* (Possessor of Immunity). However, the prosecutions did not stop, and he was fined 200 marks for a series of almost childish attacks in his articles on a police officer. It was not until mid-July 1928 that a law was passed which made Goebbels feel safer or immune from the interests of the courts, at least for a time. He was frequently pursued by the courts on many charges, but he would pack the court with his lackeys and 'Goebbels knew how to turn a courtroom scene to his advantage'.[2] He was undoubtedly reflecting Hitler who used his trial and even time in Landsberg prison to proclaim the Party's aims and himself. It was now becoming clear that Goebbels could be regarded as significant in the rise of Hitler to power.

Because of the lack of election success, Goebbels was aware that the Strasser brothers and Kaufmann were unhappy about the lack of progress, and he picked up rumours that there was ongoing chatter about forming an alternative party. While Goebbels was away holidaying, chasing women, playing with his literary aspirations, there were also problems emerging with the aggressive street riots involving the hard men of the SA. They regarded themselves as soldiers, but the politicians saw them as the amateurs and some as simply mere thugs. Goebbels had always used the SA for marches, parades and as agitators at his challenging meetings. He enjoyed their marching parades and the sense of threat they carried for the opposition, and they were good for dealing with the agitators and often praised them to their delight. In this way he found himself caught in the arising tensions between Hitler and the SA. The problem for Hitler was his characteristic jealousy over his leadership role and he was acutely aware of their existence and irritable about the SA leadership, for several possible reasons. He saw Röhm as becoming all too important in his own eyes, not least when Röhm started to suggest it should be he who should oversee the military. Hitler may have felt that since he was trying to appear respectable in climbing the electoral ladder the SA's thuggery was not helping, and with his long term plans he needed the traditional varieties of the military components onside with their professional experience. For Hitler he had long started to accrue doubts about the SA, and so Goebbels felt obliged to tread with care between the sensitivities of his master's wishes in Munich, and wanting the SA power for his Berlin manoeuvrings.

Goebbels continued to use his propaganda skills, especially with the death of Horst Wessel in 1930. Horst Wessel died in a street brawl which had absolutely nothing to do with the Party, but part of what is best described as local gang warfare. Most historians believe that Wessel was a mere pimp who died at the hands of another pimp called Ali Höhler.[3] The nature of Wessel's fight and death belong to an even more shadowy side than political street brawls, but Goebbels had met him and knew him as a minor SA leader.* One historian noted that it may even have been a shoot-out with two communists, but the real subject of the fight was rent and a landlady.[4] More simply it may have just been a fight over a girl between a communist and fascist youth, Wessel had opened the door and was shot in the mouth. He died a few days later, but 'Ali Höhler's bullet was more directed at Wessel the lover than at Wessel the Nazi'.[5]

However, because he was a member of the SA, Goebbels capitalised on this and built him up through the means of *Der Angriff* to become the legendary Party hero and martyr. Goebbels had taken a possible street criminal and turned him into a Nazi hero. It was in his sense, with his early religious background, he probably perceived the need that the Party needed a martyr at this time, which provided the necessary hallowed backdrop for the infamous Horst Wessel song, and it was prepared almost as a hymn and remained popular until 1945. It was a clever piece of showmanship, fabricated on a total falsehood, which became Goebbels' hallmark for years to come. The police tried to control the funeral, and the communist protestors caused problems before and during the funeral, which Goebbels welcomed because there were the sorrowing Nazi members attacked by the nasty unsympathetic communists which played into his hands. The Horst Wessel song was sung at nearly every rally and on many other occasions. Earlier Goebbels had tried to make something of the funeral of another incident around a character called Kütemeyer, but it had failed to attract attention. Horst Wessel was different and set the stage for many other similar dramatic almost pantomime funerals, even flying a plane over the

* He commanded Storm 5 and his girlfriend was called Erna Jaenicke.

area dragging swastika flags. This visual spectator propaganda was always exploited as it often appealed to the emotions. One biographer aptly wrote that it was always based on deception and constantly in bad taste, 'no one could match him [Goebbels] when it came to 'roaring his anger into the grave'.[6] As Goebbels took more control the more propaganda funerals he managed, and 'he was not pleased when the people dubbed him with the title "Reich's Corpse Orator."'[7] Even as Wessel 'had lay dying in hospital, Goebbels turned a private feud into a political assassination by having Wessel's song sung at the conclusion of a meeting in the Sportpalast', and according to Hanfstaengl the melody was based an old Vienna cabaret song and it lasted throughout the Nazi era.[8]

Despite now having a martyr for the cause, the individualistic policies of Hitler and Strasser continued to cause tension. Strasser was much more the revolutionary leaning towards the left wing and communism, which reflected Goebbels' original thinking and hopes. Hitler, on the other hand, as noted above, was seeking a form of legitimacy with the support of the traditional wealthy elements to broker his way to power, and 'indeed, Hitler needed money at that moment more than anything else'.[9] Gregor Strasser was now working in Munich but it was Otto Strasser in Berlin who became the main point of contention. The protagonists Hitler and Otto Strasser decided to meet, but their differences were not resolved, and Goebbels was ordered by Hitler to sack him from the Party. Otto Strasser consequently established his own group called the Black Front.

In the 1930 elections, Goebbels' abilities with propaganda, his organisational skills and oratory were more than apparent and noted by Hitler. He stirred up questions of nationalism which can be all too popular at times, and the absolute need for rapid changes in Germany. Hitler had constantly attacked the Treaty of Versailles which had caused so many problems in postwar Germany, then the Jews, the communists, and he promised he could find the necessary resolutions for a better future. The Nazi vote sprang to over six million and their 12 seats became 107. The Nazi Party had become a force overnight and considerable significance must be given to Goebbels with his organisational skills, his ability in public speaking, his clever exaggerations, prefabrications or lies, and his journalistic skills.

Despite the success the ongoing problems within the Party did not disappear, as the street brawlers, most especially the Storm Troopers, who were made up from the unemployed or unemployable suddenly felt they were now being ignored. Even Goebbels' offices were raided by some disgruntled street fighters, and he was obliged to call in the hated police force to restore order. Hitler attempted to bring them under control by making himself their Supreme Commander and appointed Ernst Röhm merely as Chief of Staff. For Hitler it was essential that he was always regarded as the only and legitimate national leader. The SA had helped Goebbels create the sense of gang warfare in Berlin, terrorised and bullied Jewish people and fought the communists on the streets, and he was less concerned about them than Hitler. The government had tried several times to ban the SA, but Goebbels always found a way through the problem. On one occasion he ordered them to appear dressed in white shirts and when a policeman stopped one for wearing brown trousers, he took them off and walked away in public in his underpants.[10]

During this period Goebbels became a trifle uncertain about Hitler concerning his decisions about other right-wing groups, and his soft handling of the Strasser brothers. However, he stayed attached to his admired leader, and always waiting and hoping for Hitler's praise and promotion. It was clear by this stage that Goebbels did adore Hitler, as it even meant Goebbels had to change some of his views, but there is no question that pure ambition had driven him this far, and it remained a personal driving force. It was during November 1929 that he met Heinrich Himmler for the first time, who was the deputy director of Reich propaganda. He also met Göring in November 1929 when they both gave speeches at a commemorative ceremony for veterans. It was this point in time that his father died, and Goebbels was distraught even though he had frequently criticised his father in his diary, angry with him because he wanted his son to be a priest. At the political level there was an ongoing debate about a plebiscite on the American Young Plan of which Goebbels was critical, always deriding the nonsense of the democratic system. He attacked it in his newspaper as well as von Hindenburg asking about the 82-year-old President, 'is Hindenburg still alive?'[11]

Goebbels had overseen the campaigning and propaganda working between Munich and Berlin during the election. He was occasionally stopped by various court cases because of his inflammatory statements and for inciting violence and public unrest. Goebbels also faced unrest in the party because whereas Hitler was trying to win by gaining conservative support by legitimate means, Goebbels, with memories and remnants of his radical socialist past was sometimes regarded with suspicion in Berlin because he was always causing or stirring up trouble. This time the elections were more in favour of the NSDAP with an 18.3 per cent of the vote at last making them a mass movement in the German political scene. Their growth in power also meant Goebbels' immunity from court cases was restored.

The Storm Trooper problems had not improved despite Hitler's efforts, and suspicions arose when Captain Walter Stennes, the SA leader in northern Germany, joined Otto Strasser's *Black Front*. This Captain Stennes had threatened rebellion in 1928 and in 1930, and he had brought the NSDAP close to a crisis. This SA issue left Goebbels in a delicate position because his need for public agitation needed the SA to help, and by boosting morale with their parades. Stennes and Goebbels often worked closely as friendly comrades, but they were soon involved in serious clashes of opinion. This was a characteristic of Goebbels which was exposed later with both Göring and Himmler, at first friends and comrades, then friction, followed by rapprochement and renewed mutual respect to be quickly followed by more personal conflicts. There were some in the SA leadership who wanted places in the election as if by right, others appeared as if they were seeking more power status, and for some in the NSDAP it was felt that their own thugs wanted to seize the reins of power. Goebbels recognised that he was potentially in a dangerous space because of his closeness with the SA. He recognised that in Munich that those surrounding Hitler were becoming more and more critical of the image conveyed by the SA. It was for Goebbels a matter of 'hunting with the hounds while running with the fox'. Göring was not helpful at this stage, and Goebbels was so annoyed with him that he let it be known that Göring was back on his morphine. It was a difficult time for Goebbels, who was trying to control two horses at the same time, trying to dissuade Röhm from dismissing Stennes, but knowing that he was seen by those in Munich as the man of Berlin out of step, so he tried to create a picture of himself as the man on the frontline. It was at this time it appeared that there was an obstructed attack upon Goebbels, but there is the raised question as whether the attempted assassination by a parcel bomb on 13 March 1931 was a connivance by Goebbels himself, to demonstrate to his inhouse critics that they should see him as comrade in danger. It has been suggested that he fabricated the incident and then believed it himself, which offers some possible insights into his corrupt personality. His position was becoming delicate, he was suspected by Stennes and his men as well as the Munich people, and much of this he brought upon himself in the belief that he was untouchable, as he had Hitler in total support. It eventually transpired that it had been Stennes who had organised the raid on Goebbels' office by a rabble, and so he was eventually dismissed by Röhm.

The Reichstag for a variety of reasons during these fraught months suddenly amended its rules and Goebbels suddenly lost his immunity. He was fined for his continuous abuse of Weiss the Deputy Chief of Berlin Police and had to find assistance to pay the various fines. A trial against Stennes for violence brought both Goebbels and Hitler to court on the grounds that the SA violence had stemmed from the top command, which was not unreasonable. There seems little doubt, albeit speculation, that Goebbels' radical approach would have made Hitler uneasy, as he was seeking legitimate means to secure the power he desperately wanted. Goebbels did not help himself because during this time he was having moments of conflict with Göring and Himmler, the latter whom he accused of spying on him. These were the clear signs of power struggles of the ambitious leaders within the Nazi structure, namely Röhm, Göring, Himmler and Goebbels all establishing their own way to be near or at the top.

Having always being of a radical and having an inquisitive inclination, Goebbels turned his attention to another area. This time he remained busy ensuring the film *All Quiet on the Western Front* had to be taken off the market to avoid the unrest he claimed it perpetrated. 'In the end the film was banned on the grounds that it was a threat to German prestige, for Goebbels this was a triumph'... later writing 'the Republic is enraged by our film victory...in the eyes of the public we are the men of strength'.[12] To ruin this film Goebbels had purchased blocks of seats for the SA who released stink-bombs and white mice and sent the centre into chaos, demonstrating the way he used the uniformed thugs, and after five days the film was removed from viewing.[13]

Goebbels pursued his radical aggression, and he was behind the events of the 13 October when the new Nazi deputies arrived in the Reichstag, Jewish shop windows were smashed by Storm Troopers in civilian dress which creating sheer mayhem. Goebbels was accused of organising this after he had organised a walk out by the Nazi representatives in the Reichstag, and it amounted to a forerunner of *Kristallnacht* in November 1938. His influence was growing which suited his ambition, but it also revealed his character, of using anything however immoral to press his way forward.

For a moment there was another coming together of Goebbels with Gregor Strasser, but there was little likelihood this could happen with the brother Otto Strasser. Nor did the agreed peace between Goebbels and Gregor Strasser last very long. Again, Goebbels was uncertain as to where Hitler stood, but he always made the point of agreeing with Hitler's decisions and thinking processes. Hitler himself appeared uncertain, caught between supporting Gregor Strasser or Goebbels as both were valuable to him. The Strasser's daily paper seemed to flourish which irritated Goebbels who always possessed a jealous streak about another person's success. Eventually Hitler made his mind up, and he decided to oppose Strasser by making Goebbels responsible for all propaganda who was thoroughly delighted. He felt even better when Hitler visited Berlin, and the Gau office was extended. The ambitious Goebbels was always thrilled in winning a tussle between the other ambitious leaders.

His Personal Life

There was gossip that Goebbels had seduced one of the maids in the apartments where he lived, and although it was mere hearsay, given the overall look at his life, highly probable. To outline the personal life of someone such as Goebbels at times seems a distraction, but his personal life reveals much about his personality or character. He still tended to idolise his old girlfriend Anka, and it appears that for a brief time, she came back in his life as an unhappy wife and mother. He had a series of mistresses and probably more than can be counted with any reliability. Names such a Tamara, Pille Kölsch, Hannah Schneider, Johanna Polzin, Jutta Lehmann, Erika Chelius, Xenia, and Charlotte Streve are just a few, and there is a distinct impression this was just scratching the surface. Goebbels' problem was that he saw these relationships as love-relationships when they were undoubtedly mere sexual occasions. In the personal side of his diaries, he gives the impression it was all love, and that women fell in love with him. His behaviour and attitudes towards women were simply appalling even in an open society, disclosing a man who was egotistical, taking what he wanted with no care about the pain he created. He was a sex addict which is often overlooked in the various biographies. His love or sex-life was personally disruptive which reflected his machinations in the Party's rivalries.

Magda Quandt

Even though Goebbels was involved with many women he became absorbed with a divorcee called Magda Quandt.* Her maiden name was Maria Magdalena Ritschel born 11 November 1901.This woman had been married to an elderly rich businessman twice her age, and later she was almost to become 'the First Lady of the Third Reich'.[14] It was not a happy marriage given their age difference, and her first husband divorced her having allegedly discovered she was having an affair with a Zionist student called Ernest. At one point there were even rumours that she was going to marry President Hoover's nephew, but despite her self-made promise that she would remain single, Goebbels appeared on the scene.

In 1980 biography of her life was translated into English which outlined in considerable detail her life and her relationship with Goebbels.[15] The author of this life of Magda was the son of Dr Otto Meissner, once famous in his work for Presidents Ebert and von Hindenburg. This status level meant her biographer was brought into 'close proximity with Magda at the time of her marriage to Günther Quandt, and then later during her marriage to Joseph Goebbels. My connection with Ello Quandt, Magda's sister-in-law and best friend, dates from this period'.[16] He even met Hitler at a meeting once, writing 'on one occasion, through the good offices of the Führer's adjutant Schaub, I was fortunate enough to receive the rarely given summons to the Führer's large round table in the winter garden of the Reich Chancellor's palace'.[17]

* When she met her first husband, Magda was 18 and Quandt was 38.

Not surprisingly the biography is full of immense personal detail, and being a somewhat sceptical historian, this writer approached it with care, and while much of it rings highly likely some portions raised doubt. However, the biographer, Hans-Otto Meissner, was around at the time and it made interesting reading about Magda Quandt. He also managed postwar to gain much information from Ello Quandt who was Magda's sister-in-law and one of her closest friends, always ready to rush to her aid or defence.

When Magda meet Günther Quandt he was thought to be worth some 10 million marks. 'By the end of the decade he owned taxed property to the value of 70 million, which at today's values would amount to some D.M. 50,000 million'[18] On 4 January 1921, Magda married Günther Quandt in church. The wedding took place in Godesberg, followed by a small party in the Hotel Godesberger Hof. They honeymooned in Italy, a typical country in those days for the wealthy to take their holidays. Magda and her first husband had a boy called Harald (born 1 November 1921) over whom Magda had total control until he was fourteen, as well as a substantial alimony whilst she remained single.* She also had two stepsons and other family children to care for and was known to be a caring mother. Günther was twice her age, and he was dedicated to his work, and it was not surprising that the marriage became strained. How far she was 'in love' with her middle-aged husband is not known, and when she met a young man called Ernest, at a ball at a friend's house, it developed into a love affair. Günther was able to use this as an excuse for a divorce, though he was not bitter, gave her the oversight of their son and made sure she was well off. The young lover Ernest was happy to marry Magda, but she was not interested in another marriage, and he was only a student living off family financial support, but he was much younger than Magda. He was merely the ideal partner for a romantic affair, she seemed to love him, but she evidently saw his limitations as a husband in terms of economic support.

With evident time on her hands, she had noticed the hustle and bustle of Nazi activities with whom her friends would hardly have expected her to find common ground, but she decided to attend one of the Nazi Party meetings. She was curious and prepared to be bored, 'nevertheless, the

---

* Quandt already had two sons called Helmut and Herbert by a previous marriage.

speaker of the evening drew her fascinated attention. For the first time she now saw Dr Goebbels as, short and puny, he limped down the long gangway through the ranks of the brown-shirted SA men, beneath hundreds of outstretched arms and a forest of banners. As he mounted the platform his physical handicap was clearly evident', but she was struck by his speech and something about him as a person.[19] Magda was known to have no interest in politics, her first husband Günther had no time for the NSDAP (for which one day he would be regarded with suspicion) and it must have been a surprise to those who knew her that having seen Goebbels and the rally she then gave her name to become a member of the NSDAP, and read Hitler's *Mein Kampf*. She even took over the leadership of the NSDAP West End Women's Organisation, but there was a degree of 'envy and mistrust surged against her. The women in this group greeted the sudden if genuine idealism of the new leader of the local Women's Organization with scepticism. To them Magda Ritschel, formerly Quandt, was a mysterious person, a scented lady who was busying herself with politics out of boredom'.[20] It did not take long for Goebbels with his passion for women to spot this attractive figure and found out about who she was, heard of her wealthy ex-husband, and he cunningly organised a meeting and offered her the post of looking after his personal archives.

She told Ernest about Goebbels who was not impressed, and 'he considered that Magda had fallen in with a comedian or charlatan. In any case he thought Goebbels no more than a political ranter of purely passing significance'.[21] This was the end of their relationship which finished with a fierce argument. She and Goebbels were soon showing an attraction for one another, some claiming this often happens when one of the two, man or woman, are in an important position, but it is just possible that Goebbels did have something attractive about him for women, but the truth will never be known and must remain speculative. In the late summer of 1930 Magda's friends heard of her engagement to Dr Joseph Goebbels. 'She took to wearing what was obviously an engagement ring, although no announcements, at that time still customary, were sent out. The betrothal naturally created a sensation in National Socialist circles as well as in Berlin society, and the news of this at first hardly credible event soon spread at lightning speed'.[22]

There followed the usual type of Goebbels' 'ups and downs 'of quarrels, partings, and renewals of love. Goebbels was disturbed to find she had at least one other lover from whom she appeared to have emotional difficulty extricating herself, namely Ernest. Goebbels felt he was in love with Magda, but like many other work fanatics made many references in his diaries that the Party had to come first. Magda had shown an interest in the NSDAP having joined the Party earlier in the year.

Goebbels felt close and comfortable with Hitler, but when introduced Magda it soon became clear that Hitler was attracted to her, causing, according to some observers, a degree of concern. Goebbels was unhappy but his anger was more directed at Magda than Hitler. However, Magda had chosen Goebbels, whom Hitler congratulated as a good friend. It is mainly irrelevant to history but there was an intriguing insight into the Hitler-Goebbels-Magda triangular relationship. The historian Reimann mentions in his early biography of Goebbels that a Major General Dr Otto Wagener kept diaries, which can be found in The Institute for Contemporary History in Munich. In these diaries it appears that Hitler fell for Magda and viewed her as his 'female balance' in his life, but such a female needed to be a married woman. Major General Wagener claims he spoke to Magda about Hitler's wishes, and she promised to think it over and in less than two weeks the marriage was arranged.[23] Reimann then proceeded to suggest that this arrangement might go some way to explain Goebbels' attitude toward his wife. Later, at one stage Magda was certainly critical of Eva Braun, which explains why she was kept from Hitler's public arenas, and the two women only met briefly in the final days of the regime. Whether this was true or not is difficult to ascertain, but there is no question that the Hitler-Goebbels-Magda relationship was unquestionably strange.

There were also domestic issues when Goebbels discovered that Magda's mother was not married at the time of her birth, raising the question as to whether Goebbels should marry a person with this tainted background. Given Goebbels' moral behaviour, it seems ridiculous, but he sought Hitler's advice.

The historian Peter Longerich mentioned the rumour and possibility that the mysterious suicide of Hitler's niece Geli Raubal may have related to Hitler's hopes for Magda. It seems on reflection unlikely, if it were true that Hitler was away when Geli Raubal killed herself with his gun. It is known that they had been constantly quarrelling, and either she saw death as her only escape, or she was murdered when Hitler was safely out of the way. It was also possible she was in love with a young man on Hitler's staff. The opposition had a marvellous time in the press reports about this and Goebbels' wedding, some spreading rumours that Magda had Jewish blood in her background. Goebbels gave her an expensive sports-car, and it has been suggested that the payment for this gift was dubious and could have brought the Party leadership into question. Much of the above paragraph is reliant on the rumours of the day, and this warning must be kept in mind by the reader.

Later Hitler was the best man at the marriage ceremony on 19 December 1931 when Goebbels married Magda (taking her 10-year-old son Harald as his own) and they also had a religious service after the civil formalities. 'The civil ceremony was followed by one in the church, at Magda's wish, Joseph Goebbels being pleased to accede to her whim; Ritter von Epp was the first witness and Adolph Hitler the second. The altar was decorated with the Nazi swastika flag, draped around a crucifix'.[24]

Quandt asked Magda not to turn his property where she lived into some sort of headquarters for the Nazi leadership, but she no longer felt she needed to respond to his views. She now always obeyed Goebbels, who knew how to use his newly acquired accommodation for himself and his beloved Führer. This new upmarket property allowed him to entertain many guests at the same time. The large and exclusive type of apartment soon became the private headquarters of the Party leadership. There it was possible to meet without constraint, to speak without being overheard, unless Goebbels had places bugged.

Outwardly the impression conveyed by the Party leaders was one of almost strict military type efficiency, the Nazi leaders were trying to demonstrate what they demanded of their followers. Goebbels was financially now much better off, and Magda had brought to the marriage this large and well-appointed residence. She had been a voluntary worker for the party, and it was rumoured that she was not the brightest person according to some sources, but others found her clever and intelligent. In his memoirs, Günther Quandt was forced to accept what was happening to his property which he had generously allowed Magda to use. 'In his memoirs he records

that he was arrested on 3 May 1933, shortly after Hitler was made Reich Chancellor, and kept in detention for three months. His arrest was obviously not connected with Goebbels' intimidation over Harald [since by law his son should come to him, but Goebbels ensured this would not happen]. Quandt had no idea why he was imprisoned at that time, neither did he discover why even after his release. 'No charge was made, and no trial took place', but his divorced wife had placed him in a precarious if not dangerous situation.[25] On the other hand, when Goebbels was enraged by rumours about Quandt's views of the Nazi Party he threatened to have him brought before the People's Court (*Volksgericht*) which would have amounted to a death sentence. Magda met her first husband and asked him to be more careful in what he said, and then used her influence on Goebbels, showing herself to have a degree of measured humanity and common sense.

A mutual personal relationship grew between Hitler and the Goebbels family. It was clear to many observers, that like her husband, Magda all but worshipped Hitler and it has been suggested that Hitler always wished that she had been his partner. It is, however, whatever the rumours and speculations, quite clear that she was evidently a total Nazi fanatic. Their new home was on the *Reichskanzlerplatz* later to be renamed the *Adolf Hitler Platz*. Goebbels was by this stage becoming a national figure, seemingly happily married, he was well-off and appeared to be going places, which had long been his personal driving force. As will be explored later his sexual addiction never left him, and when he oversaw the film industry, he never stopped his fascination for sex with women and did do so with beautiful young women who wanted to be film stars.

Nazi Rise to Power

Goebbels became Hitler's major campaign manager in today's terminology. As one historian noted, 'It could be reasonably debated that Hitler might never have gained the position to manoeuvre himself and the party to power without the outstanding ability, tireless energy and the political acumen' of Goebbels.[26] It is well-known that Hitler spent considerable time in Goebbels' flat in the *Reichskanzlerplatz* discussing the various ways of winning. Nevertheless, the tensions and internal conflicts continued, with the SA holding a notorious protest action against the government on the *Kurförstendamm* in September 1931.* Goebbels would have portrayed this event as a natural form of radical protest, but it amounted to serious racial street brutality. The government ignored Goebbels' views, and there were arrests, some twenty-seven, against which Goebbels protested at every possible level.

Goebbels encouraged aggression at all levels while Hitler was playing the 'decent politician' role, and in October 1931, he met Kurt von Schleicher (State Secretary of the Reichswehr Ministry) a close friend of Hindenburg. Goebbels and Hitler spent time together during the various elections and attended a meeting at Harzburg in which Hitler, curiously, after watching the SA march by, walked off the platform as the Stahlhelm followed. He felt apparently that he was not the major leading figure amongst those who had gathered. Hitler appeared happier than Goebbels in uniting with other parties if it provided an opportunity to challenge or bring down the Brüning government. The government had banned uniforms with political badges and were becoming all too aware and understandably deeply concerned about the right-wing pressure groups. Brüning was under immense pressure from many angles, but he somehow held onto Hindenburg's support.

Hindenburg's own election was due, and Hitler was unsure about opposing him, but Goebbels and others ensured Hitler stood against this well-known national figure. Goebbels produced his now traditional powerful and vitriolic speeches, one in the Reichstag, which was so insulting he was ordered to stop at once. Driven by his ambition and self-importance and using his propaganda skills he distributed some 50,000 gramophone records, and a 'speaking film' which portrayed himself as the central figure advocating the main themes of the NSDAP. He worked on the figure of the young leader Hitler as the saviour of the country, the Führer in embryo. Both Goebbels and Hitler travelled everywhere of electoral importance giving many speeches, but this first round of the presidential election was disappointing because Hindenburg won the necessary majority. Goebbels suffered criticism for this failure, but it was decided not to give up. The NSDAP had gained more votes, but Hindenburg won. The government followed this election with various bans on the party, as well as Goebbels' *Der Angriff* while also searching for

* The upmarket social area of the Kurförstendamm was to become a hunting ground for the SA.

the SA hooligans. In early 1932 the NSDAP failed to gain the support of the German population. The SA and the SS were banned yet again, but they circumnavigated the problem by a change of dress, and their meetings were held as sports clubs type events. It was dawning on the NSDAP that they could not gain power by SA marches or even by elections. They realised that they needed to work with other groups, but there were obvious limitations with this policy which Goebbels was always quick to announce, but he was finding it embarrassing that their voting results were always low in Berlin.

Various plots and ploys appeared, the major one being a temporary alliance with the Centre Party (but excluding Brüning) and having a willing Kurt von Schleicher on side thanks to Goebbels' influence. In May one Reichstag meeting fell apart when some NSDAP thugs beat up a news reporter, and the police were brought in led by the policeman Weiss, Goebbels' frequent target whom he was always attacking. Heinrich Brüning, with Schleicher working against him, and with Franz von Papen as his proposed candidate, was becoming more isolated. This caused a good deal of concern and excitement with both Goebbels and Hitler who perceived that in general terms they were coming close to their goal of power. For a moment Brüning almost appeared to have a winning hand in so far that he proclaimed that the victorious powers had agreed to end German reparations and the right for rearmament.[27] He went one step too far, proposing the State would purchase some of the large but poor East Prussian estates for agrarian purposes. This sounded like common sense for some, but he fell out of favour with Hindenburg and many other influential figures who owned such estates. Eventually Brüning reached such a point of enmity that he had little choice but to resign. This debate gave the NSDAP the timely opportunity to appeal to patriotism and the fight against communism which appealed to anyone who had anything to lose. It could be claimed that 'with Brüning's fall the die had been cast in favour of a dictatorship'.[28] Within twelve months the Nazi Party fought five elections, there were two ballots for the Presidency in the March and April of 1932. On the 23 April, in the State elections the Nazi Party became the major party of power within the Prussian Diet. They were not so strong elsewhere, especially in Bavaria and Hamburg. Hitler and Goebbels were convinced of one thing, namely the struggle for power had to be brought to a head while they were in the ascendancy. It was now more than apparent that Goebbels was the main support for Hitler in political elections, with his oratory, his articles, propaganda, but his continuing use of the SA which would soon cause some problems. It was already emerging that the SA 'objected to Hitler's course of action, which aimed at coming to power by legal means; they saw in this a betrayal of the revolution'.[29] For Goebbels who had used them to full effect in their demonstrations, he believed that they were part of his success.

The next election was called when von Papen, now Chancellor, was proving to be weak and his own Centre Party had stopped supporting him, meaning he had to rely on the NSDAP. There were many discussions on how they could achieve success, and Hitler and Goebbels travelled the country making speeches. It was Goebbels who convinced Hitler of the value of flying around the country in the developing tradition of 'whistle-stop' election campaigns. The new energetic leader Hitler showing the population he had the willpower and energy to win, and that he could offer a more inspiring leadership than the weaker traditional parties. Even Göring and Goebbels set aside their usual personal aggravations with one another to oppose Gregor Strasser who appeared to be growing stronger. It was Strasser who gave the first radio political broadcast to Goebbels' consternation, the problem being that Hitler refused to have his speeches checked. Not long afterwards on 10 July Goebbels gave his first radio broadcast, finding the silent studio a difficulty as like Hitler he loved the cheering crowd, even if they had been instructed to cheer, but Hitler found it an impossible task, as they were both accustomed to the rapturous applause.[30] Later Goebbels soon adapted and he was to make full use of radio propaganda, a tool never properly utilised by the opponents of the NSDAP.

In the 31 July General Election for the Reichstag, the NSDAP won 37.4 per cent of the vote (in Berlin only 28.7 per cent) which gave them a governing majority making them the largest party. Göring was made the Speaker, but the Social Democrats still held the general sway in matters of voting. The Party leaders, including Goebbels, knew that they were beginning to achieve their goal. Hitler always promised Goebbels more promotion as he had long realised that Goebbels thirsted to be closely associated with power, as well as his need for Hitler to like him. It was clear Goebbels hoped to have a major governmental ministry in which he would oversee Germany's education at every conceivable level. Hitler and his henchmen now started to think of Hitler as Chancellor and the means and ways of making this a reality. Hitler was offered the possibility of being Vice-Chancellor, but both he and Goebbels thought this was almost insulting.

All too typically the SA had murdered some of the opposition members in Upper Silesia in some notorious violence, and five of their members were sentenced to death. This not only clearly indicated the vicious violence of these campaigns but exposed the attitudes of the NSDAP leadership, including Hitler and Goebbels, who supported these criminal perpetrators, with Goebbels blaming the incident on the Jews. At the electoral level Strasser favoured a coalition with the Centre Party with the idea of Hitler being made President, and in the following weeks all kinds of devious underhand machinations and bargains took place. Hitler, Goebbels, Göring and Röhm met to discuss plans for coalitions which would allow them to topple the President. It was during this stage of events that Goebbels planned to bring down his old friend Gregor Strasser. In September, there was a vote of no confidence in von Papen in the Reichstag, and it appeared that the whole house was against him.* The Reichstag was dissolved, and a new election was called for on 6 November. Goebbels became busy on the electioneering campaign, and using his propaganda expertise he grasped all the control of all films and radio handed over to him by Strasser. During this election the Nazi Party lost votes, but they still managed to remain the largest single party in the Reich government. Their voting numbers slipped to 33.1 per cent and Goebbels saw this as a poor result, blaming it on their close association with the Centre Party.

During this year there were signs of economic recovery with the number of unemployed falling which was not a good sign for the NSDAP. It is often seen as a feature of democratic life that financial stability and employment makes any government in power reasonably stable and able to survive. If, on the other hand, a financial crisis occurs and unemployment rises the discontented will vote for a change, usually to one of the extreme wings anticipating a beneficial radical change. Gaining the popular vote was critical,

* A surprise vote because it was put forward by Ernst Torgler a communist member which did not prevent the National Socialists voting with their main enemy.

and it was up to Goebbels to manipulate this popular vote towards Hitler. He had become a sound if not natural political agitator and was within an environment and a time which suited his peculiar traits and personality.

Von Papen resigned as Chancellor in November and there followed the well-known political contest between Hitler and Kurt von Schleicher. The latter was Chancellor for a very brief period, and on 30 January 1933 Hitler was appointed Chancellor. Schleicher had offered Hitler the opportunity of becoming Vice-Chancellor, but he had turned it down, and then Strasser was asked. He also turned it down but said 'he would put up his name on the list in a future new election.'[31] The brief von Schleicher ascendancy was blamed on Strasser by Goebbels, and this has often been accepted as quite possible. However, there is no safe evidence to support this claim, and Goebbels' diaries and other works indicate that on this issue there was some doctoring on what happened.[32] It was known as the 'palace revolution', but Strasser resigned from all the Party positions he had held. Strasser had been second in the Party to Hitler, and if he had been more aggressive and determined he may have won, but he had no control over Goebbels. Otto Strasser sometimes described as the left wing of the Party, had been expelled by Goebbels on Hitler's orders in June 1930, and Gregor had taken his place. With him off the stage many still regarded Goebbels as that left wing, but Goebbels had long reached the point that whatever Hitler wanted he always agreed. For some observers at the time it may have appeared that Strasser had been treated unjustly. According to the early biographer Helmut Heiber, Strasser was supposed to have said to some friends that Goebbels was 'the devil incarnate'.[33] Reimann even wrote that 'Gregor Strasser might have given German history a different turn'.[34] It is one of the many mysteries of that time, but Strasser was to be killed in the Night of the Long Knives by a Party he had helped establish.*

Goebbels was of course delighted by Strasser's departure but during this time was concerned about Magda's health, as she had been hospitalised being in a state of ill-health. He visited her but as he had once promised, he always put his work first. Hitler visited her as well, sometimes alone.

* Not until a trial in Munich in 1957 were witnesses coming to light about the Night of the Long Knives. See Shirer, William L., *The Rise and Fall of the Third Reich* (London: Mandarin, 1960), p.222 footnote.

Goebbels at this Juncture

Goebbels was directly involved in the top discussions of the Party, and he was regularly informed of changes and information because he was needed for the news-broadcasting or the necessary propaganda material. When Hitler was in this final ascendancy to power Goebbels, the one-time left-wing leaning radical, began fully to accept all of Hitler's policies and statements. It was during these months that 'he had finally realised that his ostentatious posturing as a radical was a hinderance both to the Party and to his own career'.[35] He now realised that he was totally dependent on Hitler, and so from this point onwards was the time that he propagated the 'Führer cult' in Nazi propaganda, which was a dangerous but enticing myth for many.

Many, especially some major military figures, were opposed to Hitler, but the political machinations of the Nazi Party were becoming popular and persuasive. It is generally believed the Nazi success was often because of Göring's style of projecting himself, and Goebbels' clever propaganda. This was a critical period for the Nazi rise to power, and the support of some industrialists and money brokers helped. These people were manipulated by Hitler who was now even the more dominant figure, and who knew he needed their financial support. For many of these wealthy and sometimes important backers it was a gross miscalculation, as they were badly mistaken in their belief that their money and influence would always control Hitler.

The historical picture is not always clear and often distinctly dark and mysterious. Hitler's private armies of the SA and SS had their own internal problems with infighting, and in April there had been many attempts to outlaw these quasi-military organisations. It was a complex web for Goebbels caught between wanting to be seen alongside Hitler, but he also needed the SA thuggery for his aggressive approach. The bans were lifted only for political reasons, perhaps to placate by trying to bring the National Socialists more onto the conventional side of the then German life. Many politicians of the day, including von Papen were out of their depth with a man like Hitler who was using and abusing the democratic system to assume total power. The party headquarters have often been seen as in the Kaiserhof Hotel, but the tactics and overall strategy took place in Goebbels' new apartment. It was Goebbels who organised the propaganda, the political rallies, and with his oratory skills travelled far and wide to bring the Party message home to those voters who remained uncertain, and according to his diary it was Goebbels who proposed that Hitler should run for President.[36]

It was Goebbels who arranged the major meetings at the Sportpalast, referring to this arena as the 'platform for the people', and where both he and Hitler raised the political temperature and the hopes of those who attended. There is no question that Goebbels adored Hitler, regarding himself as his messiah's forerunner. Goebbels was not looking towards a heavenly Jerusalem but for personal power alongside Hitler. In his diaries he constantly flattered himself with self-adulation, noting the response of the crowds to his political speeches and his friendship with Hitler, amounting to almost childlike self-adoration. According to his diaries Goebbels considered himself Hitler's top man, though he allowed Göring some small praise 'as being useful'. One egotist giving another a little room. As is frequently stated Goebbels had become the master for Nazi propaganda and there is no question that he was a major factor in bringing them to power.

It is understood that all countries use propaganda to one level or another, most especially in war, and sometimes it is used to deceive and sometimes, as with the British D-Notice system news is simply blanked out not just for military but often for political reasons.* Like many other Nazi and many politicians Goebbels had little sense of morality in the way he manipulated propaganda. To him it was 'a political art'.[37] For him propaganda was about winning even it meant producing bold lies, demonstrating his Machiavellian personality. This type of propaganda makes it almost a dirty word because it distorts the truth, telling one side of the story to influence the masses in the required direction, which never concerned Goebbels, who always regarded this as an intellectual art form.

As early as 1932 Goebbels was working out means and ploys to take control of every form of the media, the press, the radio and films, as he wanted full public attention, both for the cause and for his ego. When the Nazis came to power Goebbels had extensive access to the radio, and he soon became an expert in broadcasting. During these elections and the in-

---

* The usual method was often referred to as a *D Notice* established in 1912 and revised in 1993 as the *DA*, the Defence Advisory Notice, namely official amnesia.

party battles of 1930–33 he simply told lies to bring Hitler to power, making promises that would rarely be kept. In some ways he was ahead of his time and some of his methods have since been adopted. He had challenged Brüning the Chancellor to a debate on stage, and when he refused, he had his helpers unpack suitcases supposedly containing Brüning's speeches. He then attacked them point by point, and in doing this he was entertaining, devious, and clever, as he only used the points he needed. It was clever and even an entertaining ploy as it held people's attention.

Goebbels was always into political agitation, moving to the election areas with Storm Troopers and causing disruption, often bloodshed, ensuring the Nazi message was heard. His driving ambition meant he worked hard, travelling away from Berlin when his wife was in hospital. He saw the value of ceremony at the Nuremberg rallies, and he always ensured that before he arrived on the speaker's platform there were enough uniforms and drums to impress the crowd. The Nuremberg rallies became the quintessential symbol of the Nazi Party, as 'here there was no reflection, no discussion. Only the attentive listening, screaming applause, marching, singing, saluting, and standing to attention. The person was drowned in the mass and individuality disappeared', it was once described as cerebral concussion.[38] As mentioned above he saw and understood the value of the joy of spectators soaking in the scene and being influenced through their emotions.

He revelled in funerals of any Nazis who had been killed in the street brawls. The ceremony and pageantry preceded and continued throughout the service by the graveside, and his speeches were always emotional and politically based. The Horst Wessel song mentioned above was always used, as Goebbels always made the most of Nazi deaths, and he all but canonised them as martyrs in Hitler's cause.

He was always seeking conflict with the communists who could be found in most working-class areas. He knew they were a powerful driving force, and from his point of view had to be confronted. He always tried to arrange meetings in communist strongholds and relish the inevitable street brawls. Goebbels was one of the chief instigators in having the communists ejected from their seats from the Prussian Diet, but he was not always successful, and when he visited his old hometown of Rheydt he had to leave with speed when he was stoned by angry residents. Goebbels was shrewd and managed to convince the more moderate parties that the attack on communism was justified because otherwise the sheer number of German communists would take control of Germany, which seemed to many that the alternative Nazi Party was the best choice. Goebbels agreed with Hitler that speeches were more effective than written articles, and this was especially true of the many who were more ready to hear than could be bothered to read. This was a true reflection of human behaviour and remains a continuing problem with most democratic elections and referenda to this day. Goebbels' political ranting from his speaking stand managed to work up popular feeling against the communists, the government, the Social Democrats and the Jews, mainly consisting of whipping up hatred. He was effective by many accounts, and in his diaries, as usual, he applauded himself consistently.

During this whistle-stop tours to elections in communist areas he seemed to ignore his wife Magda, who was still detained in hospital. In September 1932, Magda gave birth to their daughter Helga. Goebbels was busy, but Hitler continued to visit Magda when she was confined in her hospital bed. Goebbels was obsessed with success and was devoted to Hitler in a way which is best described as fanatical devotion. However, it has been noted that 'his loyalty to Hitler was without doubt linked sub-consciously to the same instinct to gain power and glory for himself'.[39] There is little doubt that Goebbels was always self-seeking. His extreme vehemence and his aggressive tactics paid dividends when Hitler became Chancellor on the 30 January 1933. There were only three Nazi representatives in Hitler's Cabinet, but now he was in power he was close to total power which he lusted for, so this was not seen as important. Goebbels saw himself, possibly with justification, as being responsible for this successful outcome. In many ways it could be argued that Hitler was in the dying days of the Weimar Republic projecting himself as an uncluttered person playing by the rules and only seeking election by the people. As the following years would clearly show he was in fact deeply racist, bigoted, had his own set of morals, and acted in a criminal fashion wherever he felt it was needed. During the end days of the Weimar Republic, it could be that he saw Goebbels as his alter-ego, more able to present the venom and hatred he believed was necessary, while he out of necessity had to play the role of a normal well controlled politician.

Chapter Four

Nazi Rise to Power

Coming to Power

The following weeks after Hitler assumed the position of Chancellor it soon became a matter of demolishing all the principles and values of the democratic system, so the authoritarian reign of Hitler could be established under his autocratic rule. The historian Reimann rightly pointed out that first and foremost Hitler had arrived in power because of Goebbels' electioneering techniques. This was especially true in a small place called Lippe which had turned towards the NSDAP and consequently influenced other areas by its sheer success. Goebbels behaved like many politicians promising every sector of society that they were the ones who mattered, and their problems would be resolved with the NSDAP in power. This rise to power was also assisted by von Papen's ambitions, the industrialists who backed Hitler, and Hindenburg's encroaching old age and senility.[1] All these factors and many others were relevant, but there is no question that the role played by Goebbels was highly significant.

Reichstag Fire and its Ramifications

To achieve this desired goal of total authority some dramatic national disaster was needed which was soon provided by the well-known Reichstag fire on the 27 February 1933. It provided the necessary opportunity to outlaw all the communists who were immediately blamed for the fire. This was essential for the NSDAP as the communists remained popular as a desired and possible alternative. The responsibility for the fire was eventually focused on a young Dutch communist called Marinus van der Lubbe who had learning difficulties, and there were also rumours, but they were only rumours that he may have been Jewish.

This was precisely what the Nazis needed, but the true origins of the fire have long been debated, and it suited the purpose of the Nazi leadership, which many at the time and to this day accepted as possible, namely the Nazi helmsmen were the organising hand behind the disaster. One biographer noting 'there can be no doubt at all that Goebbels himself was implicated with Göring'.[2] There is no reliable proof one way or the other, and although Goebbels cannot be trusted, he was too cunning to be caught up in this fracas of investigation. The historian Padfield suggested the Reichstag fire had been started by an SS team from Munich.[3] It has been submitted that there was an underground passageway from Göring's palace to the Reichstag, and the same writer who was a Nazi diplomat at the time suggested that 'no Berliners believed that communists started the fire', but by this stage it would have been too risky to raise this question of doubt.[4]

According to his diaries, Goebbels was having a meal at his apartment with Hitler when the news broke, and other sources suggest various other combinations trying to explain where the other likely candidates for the fire were. When the news broke of the fire, they went immediately to the scene to find Göring already there. There is possibly some historical sense that one or more of these accounts is correct, and that the SA in Berlin led by Karl Ernst had been behind this incident, but much of it will remain speculation because of the lack of actual evidence. One interesting insight was in *Der Angriff* in which Goebbels produced an article the next day which in the opinion of one historian 'was altogether too well-rehearsed to have been written in the heat of the moment'.[5] During the Nuremberg trial Hans Gisevius claimed the fire had been Goebbels' idea, but most of the likely candidate were dead at this stage, and it was therefore safe and all too easy to blame them. Had he come up with the idea there would undoubtedly have been some hint of this in his diaries. Nobody at the time suggested it was Goebbels. It was for the NSDAP and Hitler an outstanding piece of good fortune, so lucky in fact it has fuelled with some credibility the belief that somewhere behind this incident was Nazi manipulation, but whether Hitler may or may not have known will remain elusive. The truth was never discovered at the time and will undoubtedly remain a mystery, but common historical sense indicates some Nazi involvement. It was from their point of view just too good to be true, 'but even now, the Reichstag fire is among the clouded chapters of that period'.[6]

It was Goebbels who helped suggest and outline the best possible propaganda after the fire and started a full media effort to blame the communists, and posing the Nazi Party as being a stabilising force for the country, pointing out that it was all a larger plot by the communists, of which, he warned, more would occur to try and undermine the country. This was a clever attempt to give public warning that having communist sympathies could be personally dangerous. It provided just the right excuse the Party needed to wipe out major elements of the opposition especially the home communists, the KPD (*Kommunistische Partei Deutschland*).* It helped boost the next election for the NSDAP who used the Reichstag fire to create a sense of fear which Goebbels had started in his propaganda.

The communists were caught entirely by surprise by the Reichstag fire. They soon became a spent force as any opposition against the Nazi Party was extremely dangerous. The Reichstag fire had ensured that Hitler was able to eliminate his political enemies. Hindenburg had agreed to the infamous emergency decree demanded by the NSDAP, and this law never left the statute books.

Later in the year after the so-called trial of the young Dutch communist Marinus van der Lubbe, who was unquestionably innocent, Hitler held a plebiscite (a referendum), which were to become a common feature, to endorse all that the government was doing and to enhance his own reputation as the Führer. It was rigged with the polling booths closely monitored by Nazi supporters in and out of uniform. To have voted against would have been dangerous. At the end of the exercise, it was claimed that some 91.3 per cent of the electorate had voted in support. The year before that vote for Nazi support had been a mere 33.6 per cent and nobody in their right minds, including Goebbels would have believed in the validity of this popular raincheck of public opinion.

To ensure the continued success of the plebiscite the following Christmas a major party was held in Berlin and SA men offered gifts to over 1,000

* The KPD was a major political party between 1918 and 1933 which re-emerged postwar and was banned in 1956. During the 1920s they were called the Spartacists forming part of the Spartacus League.

children. It was a cleverly devised public relations scheme and was undoubtedly produced to block questions over the recent 91 per cent vote. Goebbels also managed to convince Hitler to pardon a few hundred communists who were released from prison.[7] Goebbels managed a false touch of humanity, which along with the Christmas gifts was a clever ruse to convince the public that the Nazis were really 'good chaps' when all was said and done.

On the 14 March, a few weeks later he was appointed as Minister for Propaganda and Public Enlightenment. According to Dr Wagener (mentioned earlier regarding Magda Goebbels), Hitler had made a promise as early as 1932 that this appointment would happen.[8] There is little doubt that Goebbels would have preferred more power, although he was to remain Gauleiter for Berlin to the day he died. Goebbels felt important enough to appoint a deputy Gauleiter, a man called Artur Görlitzer, which gave him more time to involve himself in what he described as the Cold Revolution, namely his way of proscribing other political institutions which might be seen as a threat to Hitler's rising power. Goebbels returned to his hometown of Rheydt which a few years before had been amalgamated with Mönchengladback against its wishes. He was now able to reverse this decision and was delighted in his own popularity, as this time there was no stone-throwing which would have been a further boost for his ego.

Goebbels also cleverly mimicked the Church's liturgical calendar and drew up a similar guidance for the NSDAP. The Nazi liturgical year started with 30 January the day Hitler assumed power. On 21 February, the day of the foundation of the Party, and 1 May which had once been the worker's day became the Day of the People's Unity. In June, he started a mid-summer festival, in September the Nuremberg rally, in October the Harvest thanksgiving, the famer's equivalent of 1 May, 9 November was Remembrance Day. It was all based on 'the national socialist year-cycle of feats as Goebbels sought to anchor the National Socialist regime more and more firmly in the people's consciousness'.[9]

Goebbels remained vociferous against the surviving communist elements, and using his usual cunning took over 1 May, the usual day for communist celebrations, by personally organising a special day when workers and delegates on this newly named public holiday could celebrate the work of the new Reich. They held a major rally in which his own stepson presented flowers to President Hindenburg as he sat alongside Hitler. There were rallies, speeches, the usual banner and drums and the Horst Wessel song. However, as a warning to the more perceptive two days later the Trade Unions were closed, and the new German Labour Front under the infamous Robert Ley was brought into existence. Some of the well-known trade union leaders found themselves under arrest, no doubt wishing they had not been so well-known as it marked them out for persecution. During the elections the NSDAP had made many promises, and this aspect seemed to indicate a complete change of mind and policy, warning of the NSDAP's ability to tell lies. Goebbels also inaugurated two other national holidays, one on 21 March for the Day of the German Uprising and the last Sunday in September as the Day of National Honour.

An important occasion was made for the re-opening of the Reichstag at Potsdam on 21 March 1933. Potsdam was deeply associated with the monarchy and the traditional military. Goebbels and Hitler avoided the preceding church service by making a dramatic visit to some SA graves. Hitler appeared in conservative dress and top hat; he shook Hindenburg's hand and bowed perhaps a little too deeply. Hindenburg himself was dressed in the uniform of a Field Marshal from the time of the Kaiser. As soon as the necessary pomp and ceremony had finished the Cold Revolution continued with the passing of further emergency legislation which mainly dealt with punishing the slightest opposition.

Goebbels always regarded himself as a radical, and a man of the people so he started, according to him, the Relief Drive or a war against hunger and cold. This was his sense of the radical socialist, an attitude he maintained for some time, but duly changed as he became more dependent on Hitler and was obliged to adapt to his master's thinking. The plan for winter relief was put into force in September 1933 just after the Party Conference, with Goebbels as the nominal head. It was run by the National Socialists People's Welfare organisation, but it pleased Goebbels to be seen as a man of the people. Many times, he would do his best through his various schemes and personal visits to try and present himself as a person who should be appreciated and liked. It has also been proposed that 'the aim was to portray the national community in action, displacing Marxism' and putting the churches in their place.[10] There is a story that it was Goebbels who came up with the idea of 'one-dish-meal Sunday' because he had eaten too much at a banquet and was ill, but it was probably just a humorous story.[11]

On the anniversary of seizing power, the Reichstag passed the Act for the Reconstruction of the Reich, which essentially abolished the authority and any sovereignty within the federal states. It was an effort to centralise national power in the Führer giving him total control over the whole country without any local dissent. As this stranglehold over the edifice of the German constitution continued, Goebbels used his skills at providing the Third Reich with the appropriate image. This move seemed to indicate that even in 1934 the NSDAP had yet to gain a full grasp on the heart and mind of everyone, which Goebbels was busy trying to achieve. There were still occasional and cautious criticisms in some newspapers such as the well-known *Frankfurter Zeitung*, which demanded some considerable courage by the editors. In April 1934, an article in the Sunday newspaper *Grüne Post* led to the paper being banned for three months and the editor, an Ehm Welk found himself in a concentration camp, he was obviously a courageous man as there had been plenty of warnings. Goebbels scanned the newspapers whether local, national or political, and when he could, he automatically blamed the Jews, but he also started a campaign against all 'moaners and grumblers', to ensure there was serious opposition or even different opinions.

Goebbels Starts to Dominate

As Hitler rose to total power Goebbels had been elevated to the position of Minister for Propaganda and Public Enlightenment spreading his influence across the entire landscape. The times had changed for Goebbels because the Party was now in power and he could not, as was his habit, attack the government and the State anymore.[12] However, the country was not yet as fully totalitarian as he wished, and this gave him the first intentions for his propaganda. At this stage he was only 33 years of age 'the youngest Minister in the world, as he liked to remind himself and others'.[13] He was to construct his own propaganda so that for many people his name and the word propaganda are often linked. For him propaganda had nothing to do with morals, or telling the truth, but was his form of art or expression to bring success. 'The little man from Rheydt was to see to it that during the brown 'thousand years' the people were not to 'go their own way', were no longer merely to be controlled but were to be encompassed'.[14]

He tried to dominate German life at every level but with little success abroad, as overseas observers who knew about his efforts were becoming quite cynical about him. His new headquarters had once been a royal residence in the Wilhelmstrasse, which against the advice of architects and planners, he tore it apart to give the building a sense of modernity and efficiency. This building, like most public buildings in Germany, was covered with swastika flags and banners announcing the new era. Goebbels ran his growing ministry with his own form of efficiency, using charm but often fear to make sure he was obeyed in everything he wrote or said. Most people found he could be bitingly cynical, unpleasant or charming, and was able to turn on or off these personal features like a light-switch. As mentioned earlier one of his stranger characteristics was his insistence that only he in his huge organisation (probably around 1,000 personnel) was allowed to use green ink. It was a colour much feared by those who worked under him and quietly became something of a joke. The biographer Heiber made the interesting observation that it was the tradition of the Prussian and Reich administrative offices that green ink 'was the sacrosanct privilege of a minister'.[15] It also happened to be a habit used by the head of the Secret Intelligence Services (SIS) in Britain.

Goebbels' Increase of Power Through Propaganda

In the early part of this period of their ascendancy towards total power, the Nazis ensured that at any level of government employment they made their own appointments at every level, and the current holders of the post were often obliged to leave if they were not sound Party members. This was all consistent with Goebbels' Cold Revolution, and he saw this as part of his task. He always ensured that the public were either unaware of such changes or accepted them as necessary progress for the new Germany. His increase in personal powers meant he was able to suppress nearly all the communist and Social Democratic newspapers, meaning that any form of opposition had no public voice. By the end of spring 1933, most papers were Nazi sponsored or inspired, and being critical of the new government was soon proving dangerous, either at a financial or personal level. Hitler had demanded what was the well-known Enabling Bill on 20 March 1933 which increased his powers to that of a dictatorship. The newspapers which may have raised this as a problem had virtually disappeared or were in the process of being closed. The speeches and the Nazi press promulgated the policy of *Gleichschaltung*, a German expression basically meaning synchronisation or 'bringing into line' meant that everyone had to share the same mind-set as the Nazi regime. It was Goebbels' intention to be in control, and he worked at this policy throughout his life as he was intending to control the public mind.

He was especially interested in what he termed cultural politics. He instituted a prize giving system whereby pro-Nazis were given all the prizes followed by the drumming of the propaganda machine. In grasping as much power as he could he often fell out with other major party members, not least Göring and Ley as well as Rosenberg. This was especially true when Rosenberg was granted supervision of the intellectual and ideological training and education of the National Socialist Movement. Goebbels' ambitious pursuit for power with the consequent alienation from most of his equally ambitious contemporaries was a constant issue for most of his life. Such was Goebbels' nature there were few of his colleagues he trusted, and the feeling was mutual. When he had to work with them and appeared convivial it was usually because this followed Hitler's wishes or directives. Rosenberg as head of ideology started his own campaign against Goebbels, writing letters of criticism to him, trying to undermine him, and concentrating on some of the musicians that Goebbels had nourished, mainly because they were suspected of being Jewish or having Jewish connections, or that their work was ideologically unstable. Rosenberg even criticised Goebbels' newspaper articles as being out of place in the new scheme. For his part Goebbels always felt 'Rosenberg's ideology factory to be an intruder in his own domain'.[16] In June 1935, Rosenberg had used a conference to launch an attack on the Propaganda Minister. As the years passed during the 1930s, Goebbels' life remained a matter of increasing his influence and responding to challenges set by Hitler. He was, for example, keen on attacking the churches and ridiculing them in the public eye and using considerable energy in resisting Rosenberg's efforts to take over his own command area, namely all things cultural and the mind of the people. The attacks on the Jewish element remained consistent, but they were restricted or moderated when external factors such as the Olympics or international relations demanded a cooling off period for the sake of international respectability.

During 1937, there were some major modifications at all levels of the Party, and this was reflected in Goebbels making considerable changes in his own ministry, mainly to reflect his own importance within the structure of the regime. According to many sources he was an unpleasant employer, dominating, interfering, and he could never be wrong, and often his cynical criticism worried or crushed those who worked with him. It was known that he would suddenly send employees off to manual labour or sack them, creating a sense of fear. He was often in discussion with Hitler over proposed changes in the Party, undoubtedly hoping for greater power himself. He objected to Ribbentrop's change of role to Foreign Secretary, but he also had to suffer the appointment in his own ministry of Hermann Esser as head of a new tourist department. His diary entries paint a picture of the man in charge, but this was not always the reality, and undoubtedly a source for his personal frustrations. The overall scheme of his propaganda fell under many headings which will now be explored in the following chapter.

Chapter Five

Methods of Propaganda

Propaganda

In any British election, foreign policy is rarely up for debate and discussion, and any political party propaganda, unless there are promises of better pay and living conditions, rarely succeeds in catching the public's attention. There must be matters of very serious concern for a country's public to be fully attentive because elections tend to revolve around the hopes for a better economic future of the voters, before any other propaganda finds a significant role. Hitler's major themes were the unfair treatment of Germany by the Treaty of Versailles, the fear of Bolshevism and the belief there was a worldwide conspiracy by the Jews. This would have attracted many traditionalists, but the factory worker, the bulk of the working class only wanted a better future in terms of living conditions. To accommodate this issue, it was about 1920 that it was decided to appeal to the masses, by the Party preparing a principal known as *Gemeinnntz geht vor Eigennutz*, the 'Common good before the good of the individual' with a leader to take the German community forward. This was meant to sound more attractive than the various Weimar government policies of fighting inflation in some distant world of economics. The care of the *Volk* was made a major and attractive theme, based on the community, and Hitler promised to unite the social classes under this policy which sounded attractive to the masses as an electoral policy. It was matter of manipulating the feelings and opinions of many in the election debates as still happens today, and Goebbels grasped the essential need to convince everyone that the NSDAP led by Hitler was the answer they were seeking, appealing to the people wanting a better economic future and to the traditionalists who wanted the restoration of their concept of German greatness. He grasped the essentials of propaganda which seeks to convince people that there is one way forward to a better future, postulating a people's government which follows their will. Goebbels had grasped that some will read the written word and examine it with care, but the vast majority were more taken in by what they could see, thus the importance of parades and rallies, and what they hear, thereby for him the importance of speeches and radio. What was essential to Goebbels' way of thinking was to take control of the public corporate mind, gaining a consensus of feeling in support of the regime, and later using coercion, offerings which were first welcomed, then given no choice but accept them. There was not a sector of society which Goebbels' propaganda machinery did not try to influence, from children to workers and housewives, to the middle-classes and upwards. The Nazi Germans later also extended their propaganda to occupied Europe, offering both reason for their actions, hope, but naturally stressing obedience and emphasising the sense of coercion. The whole drive for complete propaganda was started by Hitler and taken over by Goebbels who cleverly used his intelligence and intellect to turn it into its own form of triumphant success for the rise of the regime, and even during the end days encouraging Germans to fight to the last man and to the doors of Hitler's bunker.

However, it must be recalled that propaganda was not just limited to Germany, but it was used in all countries in one form or another, especially during major conflicts such as war, some more basic or simple than others. Sometimes it was and still is utilised to boost a nation's morale, especially in defence, at other times to denigrate the enemy to inspire hatred to encourage beating the enemy. In Britain Churchill's speeches inspired the population to be courageous, and when the tide turned against Germany their form of propaganda was doing the same thing. Different messages of hope, resistance, community solidarity, trusting the political and military authorities were issued as and when required. All such propaganda on a worldwide basis was used, doing as Goebbels had done, seeking the corporate emotional strands of the people, deploying any necessary psychology, and boosting moral in defence and even in attack. Goebbels' major success was turning Hitler into the nation's ideal leader, but when their warrior priest faltered in success, his next step, which was more coercive, was to rush to his support.

During the 1930s, Hitler appeared to achieve some promises, and even with the onset of war which disturbed many Germans, he appeared at first to succeed without too much bloodshed. For all the major events taking place in Germany there was a desperate need for a perceived consensus, not least because the nation had to be mobilised. This came to fruition in their many plebiscites which was democratic on the service but now known to have been fiction, as they were strictly monitored and controlled. The desired consensus had to include every class structure and all forms of intellect as possible to give that essential sense of solidarity. It was no surprise that some sectors proved more difficult than others, many in the working classes were either inclined towards communism or just left alone to survive with their families, and Church committed Christians need coercion more than encouraging propaganda. It could be claimed that even Goebbels brilliant propaganda machine showed signs of failure at times. No amount of propaganda could change all sectors, as the British discovered when dealing with sincere conscientious objectors. When Goebbels' attack on the Jews started many people accepted this because there was already an ingrained form of anti-Semitism which had spread widely across Europe, even though many so-called Aryan Germans relied on Jews for business reasons, as was felt after *Kristallnacht*. Nevertheless, Goebbels found this attack could be more vociferous and open, but he trod with more care in matters involving the Roman Catholic Church. Regarding the Church, Goebbels could not condemn them out of hand as he did the Jews, but he simply tried to undercut them, as he was aware that many Germans, including those in the military were Church followers. When the war started to turn against the Nazi regime propaganda became more difficult to manipulate, though by this time the word 'coercion' had become more active. Goebbels, who controlled German radio made sure it was broadcast in the factories and public streets, blaring out across the café and restaurants, but for any member of the public to listen to a foreign broadcast could end with a death sentence. When wonder weapons were mentioned to inspire a sense of hope it was met with hope, but others were becoming more sceptical by the day, their views becoming more widespread as the bombing of cities increased despite Göring's promises that no enemy aircraft would fly over Germany. There is no doubt that many of the military commanders were critical about the propaganda, and when Goebbels had to comment on Hess' departure political eyebrows were raised. His early efforts had been sound in terms of their overall effectiveness, but it proved more difficult as the war progressed. As the Nazi cause was becoming lost, so the propaganda was less effective. There is no question that Goebbels was clever with his manipulation of the public with his propaganda and because he lived in an extreme autocratic country under Hitler, he was able to use every means available to fulfil his tasks, which shall now be briefly explored here starting with the value of the radio.

Radio

Goebbels realised the importance of radio and began his interest in how to use it on behalf of the Party. 'Radio remained a highly convenient medium for bringing the regime's message home to large numbers of housewives and families, and it was used especially to publicise major campaigns and projects launched to promote autarky, for example 'the campaign against waste' (*Kampf den Verderb*). In November 1937, the intensification of waste-paper collection, with exhortation to save paper on packaging, was introduced by a special appeal from an Else Vorwerck on radio'.[1] Goebbels had long accepted the view that for the Nazis the spoken word carried more weight than the written. In this era the radio was as a central to people's lives as television is today, with whole families sitting around the radio listening to the various programmes. There had been a time when Goebbels had derided radio-listening as a means of keeping people from work, but he was now understanding its potential as a propaganda tool. Napoleon had once called the press the seventh greatest power, so Goebbels called the radio the eighth. It would prove to be a productive source which for Goebbels meant using any means, including deceit to spread the power and message of the Nazi Party. He had hardly been in post a few days before he was addressing hundreds of broadcasting employees cynically commenting in his diary noting that 'many of them would have to go'.[2] Goebbels always avoided using Hitler on the radio until he had rehearsed him, which was a difficult task as the radio lacked his magnetism and force, and it was felt that 'in fact his voice sounded rather unpleasant'.[3] There was no commercial radio in Germany and the provincial stations in 1928 had come under the control of the German Post Office, which was a national company, which

Goebbels ensured came under the authority of his ministry. To make the radio an effective and useful tool he made sure that people were able to purchase cheap sets (*Volksempfänger*), and by 1939 nearly ten million Germans owned such items, and they proved very popular in many households. He therefore had a large audience at the click of a switch. He also established public loudspeaker systems in factories and schools, and so over the airways at home and at work the Nazi Party message of race, blood and nation had to be listened to whether one wanted to or not.

During his twelve years in office Goebbels changed his Chief of the Radio Division five times. Hans Fritzsche was his last appointment in 1942, and he was to become a familiar voice on the airwaves known as 'his master's voice'. Typically, Goebbels was constantly in disagreement with Fritzsche, and with Dr Dietrich, the Reich Press Chief, all of which demonstrated the personal animosities which were a constant characteristic of the regime, especially when Goebbels was involved. Hitler cared little about this situation, mainly because he based his usual strategy on 'divide and conquer'.[4]

During the years of 1936–7 Goebbels made further changes to German broadcasting creating a new office of Reich director for radio and appointed a Heinrich Glasmeier. He also demanded more light entertainment in the evenings, and in July 1937 boasted to himself that he had provided the right level of light entertainment for the nation. In 1938, he also decided that more serious music and opera should be transmitted. More to the point he organised that incoming fees should be shared between his propaganda and the postal ministries. The public could not avoid his propaganda whether at home or at work, and it must have been like living in George Orwell's world of the 'Big Brother' syndrome but not reckoned as such at the time by most. Curiously Goebbels allowed the radio a trifle more freedom than the press on the grounds that 'the spoken word is evanescent and can scarcely be pinned down in the same manner as the written word', which was all too true.[5]

Theatres

Goebbels' ambitious nature meant he wanted to take control not only of the arts and all forms of communication but the overall education of Germany. It appeared as if he wanted to control peoples' minds, what today would be called a 'control freak'. He finally secured Göring's agreement that he should oversee playhouses and theatres, but he was disappointed that Göring maintained his authority in this area over Prussia.[6] This broad spectrum of control over every aspect of German intellectual life illustrated his desire to increase his power over the mind of the nation, as well as enhancing his status. He often travelled with Hitler to various festivals of art, on 14 October 1933 they went to Munich where the Festival of German Art was central, and where the foundation stone for the House of German Art was established.

On such occasions Goebbels tended to speak with less aggression and with a sense of intellect and reserve to suit the nature of the situation. He was intelligent and adapted his rhetoric to the new scene. He became obsessed with the idea of a Reich Culture Chamber, and he appeared to try and dictate the theatre life (although he was not as successful as he was with films) and on 15 October 1933 proclaimed the *Day of the Theatres* which was designated to be a school day to study theatre. His second step was creating *Reich Theatre Weeks* which travelled from town to town, and finally 'the crowning idea of a theatre closely allied to the people was the *Weihespiele*, open-air performances, called *Thingtheatre*, which, as Goebbels hoped, would go into theatrical history as National Socialism turned to Stone'.[7]

It was no surprise that on this issue of theatres that Goebbels and Göring were constantly at odds with one another because of Göring's need to control Prussia which included its playhouses and theatres. Against Göring's overwhelming control Goebbels held little control, but it has been claimed 'he snuffed around it like a greedy wolf'.[8] However, to keep the peace, Goebbels agreed Göring could keep some control of some of the Berlin theatres.

The famous Playhouses, which had been a feature of 1920 Weimar Germany, were soon under attack. The Gestapo pointed out that two cabaret venues, the *Katacombe* and the *Tingel-Tangel* were offering hostile entertainment, and dangerous for the Party, with their entertaining political humour. Goebbels stepped in and people were arrested and these places shut down, but curiously he was annoyed at the interference of the Gestapo looking inside his territory.

Goebbels often interfered with several productions where he believed that his beloved Führer would take offence at a performance, or he had already been critical with his own views. As in other areas of culture, Goebbels had his own tastes and when the National Socialist Rudolf Billinger put on a show of National Socialist leanings, Goebbels found it boring, preferring writers such as Friedrich Schiller, and strangely he enjoyed Shakespeare and even George Bernard Shaw.* He established his own theatres as showcases of what he judged to be the best. In 1938, he had gained control of two important Berlin theatres, the Nollendorftheater and the city owned Schillertheater and later two Berlin operetta theatres.

In late 1938, a time when Goebbels had become ill, he distracted himself by attacking some of the playhouses where political jokes were still in vogue. This was mainly because Hitler had raised the issue, and his servant threw himself into the task with all his energy. Berlin had once been known for its political wit in its night clubs and show-houses, but under the new regime 'politics had become so holy that it could not be subject to humour'.[9] Goebbels swiftly called the political joke a Jewish connivance and ensured that the cabarets and playhouses which managed to stay in action were harmless, and he even personally checked some of them. It is not difficult to imagine the sense of horror that would have pervaded behind the stage curtains and management on seeing Goebbels sitting in the audience.

It was at this time that Goebbels increase his attack on all the so-called enemies, including the Jews, clergy, the 'moaners and groaners', and he took on the intellectuals and even those spoiling his projected urban scene by being known to complain about the way life was unfolding. There were occasions when he had various intellectuals called to his office to stand before his desk while he attacked their views. On one occasion the writer Ernst Wiechert was hauled before him because he had claimed he would not be giving money to Nazi welfare charities but was sending it to the wife and family of the incarcerated Pastor Niemöller. Wiechert was then sent to a concentration camp for three months, and Goebbels recorded in his diary that next time it would lead to Wiechert's physical destruction, indicating his personally cruel nature.[10] This was a clear indicator of what one may call propaganda becoming coercive.

---

* Strangely Bernard Shaw's plays were permitted for a time because he appeared to lampoon democracy and made fun of the English. His wit and left-wing views escaped the Nazi intellect.

Film Industry

The showing of films to young people and to the elderly is always good because it is a pleasure for them to watch, it is usually outside the classroom or home, and as people tend to believe what they read in the headlines of a newspaper, so when they watch what purports to be a documentary film it can also be seen as believable if not convincing. As propaganda the Nazis soon deployed this means of delivering their message. 'As far as film was concerned, the most important weapon was the 'Film Hour for the Young' (*Jugendfilmstunde*) arranged by the Hitler Youth for its members. Within the training schedule of the Hitler Youth there were clearly defined and carefully controlled duties and attendance at the *Jugendfilmstunde* was extremely important'.[11] Film producers were encouraged to make films for young audiences which were shown in schools, Hitler Youth gatherings, always at a low admission price which proved frustrating for the professional film makers, as there were always high attendance ratings. For rural areas the Propaganda Ministry created over 1,000 mobile units to ensure that young people in the remotest areas could be influenced. A typical film was *Soldaten von morgen* (*Soldiers of Tomorrow*) produced in 1941 which was regarded as an excellent production. It was a clever Hitler Youth performance and acted as a form for anti-British propaganda, and it was made at a time when German troops were always winning. As with major films, they played on the emotions which Goebbels had long recognised as a significant way even into the most human rational mind.

Goebbels' major personal interest was the film industry over which he was dangerously obsessive, but 'he had to reckon with Hitler, who was a great film fan and very critical in the bargain' and his 'greatest enemy was Rosenberg, as usual.[12] The Nazi statistics had estimated that 90 per cent of all films were distributed by Jews which was nonsense, but it created a sense of fear in the industry when the regime came to power. Goebbels tried to neutralise this fear by consistently talking of artistic freedom which, under Hitler and Rosenberg, was a futile hope.

Goebbels with all his energy and bigotry praised some films, denounced others, and was always on the outlook for films which could be utilised for propaganda production, though he always promised to leave room for genuine and safe entertainment. The film industry would not take long to understand who was in charge, and under Goebbels they soon discovered they had a controlling boss. In the initial stages Goebbels had wooed the film industry speaking about freedom of expression and the value of art, but it took little time for his propaganda intentions to come to light. He told them that 'art is a matter of ability, not of will', which must have seemed encouraging for a brief time.[13] The film industry was pleased that Goebbels promised to subsidise their efforts if they were judged worthwhile. This evaluation of relying on his judgement meant that only those films which showed the glories of the Nazi and their rise to power would work. By 1935, it was estimated that up to 70 per cent of all feature films were receiving subsidies, and anyone involved in film making was obliged to join the Reich Film Chamber that Goebbels had established.

As Goebbels established his media empire he used his charm, which many knew was superficial, and any film director had to appeal to him and his staff, hoping to ingratiate themselves. Goebbels himself could be ingratiating with the modern developing film industry, but he was not always successful. One of the most well-known German film directors was Fritz Lang, and when Goebbels tried to exploit him with his various offers Lang pointed out that he had Jewish blood on his mother's side. Goebbels told him that such was his importance to the Reich this would be overlooked, but Lang was intelligent reading the warning signs, and he fled Germany once he became alert to the growing Jewish persecution.

Goebbels was ruthless in establishing and growing his ministry (which was divided into seven departments which dominated every possible aspect of media communications) and he took over the famous and powerful Ullstein publication firm. As with Lang, the Ullstein family had to find refuge abroad as rapidly as they could manage. This anti-Semitic purge by Goebbels and others was driving out of Germany not only intellectual artistic talent but also invaluable scientific ability. This also meant that the film industry started to lose much of its better talents.

Most countries had large film corporations and in Germany the most prominent was the UFA and their intention, as always in films, was to make money. Goebbels' Reich Film Chamber established its own control over this industry, and in February 1934 a Reich Film Law was passed setting

up its own censorship committee and vetting those who worked for the industry. Those who were of the Nazi mind-set were able to flourish, the most prominent figure being Leni Riefenstahl who in 1935–6 produced the well-known film *The Triumph of the Will.* Riefenstahl had informed Goebbels she had always been an ardent supporter of the NSDAP. She had returned from Switzerland to Germany after making films in that country. The film *The Triumph of the Will* was often seen as one of the best propaganda efforts for the Nazis in the film industry, but Goebbels had his doubts, not least because he had little to do with this production. Given Goebbels' propensity with females, especially within the film industry, and although recognising Leni Riefenstahl as a smart and clever person, her biographer implies that although she met Hitler and Goebbels, she always kept her distance from Goebbels, and disliked him, which she was frequently questioned about postwar.[14]

Most of the time Goebbels managed to take his chosen course, though he was occasionally challenged by the film lover Hitler, who may have been influenced by someone like Göring who had often talked with the Führer about their views. Goebbels frequently persecuted and scolded actors for a variety of reasons, ranging from Joachim Gottschalk because he had a Jewish wife to Hans Albers because he was devoted to a Jewish actress.* Both Goebbels and Hitler enjoyed films and Goebbels had film rooms not only at work but in his various homes. Today they would have been fixated by television. It has been noted that in the first half of 1934 he and Hitler shared no less than twenty-six evenings watching films together in the Reich Chancellery.[15] The use of films as Nazi propaganda dominated Goebbels' thinking as he saw them as a key to dominate and influence the minds of the German public. He saw himself as a mixture of an expert and artist, projecting himself as a man who cared. In the Berlin opening of the *Film Archive* Goebbels gave a speech glorifying his own perceived greatness and contributions. By 1936, Goebbels had taken control of the major studios. During the years of 1937–1939 Goebbels found himself under a degree of pressure from Hitler who was constantly complaining that the films being

* Joachim Gottschalk and his wife committed suicide and killed their 3-year-old child rather than live in a Nazi dominated world.

produced had insufficient National Socialist input. He made and remade some wide-ranging appointments, put himself in charge of many companies, and purchased some others. He always regarded himself as the guiding light, but this never stopped Hitler's criticisms, who was a film buff and a self-proclaimed expert.

Goebbels had a keen interest in some films, especially in his anti-British film *Ohm Krüger* which he helped edit, and in places even wrote parts of the script. The anti-Semitic films such as *Jew Süss*, and a pro-euthanasia or mercy-killing film *J'Accuse* were particularly obnoxious. Most of these films were tedious and self-evidently propaganda for any discerning audience. Before any entertainment film could be watched there were lengthy and equally tedious news films, many of which were best described as special documentaries when the audience was instructed how to think.

Films were one of the best ways of influencing the public, films such as *Triumph of the Will* and *The Eternal Jew* dehumanised perceived enemies of the regime while glorifying Hitler and the Nazis. The film *Triumph of the Will* by Leni Riefenstahl which was based on the 1934 Nuremberg rally promoted the unity and strength of the Nazi with Hitler presented as the new political messiah for Germany. The film became a foundation stone for the Party and was shown not just in Germany but in many other parts of the world. Goebbels had grasped that for many people a film can have a major impact on their emotions more quickly and deeply than a written tract. He quickly recognised that such was the impact on the public mind it could be used against the hated race of the Jews. The appalling and well-known film *The Eternal Jew* showed the Nazi image of Jewish people as parasites eating into Germany's heritage. It was distorted beyond belief, simply crude, and totally immoral, but it had a major impact on many audiences for all generations. When the war was not progressing as hoped and looking potentially disastrous, Goebbels ordered and rushed through the film *Kolberg* (1945) about the defence of this Prussian city against the Napoleonic forces asserting national morale, which he was trying to uphold while it was showing distinct signs of crumbling. Goebbels realised the power of some films, which is still true to this day, and with his love of posters and rallies he recognised that the most effective form of propaganda was that which could be seen by the spectators and played on their emotions.

Literature

To dominate and control the German mind through his own brand of education he encouraged the German Students' Association to clean out public libraries of material and books which he considered to be rubbish. Most of the books were naturally (from his perspective) Jewish authors, communists, and included such names as Marx, Trotsky, Wolff, Freud, Remarque and hundreds of other classics. There was the infamous book-burning episode on 10 May 1933 in the Opern Platz in Berlin and in other places, indicating that Goebbels 'from now on was to put German culture into a Nazi straitjacket'.[16]

In doing this, Goebbels probably made a serious blunder when it was all done in the name of Nazi *kultur*, and he announced all this as the end of Jewish intellectual influence in German life. For Goebbels it may have been a matter of pure unadulterated aggression, but one biographer suggests he was probably somewhat reluctant and may have been responding to yet more critical attacks by Rosenberg. At least Goebbels had read widely, whereas Hitler preferred technical manuals or Wild West stories written by a Karl May. Goebbels discovered he could be 'simultaneously a revolutionary and liberal, he failed in both respects'.[17] Many other countries had banned books but not with such ruthless and sheer clumsiness. In Russia and Italy and many other countries many books have quietly disappeared from commercial and library bookshelves. Goebbels' method had a sense of ritualistic melodrama, and the overseas press quickly and enjoyably made its cynical observations, and just possibly Goebbels may have realised he had overstepped himself, because it was noted there was a degree of restraint about the affair in the Nazi press.

Hundreds of famous writers were banned, and Germany was soon bereft of many of its talented writers who fled abroad. Goebbels was aware of this and did his best to encourage the famous Thomas Mann to return to Germany. He failed and Mann became an implacable enemy of the Nazi regime. Some good writers stayed, but the fact was that it was the poor quality and pedantic writers who rose to temporary fame simply because they followed orders.

Journalists

It was 'neither technically nor, from the point of view of personnel, practically possible to destroy the democratic press and replace it by a Nazi press monopoly, as a few extremists would have liked to have done'.[18] Goebbels thought he could handle the situation but extreme measures to control the press were soon introduced. Nazi press policy was complex and for those involved dangerous, even for the normally safe sports writers.

As early as September 1933, Goebbels had produced a law to create the Reich Chamber of Culture, and in October the Journalist's Law which made them servants of the State. Anyone who fell within his 'Chamber sphere' and worked under Goebbels had become a public servant with all its implications under the Nazi regime. It was his way of not only controlling people but ensuring they had to obey the demands of the new government. The once familiar and well-known Journalist Conference was taken over, and as early as October 1933 any journalist or worker within journalism had to be an Aryan and married to a person of this so-called race. The press had rapidly become an organ of the state, but Goebbels 'had to fight for twelve years to obtain complete control of the press, which he was only able to achieve shortly before the collapse of the Third Reich'.[19] During the life of the regime Goebbels, Dr Otto Dietrich (the Reich Press Chief and Max Amann (President of Reich Press Chamber) were between them responsible for the press and were always bickering between themselves. Hitler always read the newspapers carefully and was always distrustful of the press, and he forbade senior Party members from becoming newspaper publishers. This put Goebbels in an embarrassing situation because for six years he had published *Der Angriff* which in true obedience to the Führer he relinquished in the October of 1933.

By 1934–5, Goebbels made sure that journalists were not arranging their own rules, and certainly not criticising anything the government had promulgated. Even the advertisement department had to take care; one firm did not think twice about their title 'Mein Kampf-My battle against flatulence'![20] It was even more dangerous for journalists. Their job was simply to report and not comment nor criticise. Goebbels was making sure he had total control of the press and admitted this in his diary. His *Gleichschaltung* and policy guide made everyone nervous as there was always the threat of the concentration camp.

In the end Goebbels had to leave the control of the press with Max Amann in April 1935. Goebbels was responsible for Amman's administration, but he was not always pleased with the way his instructions were interpreted. By the end of 1936, nearly 600 newspapers had been closed, and by 1944 the original number of German papers of some 3,000 plus had been reduced to a mere 970.

In January 1935, no intellectuals in this sphere of the media were allowed to leave Germany without his authorisation. In that year, he abolished any newspapers which did not have his support and prohibited any criticism of the arts which had not passed his surveillance. There were floods of decrees and various laws sponsored by Goebbels as he took total control of the intellectual life of Germany.

Although in the early 1930s Goebbels had managed to obtain a strong grip on the nature of the press and its political criticisms, he never managed total control. He made major efforts during the years of 1936 to 1938 to gain a more decisive grip. The President of the Reich Press Chamber was Max Amann whom Goebbels was obliged to personally, mainly because Amann was negotiating with him for the sale of his diaries. Friction occurred with other Party leaders when it was discovered that in a proposed reform Goebbels had ensured that every directive had to pass through his personal hands. The new bill slipped out of sight because the opposition was too strong even for him to oppose.

Occasionally, Goebbels and Hitler held different views. Goebbels wanted to shut down what he regarded at the bourgeois press, especially the famous *Frankfurter Zeitung* and the *Deutsche Allgemeine Zietung*, but Hitler wanted to retain these newspapers, leaving Goebbels with mixed feelings. He attempted to change ownership and the editors, with much of it being propelled by recently published articles. Amann wanted to take all newspapers into State ownership, but Goebbels was unsure about this policy. In 1939, Amann acquired the *Frankfurter Zeitung* as a present for Hitler. Being a press owner in Germany was dangerous, and their work was susceptible to being purchased for next to nothing.

Museums, Art and Music

When it came to a question of art Goebbels tended by nature to be liberal whereas his master Hitler had his own peculiar tastes. Goebbels was a 'relativist, a man without any definite scale of values' but when honest with himself he tended to be liberal.[21] However, none of his liberal attitudes came from some inner conviction, and in the question of art and later with films he always followed his master's bidding and point of view. He had become his master's faithful servant, even turning his intellect and intelligence over to Hitler's control. Painting, music and architecture were Hitler's hobby horses, and Goebbels was relieved that Speer was responsible for architecture, but he remained lost regarding Hitler's taste in art and music. In art works Hitler favoured what is best described as concrete realism, and preferred pedestrian painters. Speer had given Goebbels some paintings by the artist Nolde, and he had placed them in his apartment until a visit by Hitler who did not like them. They were removed, as this was always going to be his problem, obeying his master more than a pet dog would ever do. Goebbels appeared to be sensitive to the freedom of art, that it should be free and unfettered with the inbuilt qualification that everyone 'accepted the laws of the new State as the guidelines of his creative activity'.[22]

By 1937, museums and art galleries came under his various explorations and subsequent purges, and he sponsored the well-known attack upon what was called 'degenerate art'. He organised an event which backfired on him, an exhibition of modern or degenerate art with the belief that people would come to sneer, when many turned out to view with admiration. He was making every attempt to govern the intellects and artistic tases of the population and instruct them how to think. As with the film industry Goebbels found himself time and time again having to remodel his own views to the taste of Hitler, which had been and would remain his constant highest priority. In 1937, he had taken Magda and the family for a Baltic holiday when he was invited by Hitler to holiday with him at the Obersalzberg, but invited only because Hitler used the time to impress on Goebbels what he should be thinking of in terms of good or correct art. Previously that year he had flown with Hitler to Munich to view the Führer Building and the House of German Art where Hitler showed his disgust at most of the works on display. It was decided to reduce the number of artworks they viewed so they might agree with Hitler's views. Hitler gave an art-critic called Ziegler the job of cleansing German art galleries of degenerate art. In January 1938, Goebbels put this requisitioning of such art on a legal basis, and soon any such artwork which was worth any money was quickly sold overseas. It was no surprise that the art collector Göring took a keen interest in all this revamping of German art. Goebbels had different tastes from Hitler, but he complied with all his wishes simply to ingratiate himself to the father of the Reich. The journalistic critics when appraising any work of art or culture supported by the regime soon learnt 'the thing that was wanted was simply to praise everything without discrimination, so they applauded their way through the columns'.[23] Because of his private literary efforts, Goebbels had every vengeful reason for keeping critics in their place which he frequently did with venomous words and actions.

Goebbels wanted to have control of people's taste in art, but it was to prove more difficult in the field of music as Hitler's taste was simply Wagner. Goebbels' adversary Rosenberg, held to strict doctrinaire policies, had forced the resignation of many of Goebbels' selected men including Richard Strauss who had been President of the Reich Music Chamber, and the composer Paul Hindemith who both decided to live abroad. Strauss was a world-famous opera composer and was in his old age and not interested nor involved in politics. He had given a speech which praised the regime mainly for its promise of money and support through the creation of a Reich Chamber of Music. Goebbels' colleague Rosenberg then criticised Strauss, and Goebbels tried to ignore this, only to find the Gestapo had intercepted some correspondence between Strauss and Stefan Zweig, in which the latter said he was giving some of his royalties to a Jewish charity. Strauss was instantly dismissed and was removed from the public arena.

Goebbels had claimed that art and music should flourish and be allowed to experiment, but Jewish artists and musicians had to flee the country as they could not find work. Göring was responsible for the State Opera and dismissed the famous Otto Klemperer and Lotte Schöne because they were Jewish. The wider world outside Germany was becoming shocked at the Nazi behaviour and attitudes, especially when the well-known Wilhelm Furtwängler was cast aside because he had apparently made some honest comments about the regime. 'The shock of his resignation reverberated around the world, resulting in rather unfavourable reactions to the German leaders'.[24] Any mention of politics which could be assumed as critical of the government became a death threat for the instigator, so those who were able, escaped their homeland as soon as possible.

It was not until 1938 that Goebbels made a bid to take control of the country's music with a degenerate music exhibition. He tried to portray what he considered to be the important elements of music, giving him the excuse to attack all Jewish music compositions. He managed to find a place for popular music in line with his thinking and that the radio should also entertain. Because of the nature of music Goebbels failed to define what German music should be, not least because it was so varied. Whether it was fine art or music 'what Goebbels brought to flower was not the spiritual or cultural life of a nation, but rather a kind of official culturism [*sic*]'.[25]

Foreign Press

Goebbels found it more than difficult to convey his influence and ideals overseas, and his relations with the various foreign press agents was rarely successful. When he offered his thoughts, the foreign press tended to point out his various falsehoods and fabrications. He used his power by expelling many foreign journalists or blocked them coming to his press conferences. Many left the country because they realised that their lives or safety were at stake. The first direct expulsion was Dorothy Thompson an American journalist for the *Time* magazine in 1939, and who was recognised as the second most influential woman in America. Later it was seen to her credit that she was expelled from Nazi Germany in 1934. As Heiber in his biography noted, Goebbels 'created martyr after martyr, who, like Dorothy Thompson achieved through such beatification a world fame that was detrimental to Goebbels and to Germany.'[26] It was abundantly clear that Goebbels had little or no understanding of the world outside Germany, and 'one notable journalist followed another, and Goebbels refused to see that he was storing up immensely unfavourable feeling towards Germany, especially in America'.[27]

Goebbels like many of his Nazi cohorts never understood life abroad. He had visited only a few countries outside Germany, and his limited international travel left him ignorant in understanding the nature of life and the politics elsewhere in the world, even in Europe. When he was attacked for his anti-Semitic proclamations, he simply denied it all as falsehoods, thereby revealing that he was a liar. He constantly attempted to influence readers overseas by control of the press and through some selected agents. He worked hard to convey the Nazi message in South America, and in North America he employed a public relations expert, as money was no issue. He ensured that his propaganda staff were attached to as many German embassies as necessary. 'In 1938 there were as many as eighty-three accredited German journalists in London alone'.[28] A free foreign press was almost beyond his perception, and the foreign press had seen the destruction of Jewish shops and the barbarity, and yet he informed them it was all lies. He certainly had little concept about the British or the Americans and their reactions, both before and during the war.

The main problem for all the efforts made in the cultural side of life through the arts and the communication systems was that because of the nature of the regime, German intellectual life was rapidly becoming isolated from the rest of the world. The actors were the people who benefitted most simply because both Hitler and Goebbels enjoyed their company. Goebbels had founded 'the house of *Comradeship of German Artists* situated in Viktoriastrasse in Berlin…and appointed himself as the ruler and protector of all theatre artists', if they were not Jewish.[29]

The usual esteem in which artists were held was disappearing with the outbreak of war when a general call-up was issued for the military. Various lists were drawn up with grades of exemption. Hitler interfered and new exemption lists appeared with lists A and B and so forth. Because of Hitler's love of fine arts, no less than twelve artists were placed in List A. By October 1944, theatres were closed and the following month the exemption lists meant nothing. The propaganda was clever, and it worked in Germany because it was supported by the sense of fear, but overseas it had little impact apart from amazement, amusement and a degree of increasing alarm.

Foreign Propaganda

When the equally ambitious Joachim von Ribbentrop became Germany's Foreign Minister, he persuaded Hitler to give him control over foreign propaganda. Hitler with his 'divide and rule' policy he never informed Goebbels who was angry when he later heard of Ribbentrop's incursion into what he regarded as his part of the regime. Since the early days of 1933, he had always presumed this to be his area of total control. The debate grew heated with Ribbentrop, and Hitler had to intervene and finally appeared to withdraw his agreement with Ribbentrop, who ignored this advice and the mutual hatred between Goebbels and the Foreign Minister continued for the duration of their limited lives. This created some pleasure in the foreign press who enjoyed baiting both men. When a biographer wrote that Hitler often had to intervene 'to separate the two fighting cocks' he could have added that this internal bickering over personal power bases was a hallmark of Goebbels as well as Himmler and Göring and many other senior leading Nazis.[30]

Goebbels was despised because of his violent anti-Semitism, especially in his pursuit of well-known individuals who were either Jewish or had Jewish friends and family. When Ernst vom Rath, a staff member of the German Embassy in Paris was murdered by a 17-year-old Polish-Jewish boy called Herschel Grynszpan, Goebbels helped instigate the pogrom in which the notorious *Kristallnacht* took place on Jewish shops, synagogues and businesses. The foreign press condemned it, bringing it to the attention of the world as an act of barbaric proportions.

Goebbels always regarded himself as the spokesman for most major international events, be it the annexation of Austria, the problems of Danzig, and he took every opportunity to be seen or heard at the centre of such national moments, but it was his vitriolic anti-Semitism with which the foreign press took issue with the most passion. He was able through sheer power and fear to avoid criticism on the German domestic front, but he had no such control overseas.

It was after the annexation of Memelland, and when the first propaganda war against Poland and Britain started, it was Goebbels who had to realise that he was not the most important figure in the political scenery when it came to propaganda relating to foreign policy and overseas.* Ribbentrop in

* Memelland was the Klaipédia Region of northeast Prussia and bordered Lithuania with Klaipédia being the major port.

1939 was appearing as indispensable, and he was granted permission in the June of that year to start a foreign language broadcasting department. The Wehrmacht had its own divisions and as war came closer their arguments for their own department appeared, to his extreme annoyance, as for him it seemed to place Goebbels on a lower rung of importance, because by April 1939 the Wehrmacht had its own establishment for propaganda. Goebbels was also set firmly in his place when he was obliged to cancel an arranged visit overseas because the international scene was becoming heated, and Hitler no longer regarded Goebbels as indispensable in all matters.

Chapter Six

Signals of Nazi Dangers

Night of the Long Knives

Hitler was becoming even more power hungry and dangerous in believing that as the leader he was indispensable if not chosen by providence, and he would not tolerate the slightest form of opposition. For him and Goebbels and the other senior Nazi cohorts the NSDAP was about total power. The inevitable clash between Hitler and the SA nearly found Goebbels on the wrong side of his demi-god, the Führer. There had long been this well-known internal conflict within the Party, which would lead to what was commonly known as the Night of the Long Knives. Goebbels was always a radical, he had often been disturbed by Hitler's needing the more conservative elements in support of his causes. There had been during the 1933–35 years some rumours and counter-rumours of the re-establishment of the monarchy and growing doubts about the intentions of others. There was even the suggestion that Hindenburg, now suffering from the weaknesses of old age, was leaving a final testament suggesting the re-establishment of the monarchy. Von Papen had delivered a highly critical speech concerning the Nazis at the University of Marburg, but Goebbels had ensured it was never printed.

Goebbels had misjudged the politically delicate situation with the SA because it had always been his belief that this was not a major concern for Hitler. His assessment of the situation soon proved wrong as it became apparent that Hitler had his critical sights on the SA and its leadership. As noted, Goebbels had used the SA at most of his meetings, and he was a friend of Röhm, who had suggested to Hitler that as the SA leader he should under Hitler oversee all the armed forces, suffering from the traditional Nazi lust for being seen as important. Hitler knew that Hindenburg and the generals would not accept such a stupid take-over. In 1933, the SA membership amounted to some 500,000 but by 1934 it had risen to a staggering 4.5 million. This was a formidable force, which with Röhm seeking more power, and it seemed to act as a warning to Hitler that his position of total power could be in danger. He was a man always sensitive to any threat whereby his dominance could be challenged or even questioned. There is no appropriate or safe evidence to indicate that Röhm was planning any form of revolt, but there was some growing unrest in the SA ranks and within the Party. When Hitler announced that he was going to act Goebbels was taken by surprise when he heard that it was against the SA, and not the politically inclined conservative elements whom he despised. However, unknown to Goebbels, the SS, the Gestapo, and even the army had been planning for such an event for weeks, but Goebbels had not been involved in any of the decision making, and he had failed to understand the complexity of the jealous domestic political situation.

Hitler was actively involved in the well-known account of the Night of the Long Knives, which took place between 30 June and 2 July 1934. It was a bloody and brutal affair orchestrated by Hitler and his other henchmen Göring and Himmler. As soon as Goebbels realised what was happening he promptly disassociated himself from Röhm, and looking to his personal safety stayed close to Hitler throughout the ghastly series of killings.[1] That Goebbels stayed close to Hitler for personal safety is the view of the historians Manvell and Fraenkel.[2] The biographer Peter Longerich pointed out that Goebbels put his wife and children in the care of the police, and added this 'meant his presence was a salutary lesson for him: Hitler made sure he was present at the action'.[3] It was also possible that Hitler wanted Goebbels out of Berlin because Göring was in charge of the Berlin massacre. Quite where Goebbels stood in all this is difficult to ascertain, some have even claimed that it was Goebbels who raised the alarm.[4] However, the truth remains evasive, though it is curious to note that Heiber also pointed out that it was definitely Goebbels who had first warned Hitler about an SA rising on 29 June.[5] The same author makes the valid point that in these risky Machiavellian moments had Röhm been the winner then Joseph Goebbels would have been among the murderers and not the murdered.[6]

Göring and Himmler with his SS and the army worked on the organisation of the proposed plan, and Hitler was in attendance for the arrest of Röhm who was caught in bed with another man. Hitler would use this question of Röhm as a homosexual against him, and the other man as an act of betrayal who 'had been exploited by a depraved and unscrupulous leadership'.[7] Hitler also excused this purge justifying the deaths by claiming that any form of attack on the German government gave the authorities the right to deal with them at once. However, it was much wider than just the SA issue, but other challenges to Hitler's power were also dealt with at the same time. Gregor Strasser was taken to the notorious Prinz Albrechtstrasse prison and shot. Von Schleicher and his wife were murdered and von Papen just escaped with his life, and even Karl Ernst who had probably assisted in the Reichstag fire was also shot. Very few documents concerning this incident survive and the numbers involved in the various murders has never been fully established, but they may have amounted to over 200. For Goebbels, his main task was to supress the news and check what was released to the public. The excuses he produced included that the dead had been, purportedly, colluding with foreign powers, indulged in debauched living, and they all had a thirst for power. There was a cynical ring about Goebbels' propaganda, but the incident was generally kept as quiet as possible.

This event made it clear that any attack or attempted reformation of the Nazi movement would be met with immediate death. The Night of the Long Knives 'ended once and for all every revolutionary and socialistic tendency with National Socialism'.[8] Goebbels had been close to Röhm, but he had quickly re-estimated the situation placing himself at the side of Hitler had saved himself from any recrimination, revealing that he was driven by personal ambition, which had to include unquestionable adoration and loyalty to his demi-god Hitler. It raises the question as whether it was Goebbels' ambition which made him adore Hitler, and the answer appears simple when all the various accounts are read. He turned to Hitler because of his ambition, changed his views because of Hitler, and dedicated himself to total obedience of his master. However, somewhere during this journey of wanting to become important he became so loyal to the Führer it became essential for his well-being that for him Hitler became his lord and master if not demi-god, which although unusual was not the first time some people had behaved this way.

Death of Paul von Hindenburg

At the end of July 1934 there was incoming news that that Hindenburg's last days was imminent. The Nazi power-grasping machine went into operation at once and a law was passed merging the office of President and Chancellor, making total power possible. Hindenburg died on 2 August with Goebbels ensuring there was appropriate mourning, even a broadcasting silence for thirty minutes. Hitler demanded another plebiscite to make it appear that when he assumed total power that it was based on the wishes of the people. There was some concern about Hindenburg's last will and testament, but it proved quite harmless, the service was held at the Tannenberg Memorial with all the pomp and ceremony making it as public as possible. Goebbels organised the plebiscite and spoke in many places, and the vote was 89.9 per cent which looked far too good by normal democratic standards, but given the way these plebiscites were organised it was not surprising. Goebbels found it quite disappointing as he wanted no votes against. There appeared to some Nazi members that the support for the regime appeared to be fading somewhat, possibly caused by the events of the Night of the Long Knives. This resulted in Goebbels turning his anger on some papers, especially those of the Catholic faith which he often suspected the most of such treachery, as he would regard such criticism.

Hitler assumed the office of President while also retaining the position of Chancellor. He was now able to turn his attention to the army. They were paraded in strength and swore their oath of allegiance to Hitler, and it was Goebbels who announced on the radio all these developments. Most countries have their military swear an oath of allegiance, in the USA to the President, and in Britain to the monarchy. It was the same in the Prussian tradition where such an oath was taken to a life and death situation.

Following the election results Goebbels and Hitler went on a series of tours trying to garner a show of support. They concentrated on the Winter Relief fund, and street collections were an everyday occurrence and badges were handed out, and it would soon be known if one were not a charitable giver which could lead to personal dangers. Massive campaigns, pageants and ceremonies were organised, but later research has revealed that not everyone in Germany was happy with what was happening, but the problem under a dangerous government was that any protest was not just dangerous but virtually impossible.

Anti-Semitism

Although Goebbels was helped and supported by Jewish scholars as an undergraduate and received funds for his education from the Catholic Church, times changed him in the new totalitarian Nazi state. Goebbels followed his master's voice and turned his vehement propaganda and vitriolic speeches against Jewish people and would also like to have done the same against the Church, but with this international body with many German adherents he knew he had to be more cautious. Anti-Semitism was a feature of NSDAP power which scarred Europe and the German nation. As in many countries anti-Semitism had an unfortunate degree of this racism ranging from social snobbery, such as in Britain where some golf clubs excluded Jews, to more venomous attacks which could be found in Tsarist Russia with its organised pogroms. In Germany it has been noted that in business 24 per cent of the supervisory positions were in Jewish hands, up to a quarter of all lawyers were Jewish, and they could be found in abundance in most of the professions, doctors, universities, theatre and entertainment. It could be argued that it was beneficial having such a gifted and enterprising people, many of whom had already proved their loyalty by joining the German military. It has been noted by some cynics that despite so many Jews being in business and professions that the Jews never exceeded 2 per cent of the German population. As immigrants, like all immigrants, they sought a successful life in any available sphere of work, and many felt they were supporting what was their host country, and which for most was their community. The Jewish-German academic Professor Victor Klemperer, famous for keeping his diaries during the Nazi regime, was always robust in declaring he was a German by birth, he did not adhere to the Jewish faith, married a so-called Aryan (which saved him), had been awarded a medal for fighting for Germany in the First World War. Many Jews died fighting for Germany during the Great War but the myth of the stab-in-the-back (*Dolchstoßlegende*) mentioned earlier in this text gave an unpleasant impetus to a rising tide of anger against all German Jews, and soon against all Jews.

Many historians and others have attempted to show that Goebbels was not as anti-Semitic as he seemed, but while this remain true of him as a young man, early diary entries indicate he was curious about German Jews. It was best described by one author writing 'though Goebbels was by no means convinced of the necessity for persecuting the Jews, he put the full weight of his mighty propaganda machine behind it. Obedience to the Führer demanded this, but it was also in his own interests to allay the mistrust of his opponents in the Party, and if possible, to dispel it altogether', but whatever the impetus for his anti-Semitism it grew to huge and vicious proportions.[9]

Goebbels' disclosures about the Jewish issue offer many insights concerning the National Socialist policy toward a final solution (*Endlösung*) of the Jewish Question, which relate to what is currently known as the Holocaust. It is generally understood, with good reason, that the whole of Nazi leadership, Hitler above all, were dedicated or better obsessed anti-Semites who would eventually organise the final solution with the extermination camps and massacres, even though it meant using valuable resources and manpower in a major war. It has even been argued that because Goebbels makes no direct reference to *Endlösung* he and possibly even Hitler had no idea that their venom had reached this conclusion. This is generally and understandably regarded as sheer nonsense by most historians, and Goebbels undoubtedly made no reference to the *Endlösung* because he knew it to be immoral and criminal. This was why Himmler in the end days of Nazism tried to cover up the horrors and denied and feigned ignorance, claiming some men had possibly gone to the extremes, and Goebbels would not have mentioned this anymore than he would have listed his many sexual liaisons.

Goebbels' venom towards the Jews was revealing in his diaries about the way Nazis regime thought and acted. Some of his early thinking in his diary entries indicate his attitudes. On the 8 April 1924, he wrote the following:

> The Jewish Question is the hottest issue at the moment. It has to be solved before one can go on to the refortification of Europe. Maybe Russia will make a start. What I already suspected – namely that the current Russian situation is only Jewish soap scum atop a heavy nationalist dishwasher – I now find confirmed in all authentic opinions. I read Henry Ford's The International Jew today. The book is very interesting and salutary. But one shouldn't let

> oneself be too taken in by the author's captivating evidence. He also writes a bit to the home crowd. All the same, a lot is revealed in the book. One can see the implications of the Jewish Question in the non-German lands. Strange: Henry Ford, the richest man in the world, makes Jewish capitalism his target. The world is a big theatre. Lenin, Trotsky, Chicherin are Jews. How stupidly one can sometimes judge political and economic processes, if one doesn't know the most necessary material. A major part of Ford's book discusses the *Protocols of the Elders of Zion*. But the text itself is missing. I have to reorientate myself about this question another time. I won't rest until I have clarity about the Jewish Question. The solution to these things may change my whole inner nature.

It did not take long for him to 'reorientate' himself, 'change his nature', as only six year later 12 May 1930, he wrote, 'Drive to Vienna. This magnificent city. But the Jews must go'. In terms of racialism there is no doubt that Goebbels was deeply anti-Semitic, not just hostile to this ancient race of people, but he was on this subject always simmering with venomous hatred. The question should be asked as to why and when this arose in him as an individual. When a youngster there had been no signs of this bigotry, and at university he had been carefully taught by Jewish intellectuals and guided by the once famous Jewish Professor of Literature, Friedrich Gundolf. After the First World War the nationalistic groups had decided that anti-Semitism had provided them with 'the best proof for their nationalistic attitude', using the 'stab in the back' myth that it was because of the Jews that Germany had lost the war.[10] One of his first major girlfriends Else had a Jewish mother but Goebbels' early aggression was mainly directed at the bourgeoisie. In his desperate pursuit of ambition, he was prepared to ditch good friends and ignore those who had helped him. He was equally prepared to change his politics, his religion, and his own personal beliefs. He abandoned his one-time support of communist Russia, later abandoning his actress-mistress because of Hitler's insistence, and because Hitler was a rabid anti-Semitic and imbued the party with this disease, Goebbels took up his anti-Semitism with all the aggressive behaviour which has since characterised his name. The historian Reimann explains Goebbels' anti-Semitism as progressing through three stages: the first serious stage was joining Hitler and typified by his attack on Weiss and Jewish journalists. The second stage was when

Hitler assumed total power and this is associated with the purges, and the third started with the war against Russia when the destruction of the Jews became a top-secret governmental issue.[11]

In an early German biography, it was stated that 'Goebbels was never an anti-Semite by conviction: he was too intelligent for that. Privately he thought all Rosenberg's racial theories a lot of nonsense'.[12] If this were the case his anti-Semitism was an emotional and self-serving change because he knew that this form of fanatical hatred was his best weapon to follow Hitler. This made his anti-Semitic attitude not only more difficult to comprehend but even more morally corrupt than the limited intellectual minds of people such as Rosenberg and Hitler.

His propaganda relied on the eulogising the myth of Aryan superiority while degrading the Jews and portraying them as the greatest enemy of Germany. Goebbels started to produce the theory of a global Jewish conspiracy, blamed them for Germany's economic collapse, the 1918 defeat, and the cause of communism. He was not the first to do this, but he built these claims up to the greatest possible extent. Anti-Semitism was rife across Europe at various levels, but Goebbels made it a central feature of the Party and for much of the public.

Once appointed as a minister he established the order of the 'Nazi-Day' in organising the boycott of Jewish shops and businesses on 1 April 1933. It never appeared to cross the Nazi mind the effect all this could have on the German economy or their nation's reputation. For Goebbels everything was subordinated to the demand of his propaganda arising from his ambition which was linked to his adoration of Hitler. Nazi SA thugs blocked active Jewish businesses, and Goebbels claimed it was to teach the Jews that their associates overseas had to stop criticising the German government. Goebbels knew overseas the NSDAP was being attacked by protest marches, newspaper letters and by foreign politicians. There was an established committee behind this boycott of Jewish businesses which included Robert Ley, Himmler, Hans Frank and Julius Streicher. For his part Goebbels publicised the details and reasons for this hatred, always authorised by Hitler. These viewpoints and policies were generally unwelcome around the globe, but unfortunately there were varying shades of anti-Semitism in many countries. On 1 September 1933, Goebbels gave a specially prepared speech at the Party Conference, having first conferred with Hitler in which he outlined the Party's anti-Semitic guidelines, which he frequently referred to as the settlement of the 'Jewish Question', and there were many other sinister elements contained in this speech.

As Hitler tried to gain some international respect for Germany the anti-Semitic attacks appeared to calm down, notably during the signing of the London Naval Treaty and later the Berlin Olympics. When the Saar plebiscite had stirred the anti-Semitism once again, Goebbels took this as a necessary sign in reading the mood of the people. The popular expression was 'racial disgrace', which interpreted meant the 'intimate relations between Jews and non-Jews', reflective of the Nuremberg Race Laws.[13] Since Goebbels had turned away from his usual social radicalism, he constantly made his target the Jewish people. The focus for this barbarism tended to be Berlin where the Hitler Youth members found it fun to harass Jewish shops. The paper *Der Angriff* encouraged the population to show its anger, which unleashed the traditional barbarity, and the foreign press announced in 1935 yet another pogrom. Goebbels was overjoyed when he managed to blame the police for mishandling situations, and he was overjoyed when the Berlin Police Chief Levetzow was replaced by his close friend von Helldorf.

At the Party rally in September 1935, Goebbels gave a speech on the nature of the Jewish menace. This coincided with an incident in New York where a swastika flag had been ripped from a German ship mast which had two immediate ramifications. The first was the elevation of the swastika above the traditional German flag on major buildings, and secondly it increased the hatred of local Jewish citizens who were blamed for this deed which had taken place thousands of miles away. At the end of the Party session two new laws were agreed upon to be passed by the Reichstag. The first was to deprive German Jewish people of their rights of citizenship, and the second proscribed relationships between Jewish and non-Jewish people. As far as Goebbels was concerned this was his new form of radicalism.

As noted above, the 1936 Berlin Olympics in Germany provided a brief saving grace for German Jewish citizens because the Nazis needed the best possible picture of Germany for the wider world. Even when Wilhelm Gustloff of the Swiss NSDAP was murdered by the Jewish student David Frankfurter the anti-Semitic brakes were applied.

In his cultural arena and all his departments Goebbels immediately started to ensure that his various staff and those reliant on them were free of Jewish family members and friends. It was not as easy as he had anticipated, and in 1937 he complained that in the Reich Chamber of Fine Arts there were still some 156 Jewish members.[14] He was never entirely successful given that many of those he protested about were only *Mischlings* (part-German part-Jewish) and often with a minimal Jewish background. He was still concerned by so-called Jewish influence in 1943 but thereafter, as the war turned, he had more pressing matters to occupy him.

During 1937 and following Hitler's demands, Goebbels started a more radical approach against German Jews. They were banned from theatres and any form of public cultural event. After the *Anschluss* the anti-Semitic heat was increased again. The German Jews suffered less when international issues were prominent, but they suffered a great deal more afterwards. In all this wretched business Goebbels played a major role by setting an example in Berlin on the way to deal with the Jewish problem. In April 1938 the anti-Semitic onslaught increased dramatically, with Goebbels interpreting this urge in anti-Semitism as a sign of popular anger. The Kurfürstendamm in central Berlin had always been a place of strolling and leisure, but there had been considerable anti-Semitic activity associated with the area. The police had arrested over 300 Jewish citizens who were only enjoying a coffee in a large café. Goebbels had sent out the message that Jewish people were mainly criminals and anti-social. This Berlin episode sparked similar outrages in other towns and cities, and it appeared to be out of any normal control. Goebbels behaved like a music conductor, proposing when to start, when to moderate or increase, and doing so from behind the scenes.

The spark which created in increase in gross vindictiveness occurred when on 7 November 1938, when a teenager called Herschel Grynszpan killed the German diplomat Ernst vom Rath in Paris because of his parents being forced out of Germany. The backlash was unleashed by Goebbels, and between 7 and 10 November, synagogues were burnt down, shops destroyed which led to the notorious name of *Kristallnacht* derived from the shards of broken glass that littered all the streets. This was not confined just to Berlin but spread rapidly throughout Germany, especially in Kassel and Dessau.

Goebbels talked to Hitler who confirmed that the action was right, thus putting the lie to the theory that Hitler was ignorant of such events.

Speer claimed it was all Goebbels' initiative, but this was 'typical of Speer's endeavours to whitewash Hitler and more so himself in his memoirs'.[15] Himmler claimed the order came from Goebbels, and at the Nuremberg Trials Funk blamed Goebbels. Later the Reich Press Chief Dr Dietrich who hated Goebbels and had every reason to attack him, stated that Hitler lost control and gave the orders to Goebbels which sounds just possible. Over 20,000 Jewish people were arrested and at the very least thirty-six were killed.* In the meantime, Goebbels decided it was necessary not to associate this appalling event with the regime, but the foreign press was not fooled. The barbarity was out of control, but Reinhard Heydrich and Goebbels tried to calm matters. However, Goebbels was very much in control, the very power he had always wanted. More on Göring's mind was to take hold of the Jewish wealth. Almost the day after the malicious fury had started to abate Goebbels met with Göring where it was decided the Jewish people should pay for the damage, and they were fined a billion Reichsmark, their insurances were taken over by the State and they were excluded from business. Goebbels suggested even more unpleasant ideas that Jewish people should have to clear the synagogue sites so they could be used for car parking. It was also considered necessary that Jews should be excluded from public areas such as parks and resorts, be removed from schools and not sit on the same benches as Germans. It amounted to an extreme form of apartheid. Some of the other Party leaders thought Goebbels had gone too far 'that it had been a bad move on Goebbels' part' but they were not prepared to fall out with Hitler.[16] There was no doubt that Hitler was extremely anti-Semitic and Goebbels had followed him, although ironically, it should be recalled that Goebbels in 1926 in the Elberfeld National Socialist Letters had scorned 'primitive anti-Semitism', just over decade earlier.[17] There is no question that by the 1930s Goebbels had become rabidly anti-Semitic but undoubtedly he was following his master's thinking to every comma. In January 1939, in the Reichstag Hitler spoke of the destruction of the Jewish race in Europe,

* Numbers vary considerably, but the true figure may have been near a hundred.

and the persecution never ceased as Goebbels always supported this view through his various channels of propaganda.

The realities of Hitler's intentions were clearly exposed following the successful invasion of Poland, where even German generals and many others were shocked at the way Poles and especially Jews were treated. Goebbels heard that thousands of Jews were to be deported to a planned reservation in east Poland, to cleanse the Reich from what he sometimes referred to as the hygienic problem. This issue now took on a more sinister tone because it was decided that this was no longer a matter for propaganda.

One historian noted that 'After the victory over France, German Jewish policy acquired a new momentum', not least because this owed much to Goebbels' initiative.[18] He decided that one way or another he was going to cleanse Berlin of all Jews. He told Hitler that the Jewish people were the criminal element and needed removing, showing him plans on the way this could be executed. Hitler agreed and they talked about sending all Jews to Madagascar which would become a German protectorate. This was not an original idea as it had occurred to some anti-Semitic Poles and had often been discussed elsewhere. The same policy was to be done with Austrian-Jews in Vienna. Eventually it was decided that they would be deported to Poland under Governor Frank whose protests at the huge numbers involved was over-ruled to Goebbels' delight. The now very familiar names of Reinhard Heydrich and Adolf Eichmann were brought into action to expedite the matter. The only issue for Goebbels was the realisation that many Jewish people were needed for the armaments industry. Goebbels knew that there had been massacres of Jewish people in Poland, but he did not want this as part of his propaganda, and he backed the proclamation that the person issuing the orders should not witness the executions in case it weakened their resolve. Himmler was behind this barbarity, but Goebbels provided the propaganda stimulus.

It was during the Russian campaign (Operation *Barbarossa*) Goebbels started the policy of stigmatising Jewish people by publicly identifying them. He claimed they needed to be seen for what and who they were, and the result of his thinking was the demeaning yellow star, cleverly linked with the growing theme of 'international Jewry'. The yellow star did not work as well as he had hoped, as he heard news that some members of the public were showing signs of sympathy to those obliged to wear this emblem.

He returned with a new argument informing the public claiming that it was 'international Jewry' which had started the war. For those aware of this development abroad it appeared simply ridiculous, and it may have raised serious doubts in the minds of some of the German public already saturated by his anti-Semitic views. Even they would have asked questions as to how these down-and-outs walking in the gutters with their yellow stars could possibly be the cause of what was looking like an oncoming global war. The mention of 'international Jewry' and powerful Jewish bankers may have helped ease such sensible doubts, but ss far as Goebbels was concerned such critics were just bourgeois and were described as 'filthy swine'. He took the next step in October 1941 by making it a legal offence for anyone to help or show the slightest kindness to Jews. This offence of showing any form of humanity could mean being sent to a concentration camp or protective custody as it was commonly called. This was not so much promulgated but made clear in the propaganda and controlled newspapers and was often repeated as a reminder. When it came to the attention of the foreign press, Goebbels was more cautious, pointing out that the Jewish people would be treated as individuals, and their move eastwards came under the heading of economic warfare and was therefore regarded as secret. In the October of 1941, his anti-Semitic measures increased dramatically. He castigated Britain and America as centres of a Jewish world conspiracy. In November 1941, he wrote an article in which he stated Jewry was now undergoing a gradual process of annihilation, which sent an ominous message around a world which generally wanted to ignore the problem. In early 1942, he was still working on ridding Berlin of its German-Jewish citizens, but he was now contending with Albert Speer who needed them for armament production.

It never seemed to occur to the Nazi leaders that they were eliminating a large potential work force, even potential soldiers and much needed clever scientists. Their obsession with destroying Jewish people was immoral and beyond reason, and it should have crossed Goebbels' mind that this was why Fritz Sauckel was employed to find labour from occupied territories. It is clear from his diaries that he read the minutes of the infamous Wannsee conference in which the Final Solution was openly discussed. He had visited a ghetto in Vilnius when trapped there by winter weather and noted 'there were frightful characters hanging around the streets, whom I wouldn't want to come across in the dark. The Jews are lice that live on civilised humanity. They must somehow be exterminated otherwise they will keep on tormenting and oppressing us'.[19] It was not long before Goebbels was aware that there had been experiments with gas vans, and new types of gas chambers were undergoing experiment. Occasionally he made references to it being a barbaric process but also claimed that 'later generations won't have the drive and the instinct for this, so it's good we are being radical and decisive'.[20] Goebbels was to make many similar observations in his diaries and verbally, noting that 'they are no longer people but beasts…it is therefore not a humanitarian but a surgical task'.[21] He later added that 'no other government and no other regime would have the strength for such a global solution as this', directly referring to what he called the battle between the Aryan race and the Jewish bacillus.[22] This had become a severe form of racism and in the postwar era would be regarded as one of the Nazi regime's most immoral acts.

His diaries reveal beyond question what can only be described as twisted immoral thinking. On the 14 February 1942, he wrote 'that the Führer once more expressed his determination to clean up the Jews in Europe pitilessly. There must be no squeamish sentimentalism about it. The Jews have deserved the catastrophe that has now overtaken them. Their destruction will go hand in hand with the destruction of our enemies. We must hasten this process with cold ruthlessness. We shall thereby render an inestimable service to humanity tormented for thousands of years by Jews. This uncompromising anti-Semitic attitude must prevail among our own people despite all objectors'.[23] Later on 27 March 1942, he wrote that 'about 60 per cent of them will have to be liquidated; only 40 per cent can be used for forced labour'.[24] This entry by Goebbels makes a nonsense of those who occasionally suggest that some of the top Nazi leaders were ignorant about the extermination camps.

When in May 1942 a propaganda exhibition was attacked it was alleged that some of the would-be saboteurs were Jewish. Goebbels promptly informed Hitler and then colossal reprisals took place, including over 100 executions. This anti-Semitic attitude had embedded itself into his mind and soul and had become part of his nature which had grown to 'daemonic proportions', and he was guilty of conveying this attitude into the minds of many of the public.

The Heydrich assassination provoked even more problems. Many of the surviving Berlin Jewish citizens found themselves under arrest, and this action encouraged Goebbels to persuade Hitler to ignore Speer's arguments, and to replace Berlin Jewish workers in armaments with imported labour. In this diary entry which Goebbels recorded this, it also became clear that Hitler was still thinking of depositing Jewish people in Africa. It has been occasionally argued that this seemed to indicate that the concept behind the Wannsee meeting about the Final Solution had not yet been finalised, but this infamous Wannsee conference was only a matter of confirming what was already underway. One of the consequences of the Heydrich affair was that the Jews in Prague suffered and thousands of them were rounded up and deported. Around December 1942, news reports started to appear in the enemy press about the mass-murders of Jewish people, and then the Allies published an official paper about the Nazi policy of systematically exterminating Jewish people. Goebbels felt obliged to inform his various agents to ignore these statements from overseas 'without, however, denying them to his staff'.[25] His counterattack was to accuse the British of their barbarity in their colonies. While it was true the British and other European countries had sometimes behaved badly in their occupied territories there had never been a State sponsored mass extermination. It also raises the question how far the extermination camps were known by the German public and whether Goebbels might have had a change of mind had he visited one, but in the meantime, there was simply no good reply that Goebbels could find or make up against such accusations.

Later, the fall of Stalingrad had many reasons, ranging from superior Soviet manpower and determination to Hitler's commands being unreasonable and faulty, but for his part Hitler announced the problems was international Bolshevist Jewry which caused yet more problems for those Jewish people within the Nazi held territories. Goebbels continued this theme in a major speech given in the Sportpalast on 18 February (after Stalingrad was lost) in which he claimed Jewry was a menace to all nations, thereby turning them into a scapegoat for any Nazi failures. When Goebbels had heard that the Berlin evacuation of Jews was to start, it was often referred to as the 'factory action' because some 8,000 Jewish people were arrested at their place of work, and Goebbels was angry that there had been some warnings, and some Jewish workers had escaped the roundup. He was also concerned when some protests at this action arose, and at one stage because of bombing raids, he asked the SD to calm matters down, so the city tension did not rise further. He was equally concerned about the number of mixed marriages, and he estimated there were some 17,000 as well as the problem of *Mischlings* (part-German and part-Jewish). Hitler had demanded the problem had to be resolved and Goebbels thought he was succeeding, writing that 'by liberating Berlin from Jews I have carried out one of my greatest political acts', an entry which portrayed his mindset.[26]

When in April 1943 the Katyń massacres in Poland became known Goebbels jumped at this to detract from his failure in his Total War propaganda.* His emphasis was once again that the Jews had been behind this act of barbarity. It was part of his anti-Bolshevik attack, but it was always the anti-Jewish element which held the priority in his propaganda. This method of blaming the Jews for everything arose again with the Warsaw uprising, which was Jewish inspired, and even when the RAF carried out their well-known 'dam busters raid' Goebbels claimed it was successful because the scientist behind the technology was Jewish. However, it was the Katyń massacre which dominated the press and was sensationally presented in all papers and publications. 'Yet what was a Katyń massacre in comparison with the German camps, the Einsatzgruppe, mass murders, gas-chambers and the like', as the kettle was calling the pot black which clearly demonstrated the hypocrisy of two evil regimes.[27] The Katyń massacre at the time and later left the world confused, the British 'refused to comment unless to point the finger at the Nazis. British officers were forbidden to participate in Katyń memorial services' and plans for a monument in London were quashed.[28] Churchill had told the Polish Ambassador in in London that 'the Bolsheviks can be very cruel' but there was nothing he could do about the matter.[29] British experts remained divided although one official report by a Sir Owen O'Malley pointed out that it was probably Soviet guilt.[30] Only

* The Nazis tried to find reluctant experts from neutral countries, and Britain and America were more concerned about keeping Stalin on side so assumed or pretended it was a Nazi crime.

fifty years later did the Russians announce the truth behind Stalin's orders, but although Goebbels had wanted to stoke up the anti-communist attack, the anti-Semitism propaganda took priority in his personal thinking and propaganda. Hitler added his own invective that his own allies should be tested by their lack of anti-Semitism, no doubt thinking of the Hungarian regime where there had been a lack of support in making themselves Jew-Free, and Italians had not been overly happy about the anti-Semitism Hitler had virtually demanded.

Goebbels never stopped from his attack on the Jews, and again in May 1943 he used the book the *Protocols of the Elders of Zion* which he had read in his youth, to add to his venom.* He was intelligent enough to know the book was only fabricated propaganda, but Hitler maintained it was true and encouraged its use. Goebbels instigated another anti-Semitic drive seeking the production of anti-Semitic novels and ensuring that the subject was always in the press. Later, it slowly dawned on him that it was beginning to show signs of being counterproductive. Nevertheless, this did not stop him in his next major speech in the Sportpalast of describing the Jewish person as a potato beetle which from sheer necessity had to be destroyed as soon as possible. By 1944, the Jewish propaganda started to change slightly. The damage had been done to the Jewish race, the Hungarians had been bullied into a similar ideology, but the propaganda pressure which had long dwelt on the war against 'international Jewry' started to change to Jewish-Bolshevism and then uncluttered anti-Bolshevism and straightforward anti-communism.

There were times during the war when people started to question the anti-Semitic propaganda. Many in the film industry had turned against Goebbels especially over his insistence that no one should be married to a Jewish person. He had heard reports that an old Jewish person's home whilst being emptied was watched by sympathetic members of the public, and there was further information that any further anti-Semitic propaganda was irrelevant during a major war, and the fear that one day the Germans would pay the price.

---

* *The Protocol of the Elders of Zion* was a strongly anti-Semitic and fabricated text purporting to describe a Jewish plan for global domination. As far as is known it was first published in Russia in 1903 and then widely translated and distributed.

Anti-communist propaganda soon became the focus, registering some success both with the public and the allies. This was the political reason in Goebbels thinking, namely that this policy might just divide the Western Allies from their Russian counterparts. This hope was to persist until the end of the war, but it only came to a degree of reality after the war when Hitler and Goebbels were dead, not that this development saved any Jewish people.

One of the best insights into Nazi anti-Semitism is given by the academic German-Jew Professor Victor Klemperer, who kept massive diaries unfolding the suffering and pain of the persecution. He had frequently in these diaries derided Goebbels, but in the following extract he pointed out the danger Goebbels had created by his propaganda, as many of the public, who at times had tried to help him, but others had been persuaded by the propaganda machine to hate people of Jewish background:

> The year 1939 for Klemperer offered no hope, the oppression intensified, in September the war broke out with Hitler now appearing all-powerful. On New Year's Day he took a taxi to a friend's house having been banned from driving, with the driver sympathising with him. He heard of the devastating news about the vicious treatment of Jews in Ulm where a rabbi he wrote 'was chased (by the mob, that is, by the people, and not just by SA carrying out orders!) round the market fountain with his beard alight and was hit on the hands when he tried to touch his beard'. Klemperer was understandably concerned that this was a public reaction and not Nazi thugs (SA) under orders. He related more promising news about another acquaintance who had been attacked, but some Aryan friends had rescued him.[31]

This extract showed that although not all Germans were persuaded to hate Jews some did, for which men like Goebbels were responsible.

Anti-Church

Recalling Goebbels' early ambitions within the Church, and the help they gave him during his early education, he was now in a very different space in his attitudes and thinking. There are a few early diary entries when he expressed concern about the Party's anti-Church stance, and he had expressed annoyance at crucifixes being banned from schools and hospitals.

Further entries reinforce this interpretation as he believed that anti-Church propaganda would cause resentment amongst many Germans, over which he was correct. There are many differing historical viewpoints on Goebbels and Hitler's views of the Church, and often the Church publicly and naturally expressed its criticisms of the regime which made it an instant target for Nazi aggression. There were some clergy of all denominations who either had some sympathy for the Nazi regime, or who felt they should try to save themselves or protect the Church, but it should not be forgotten that a massive number of priests and ministers soon found themselves in concentration camps. Goebbels realised that a major conflict with the Church in a war would be highly counter-productive, and he thought it should wait for safer times. He had left the Church during his student days, having borrowed money from them for his education. He never technically left the Church and paid his Church tax even though he had been ex-communicated for marrying a divorced woman.

However, once in power, he developed a serious distrust of all Church denominations, not least because many were a form of opposition to the NSDAP because of the way the regime was conducting itself. Goebbels' 'combative attitude towards the Catholic Church was perhaps as clearly defined as that towards the Jews, but it reveals even more clearly his split state of mind'.[32]

To keep the churches passive Hitler had appointed a Hanns Kerrl as Reich Minister for Church Affairs. The idea behind this appointment was that the Protestant churches which were varied and many would unite, it was a bold ecumenical view but started for the wrong reasons. Goebbels was in favour of this at times, but only because he saw the Protestant element as a balancing factor against the power of the Vatican. In many ways the sense of anti-Church hostility during 1936–7 arose at the time when Hitler had invited some Cabinet members to join the Party, and the Reich Transport Minister, Paul von Eltz-Rübenach refused on the grounds that the Party was supressing the Church, and he demanded a better policy towards the churches in general. This singular protest by a Cabinet Minister raised the Church problem as a serious and possibly an ongoing concern. Goebbels' observations were correct in so far that individual clergy of all denominations were still justifiably protesting about the behaviour of the government. His full venom subsequently came into play backed by other senior Party members including Himmler, Hess and Wilhelm Frick. Plans were formulated to resolve the Church issue, with Goebbels writing that 'Kerrl wants to conserve the Church, while we want to liquidate it. Our differences are not just tactical but fundamental', making his viewpoint all too clear.[33]

His initial idea was to separate Church and State and watch the former suffer from income loss so they would be obliged to seek help from the State. Hitler himself changed his views many times, having little time to bother about this potential opposition, warning he would cancel the Concordat with the Vatican and only National Socialists could be considered the real Christians.* Other times he was calmer, but this was undoubtedly more to do with his concentrating on foreign policy, and he may have realised that being seen as oppressing the Church might send out the wrong signals internationally. As with the Jews the Church did not suffer the same vitriol during the Olympic Games, or during the plebiscite in the Saarland, and other times when the regime was all too aware they were being watched from overseas. When in 1937 Goebbels had given an especially vitriolic attack on the Church in a major broadcast speech in the Berlin *Deutschlandhalle*, he recognised he may have 'gone too far, just as he had stirred up foreign opposition by his anti-Semitic speeches'.[34]

The Pope had published an encyclical with the leading title of *With Burning Concern* in which he outrightly objected to the Nazi ideology and its pseudo-religious stance. There was an attempt to ignore this, but not with Goebbels who was angry and had noticed how quickly the foreign press had picked the subject up and agreed with its contents. Cunningly Goebbels decided to reopen some old paedophile cases against clergy and make it as public as possible. He revelled in this attack on the personal morality of some priests and the Church at every given opportunity. The various openings of the paedophile cases may have been the correct thing to do, but it was all done for the wrong reasons, and he used this action as a tool to attack all clergy and the Church for this weakness, and the sins of the few, ordering all newspapers to join in the attack. There were some 400 cases, perhaps

* On 20 July 1933 Vice-Chancellor von Papen and the Secretary for State of the Vatican, Cardinal Pacelli (later Pope Pius XII) had concluded the Reich Concordat.

some were justified, others less so, but it worked in propaganda terms. Hitler was pleased with the propaganda and the NSDAP policy decided to forbid celibacy, and they promulgated that no one under 24 should be allowed to study theology, religious orders were to be thrown out, and churches were to lose their right to teach. Goebbels was happy and frequently referred to the moral decay of the Church.

The well-known and much admired Pastor Martin Niemöller of the Confessing Church was arrested for making critical comments, and was sentenced by a fairly sympathetic court to seven months, but Hitler ordered that he was to go to a concentration camp as one of his personal prisoners, where he was retained until 1945, but survived.* Trying to eradicate the churches from any form of public life remained Goebbels' fixations throughout the rest of his life.

After the annexation of Austria in 1938 the situation of the Catholic Church raised its head again. Goebbels and Hitler agreed that there could be no other authority even outside Germany which could issue influential advice or orders. Hitler spoke at length to the Viennese Cardinal Theodor Innitzer, and Goebbels even suggested the concept of a German Catholic Church without recognising the leadership of the Pope. Cardinal Innizter may have had a degree of sympathy for Hitler's Germanic ideas, or maybe pretended he had, but Goebbels' suggestion remained just a mere idea.

During the early war years, the Church had raised a fierce protest at the T4 Euthanasia programme. The Euthanasia Decree was known as *Aktion T4*, the *T4* standing for *Tiergartenstraße 4* which was the street address of the Chancellery Department at that time, prompting a reminder of Primo Levi's remark of 'the banality of evil'. The Roman Catholic Bishop of Münster, Clemens August von Galen had protested at the action as well as remonstrating about the confiscation of Church property. Local Party activists and functionaries in the Münsterland were outraged, 'denouncing Galen as a British agent'.[35] The regional leader Meyer asked Bormann if Galen should not be hanged, but Goebbels was against making the Bishop a martyr.[36] Goebbels tried to prepare public opinion by producing a film called *J'Accuse* (*I Accuse*) in 1941 (mentioned earlier under Films) about a

* First, he was interned in Sachsenhausen then Dachau.

woman dying from multiple sclerosis and demanding the choice to die. It provoked discussion but few connected it with the Nazi medical killing programme, and 'despite the public protests of 1940 and 1941, knowledge about the medical killings remained very patchy...when Wally Linden signed the receipt on 12 March 1943, acknowledging the return of her dead son Dietrich's things, she gave no indication that she doubted he had died a natural death'.[37]

The protest was growing louder and Hitler along with Bormann and Goebbels decided the euthanasia problem was to be put on the shelf. Somewhat cynically they had probably finished this degenerate and immoral policy because an estimated 70,000 people had been murdered by the state. Goebbels advised the various Gauleiters that during the war criticism of the Church should keep a low profile. There were too many believing Church goers amongst the soldiers, and it was a problem which would have to be solved after the war. In a strange twist of fate an aircraft bombed a hospital in September 1940 giving Goebbels the opportunity to broadcast against the wicked British. A highly respected Pastor Friedrich von Bodelschwingh at the hospital said, 'should I condemn the deed of the English and shortly afterwards take part in an infanticide on a far greater scale'.[38]

Chapter Seven

Towards War

Goebbels Overseas

Goebbels may have been clever and intelligent, but he had limited experience of life beyond the German borders. In his limited wanderings he 'never saw a genuine democratic country, and the same with Hitler and Himmler.[1] At one time Goebbels had planned a visit to the Great Fair of Chicago in 1933, but Hitler was furious at the idea and it was dropped at once.[2] He made some minor visits in Europe and personally desired to make a great public appearance overseas, which would have suited his demanding ego. His lack of travel, as with other Nazis, clearly indicated that most of them had a gross misunderstanding about non-Germans. It is known that they had no idea of the American potential industrial output, tending to associate America as being only concerned about cars and kitchenware, probably encouraged by America's policy of isolationism. More importantly they tended to see the traditional Western Powers of America, Britain and France as ex-enemies who had oppressed them with the Treaty of Versailles, and knew nothing about their citizens' right to have opposing opinions to the government and their legal right to oppose and criticise.

He did make a trip to Rome in May 1933 which was primarily intended as making personal connections with Italian fascism and its leaders. He was pleased in his self-important image of himself, to see a chauffeur driven car ordered for him by Mussolini. Despite his views of his own self-importance, it was not intended for Goebbels to shape the political relationships between the two countries. It was a rapid tour during which Goebbels gloried in being lavishly entertained and meeting important people. He thought little of the German ambassador Ulrich von Hassell whom he derided as *petit bourgeois*, but the feeling was mutual.* He thought highly of Mussolini,

* Von Hassell was anti-Nazi, and his diary has been a sound reference in this exploration.

and the main policy for a visit was to spread the good news of the NSDAP and improve the Italian and German relationship. However, Goebbels was not kept in the picture of the various plans that Mussolini and Hitler were already hatching, he was simply a public relations exercise though he would have viewed it quite differently.

In September 1934, Goebbels attended the League of Nations in Switzerland and its ever-continuing discussion about disarmament. While there, he exhibited an appalling exhibitionist approach of walking around with members of the SA as his bodyguard, exposing that he was out of his depth in such a diplomatic international meeting. Goebbels instantly detected the animosity of the foreign press. He held a conference in which he mentioned the Jewish issue and stating, 'I will not pretend that certain excesses perpetrated by uncontrollable elements have taken place during the national revolution in Germany'.[3] He regarded himself as a born diplomat to the amusement of many foreign correspondents, as most of them knew he was a powerful driving force against the Jews.

Germany later withdrew from the conference on the grounds that France was unwilling to disarm and became the 'isolate' in Europe, although rapidly descending to what may called a pariah state. As in Italy, however, Goebbels perceived his role to be important, but he had only been sent as a public relations exercise. He travelled on the suggestion of the Foreign Minister Neurath and spent most of his time making cynical diary entries about the international figures he met. He was never part of any decision-making process, he was just 'a diversionary tactic', his 'self-confident appearance there, which he thought so brilliant, was designed to pull the wool over the eyes of the international diplomatic fraternity', but by most accounts it failed.[4]

In February 1934, he visited Warsaw. Hitler was intent in Germany breaking free of the diplomatic isolation he had created, and he was seeking agreements and treaties where possible. Unlike Italy and Switzerland this was not a grand tour of meeting national leaders or being feted and feasted as in Italy, it was a utilitarian visit based simply on a fact-finding mission and appraising the future between the two countries.

In 1936, he took Magda to Venice and then travelled to Greece where he was given a national award, visiting the traditional famous historical sites. The Greek tour was more of an official visit, but again it was a mere public relations exercise. In the spring of 1939, when Goebbels would rather have been in Berlin, Hitler had demanded that he go on a previously arranged trip overseas. It was probably (as previously suggested because Hitler did not regard Goebbels as indispensable) that there were other factors in play. His private and casual trip overseas would send out the signal that Berlin was at ease and not a cause of concern. May be the intention of not being a cause of concern was right for the regime, but as one historian has probably correctly pointed out that Goebbels 'could not imagine that hugely significantly decisions would be maturing in Berlin during his absence, and he did not grasp that his trip was a political diversionary tactic'.[5] He did a diplomatic tour through Budapest, Belgrade, Athens, then Rhodes and Egypt where according to his own dairy entries he found everything exciting. What he found less pleasing was meeting journalists from democratic countries because he made 'no headway in his dealings with people who did not jump at his command'.[6] Furthermore, while he was away Mussolini had occupied Albania and Hitler was preparing *Case White* for the invasion of Poland. As important as he thought he was, he was not part of the then current inner Nazi circle, he was only seen as essential for his propaganda abilities.

The Saar and Danzig

Hitler was interested in the return of the Saar, famous for its coalmines but still under the control of the League of Nations. It was suggested that another plebiscite should resolve the issue, and so Goebbels threw the propaganda machine into full swing. This event has often been quoted as Hitler breaking away from the Treaty of Versailles, which a few historians have queried. However, this policy once known, enflamed international tension and became a constituent component towards the build-up of war. It would be like an American President suggesting Canada should be part of the USA and Greenland should belong to the States, a dangerous signal for the rest of the world.

However, the League of Nations by arrangement had control of the Saar for some fifteen years and it had been administered first by a Frenchman, than a Canadian and next by an Englishman. The Saar plebiscite was administered by a British administrator called Sir Geoffrey Knox. Nobody could foretell the outcome because many Germans had fled to the Saar from Germany because of the Nazi dominance. Communists and Social Democrats preferred the United Nations, but in the Saar, there were resident German Nazis who had already taken on board Goebbels' propaganda followed by the usual thuggery and intimidation. The League of Nations were aware of the tensions but too timid about stirring up the all too familiar local Nazi riots. Many who had lived in the Saar had gone to Germany to become Nazis, and it was rumoured that they threatened to invade their old homeland. Anthony Eden offered to send soldiers to keep the peace and matters cooled down a little because of this threat. The plebiscite took place on the 13 January 1935 and was overseen by judges from Italy, the Netherlands and America who declared the result fair and genuine. The result was an overwhelming 90.3 per cent in favour of Germany. In this sense it was in accordance with the Treaty of Versailles, though as mentioned a constituent part of the road to war. Goebbels was pleased not just because it validated the Third Reich, but as he had pontificated, it demonstrated that Germany would not be brow-beaten, and they would stand behind their Führer even when he was miles away. For Goebbels it also threw doubts on the validity of the Treaty of Versailles, giving him the opportunity to boost Hitler further, thereby casting into doubt similar situations, especially in the Sudetenland. This incident not only concerned the rest of the world about Hitler's expansionist ideas, but it underlined that the League of Nations would do anything to avoid conflict. For many German people it seemed to justify the Hitler theory that the Germanic people had to be united. Little attention was paid to the fact that when Eden threatened with military resources the opposition had stepped back. Goebbels ordered swastikas to be flown and draped in every possible space illustrating his fanatical sense of nationalism.

During the Saar plebiscite it was apparent to many observers that the voting had been run under Nazi control based on the ever-present sense of fear. Goebbels flew to the Free State of Danzig to repeat the so-called success. This time the results were a mere 59.3 per cent, and he had to persuade the local Gauleiter Albert Forster not to fabricate higher results over the radio. The Danzig High Court decided the voting campaign had been corrupted by secret funding from Germany, opposition parties were banned or supressed, but the United Nations exposed its traditional weakness and refused to revoke the result. The result was poor compared to previous voting in the area despite all the Nazi manipulation. It was clear to Goebbels that the Danzig exercise was a great disappointment. Despite the marches, flag waving and bullying tactics it was for Goebbels indicating a failure. The growing Nazi anti-Church tactics had been one factor in that area, but the aggressive tactics in Germany were known in Danzig and not appreciated. There was also a growing resentment about the way senior Party members behaved using their power to live in luxury and bully others. It was at this stage that Goebbels realised knew he had to pay more attention to the public moods.

The Third Reich did purposefully break the Treaty of Versailles when Göring suddenly announced the following month that Germany had a new air force (the Luftwaffe), and Hitler announced he was introducing universal conscription. During these months Goebbels was visiting boat shows out of personal interest as he loved this as pastime, and these declarations caught him by surprise. He responded with his usual rhetoric, propaganda and with many journalistic articles referring to the power of Germany and the will of the Führer.

Hitler, Goebbels, with some others were becoming concerned at Germany's apparent growing isolation as a pariah state. When news came from Poland that Marshal Józef Piłsudski had died on 12 May 1935, there was some panic because the German Polish treaty and relationship at the time was deemed necessary. Goebbels raised the matter with Hitler and together with Göring and Ribbentrop they discussed the way forward. It was Göring who attended the funeral returning with the news that the new man, Józef Beck, would keep to the treaty.

Meanwhile, Mussolini with new ideas for his 'Roman Empire' was looking towards Abyssinia which soon led to an international crisis. Goebbels warned his press not to be critical of the Italian behaviour, and Hitler in the meantime offered Britain his hand in negotiating. On 18 June, Hitler signed the Anglo-German Naval Treaty, and both Hitler and Goebbels soon started to think, quite mistakenly, that relationships between the two countries could develop into an alliance. Both men, as noted, were inexperienced in the life and traditions of other countries, appeared diplomatically dumb when it came to British relationships and attitudes. The signing of the Naval Treaty led

Goebbels and Hitler to think or hope that Germany was emerging again as an acceptable and respectable member of the international European club.

When Italy finally invaded Abyssinia there were international repercussions, and Hitler decided this was the time to rearm because Italy had diverted international attention, which suited his long-term policy. The rearmament brought more employment but cost money, and there was some public protest at the shortage and price of food caused by the impact of the war-industry. Goebbels promptly addressed this problem speaking of the needs of the 'national community' which was to become one of his stock phrases. To try and counter the public annoyance at the austerity another huge Christmas party was held, and an astonishing five million children were given Christmas presents.

At the end of 1935, Goebbels and Rosenberg were again in serious contention with one another, but Goebbels managed to keep Hitler on his side by blocking Rosenberg from intruding in what he decided was his cultural authority. Rosenberg even managed to make it deeply personal by letting it be known that he knew about one of Magda Goebbels' affairs from the past with someone called Lüdecke.

1936 Berlin Olympics

The 1936 Olympics in Berlin provided the moment for Germany's show piece, and Goebbels and Hitler spent time together at both the winter ceremonies in Garmisch, and later in the year at the full summer meeting where Germany led in many events. Goebbels was more than happy when the visiting teams marched by Hitler giving the Nazi salute, but he was cynical about the Americans using their Black athletes, and 'in general, Goebbels' sports policy was to display the winners and hide the losers'.[7]

The various Party leaders exhibited themselves by giving large, sumptuous parties to visiting dignitaries. Goebbels gave one of the grandest parties which became notorious and was known as the *Pfauen-Insel Fest* (Peacock Island Feast), with people attending if only to see the 'Mephistopheles of Europe' as Goebbels was sometime known.[8] It was full of gate crashers, the drinking was out of control, which was an embarrassment for which Goebbels naturally blamed everyone else.

Early in the same year Hitler started to think about remilitarising the Rhineland which would clearly indicate his intentions to break the Versailles and the Locarno treaties. Once the deed had been done Hitler decided on a new election would be called for by the Reichstag. When it happened there was no serious protest and reaction within the international community, and Hitler tried to justify the occupation by reference to the proposed French-Soviet Treaty.

Goebbels worked hard for the next elective vote, always speaking and writing and referring to the event as the 'People's Day'. It resulted in a claimed 99 per cent vote which delighted him and Hitler but was obviously rigged from start to finish. Hitler felt he not only had total power but seemingly the support of the people, and he mentioned to Goebbels and his other cohorts the ominous warning that they must maintain the tensions in Austria and Czechoslovakia, indicating that his totalitarian power was having some sinister intentions. Hitler also had an audience with an envoy of General Francisco Franco in Spain. Goebbels was not privy to these international deliberations, but Hitler always kept him informed.

Under instruction from his Führer, Goebbels began a series of anti-Bolshevist tirades which were to become widespread and regular. It was during 1936 that German foreign policy started to formulate emanating from Hitler's long-term plans. Goebbels was mainly excluded from this side of policy making, though he observed and made notes in his diary as if he were a critical component of government. Some of these notes have proved useful in ascertaining that certain meetings did occur when they did, and Hitler's main contention was against communism. Hitler appeared convinced that France and Spain would become communist controlled countries. The Italian Foreign Minister Ciano, Mussolini's son-in-law, had visited Hitler at the Berghof and from this grew the possibility of an alliance between Germany and Italy initiating an anti-communist block. Mussolini within weeks was speaking about the Rome-Berlin axis. Observing the likely clash between Russia and Japan, an Anti-Comintern Pact was signed on 25 November 1936, making it clear that Hitler was looking to aggressive policies, seeking the necessary alliances for his viewpoints and need for his dominance.

By 1936–7 Hitler's plans were more like a moving kaleidoscope but there were gathering features. When Mussolini visited Germany for a grand tour, Goebbels was able to meet and greet the two national leaders at the old Olympics stadium. Millions of people had been instructed to attend, with announcements in the press expecting them there. Behind this showmanship Hitler was now more openly anticipating expansion in Austria and Czechoslovakia. Goebbels was not involved with such foreign policy and the plans, but he was kept in the picture to come to terms with the necessary propaganda.

Blomberg and von Fritsch

As 1938 unfolded the Party was hit by two seeming scandals at the same time. The first was the well-known case of Reich War Minister Blomberg who at the beginning of the year had married a much younger woman who apparently had a dubious sexual background, and this was brought to light probably by Göring, who had long desired Blomberg's post. It was also Göring who produced old Gestapo documents accusing Werner von Fritsch, head of the army, of being a homosexual. The witness against Fritsch was a young man who had a record of blackmail and using homosexual liaisons as his *modus operandi*. Goebbels exhibited his usual hypocritical disgust suggesting that Blomberg should shoot himself, and expressed surprise that Fritsch was a 175er.* There was little doubt that Göring was manipulating events, but Hitler resolved the problem by taking over the military himself, and pleasing Göring by making him a Field Marshal. The trial of Fritsch took place, and it was soon proved that Fritsch was totally innocent as he had claimed all the time. The only note Goebbels made was that it must have shown Himmler in a bad light. During these momentous events it is easy to gain the impression that although Goebbels spoke to Hitler over many of the issues, he was more of an observer than his diary entries tended to indicate.

Austrian Putsch, *Anschluss*

It had been as early as 1934 when Goebbels attended a meeting in Bayreuth with the senior NSDAP Theodor Habicht for Austria, and his SA counterpart.

---

* 175er referred to the legal section outlawing homosexuality and was the popular way of referring to this so-called offence.

His diary entry is the only reasonably reliable evidence that the German Party leaders knew exactly what was being prepared. On 27 July 1934, an attempted putsch took place when the Austrian radio transmitter building was taken over, and the Federal Chancellor's office occupied. This resulted in the death of the Federal Chancellor Engelbert Dollfuss, but although the rising spread, it was quickly stopped. It was known and noted that Mussolini had been in support of the Austrian government, and the Italian press to Goebbels' annoyance made the failed affair too much a point of interest. Mussolini was nervous about having the growing power of the Nazi regime too close to his own borders.

However, during the year 1938, German power was rapidly growing. Goebbels was only an observer in the world-shattering event of the takeover of Austria, which sent reverberations through all governments and diplomatic circles. It was commonly known as the *Anschluss* or annexation. It amounted to a case of sheer bullying by Hitler and Göring of the Federal Chancellor Schuschnigg, the unpleasant tactics of Arthur Seyss-Inquart, threats of revolution, and invasion. Hitler's policy was to increase Germany and his power, and his explanation or excuse was uniting German speaking peoples. However, many foreign observers noted the apparently joyful reception of German troops as they marched into Austria on the 12 March 1938, and the Austrian troops had to swear allegiance to Hitler as their first act. It was all manipulated from the beginning to the end despite the support that the Austrian NSDAP supporters had been able to bring to the surface. The Pulitzer Prize winning journalist Edgar Mowrer reported from Paris that 'there is no one in all France who does not believe that Hitler invaded Austria not to hold a genuine plebiscite but to prevent the plebiscite planned by Schuschnigg from demonstrating to the entire world just how little hold National Socialism really had on that tiny country'.[9] It would be a difficult if not an impossible task to give a realistic appraisal of actual Austrian support for Hitler, but the *Anschluss* made it clear that Hitler had wide-ranging designs, and many of the Austrian public were happy and up went the persecution of Austrian Jews. Goebbels was in conversation with Hitler during this event, but his main task was controlling the press and ensuring the best propaganda was printed. His theme tune tended to be that Germany's only interest was the protection of what he termed 'national comrades',

Goebbels (right) at first Communion. (*Public domain*)

The happy family. Goebbels with his wife Magda and six children. At the back is Harald Quandt from Magda's first marriage. Goebbels and Magda murdered their children before killing themselves. Harald was lucky – a prisoner of the British, he survived and postwar became a wealthy businessman. (*Bundesarchiv, Bild 146-1978-086-03/CC-BY-SA 3.0*)

When they were younger and hopeful. Himmler to left, Göring to the right, Goebbels always close behind Hitler. (*Public domain*)

Hitler was always very close to Magda and her family. (*Bundesarchiv, Bild 183-1987-0724-502/Heinrich Hoffmann/ CC-BY-SA 3.0*)

Portrait of Magda. (*Bundesarchiv, Bild 146-1973-034-56/CC-BY-SA 3.0*)

Charming. (*Public domain*)

Coercive. (*Public domain*)

Threatening. (*Bundesarchiv, Bild 102-17049/Georg Pahl/CC-BY-SA 3.0*)

Goebbels with the Finnish SS. They are attentive but their faces range from grim to bored. (*Public domain*)

Hitler's left-hand attendant. (*Public domain*)

Checking the Degenerate Art Exhibition, 1938. (*Bundesarchiv, Bild 183-H02648/CC BY-SA 3.0 DE*)

Goebbels was noted for his limp (right foot) and diminutive size. (*Public domain*)

Goebbels' broadcasts came from speakers in streets and factories, and the posters could not be missed. (*Public domain*)

Goebbels preparing for radio broadcast to the nation. (*Public domain*)

Goebbels giving a speech. (*Public domain*)

Goebbels giving a street speech in Berlin, July 1932. (*Bundesarchiv, Bild 119-2406-01 / CC-BY-SA 3.0*)

Telling his audience what to think and how to act. (*Public domain*)

Showing how good the NSDAP was by giving thousands of children gifts. (*Public domain*)

Saluting a work force – spades, not guns. (*Public domain*)

Hitler often gave Goebbels flowers. (*Public domain*)

Franz von Papen with Hitler and Goebbels *c.*1934. (*Public domain*)

Goebbels, Hitler and von Blomberg, February 1934. (*Bundesarchiv, Bild 102-00765/CC-BY-SA 3.0*)

Goebbels and Göring promised that Berlin could not be bombed. (*Public domain/CCO 1.0 Universal*)

which was Hitler's main theme. When the British government made their protests, Goebbels believed that it was only Neville Chamberlain trying to appease his own opposition in Parliament. It was Goebbels who arranged for Germany to be in a state of self-celebration, with flags and swastikas flying everywhere, parades of jubilation, and then he busied himself with yet more elections because Hitler had announced the dissolution of the Parliament. It was the last ever vote and recorded 99 per cent in favour following a turnout of 99.6 per cent, with even Goebbels wondering if the election rigging had been taken too far.[10] Later Göring would explain how the rigging was done at the Nuremberg Trials but basically people who voted 'no' or spoilt their papers 'could be identified and punished, and people who took this course, or refused to vote, were beaten by the Brownshirts, or dragged through the streets with placards round their neck calling them traitors'.[11] Goebbels visited Vienna, visiting as the all-conquering hero's main representative, and following a conversation with Hitler he was determined to do something about the Jewish problem in Austria.

Sudetenland

For some time, Goebbels had been aware of Hitler's designs on the Sudetenland in Czechoslovakia.* The Party leaders of the Sudetenland had long been instructed to become belligerent in their demands, but the press was restrained by Goebbels following Hitler's instruction, mainly because he was about to visit Italy on a State tour with Goebbels as his companion. It was during this trip that it was Hitler who informed Goebbels that Magda had given birth to another daughter called Hedwig, such was the frenzied state of their lives.

Ribbentrop was concerned about the brewing trouble in Sudetenland, but Goebbels who detested Ribbentrop was less certain and knew he had Hitler's support. However, on their return from Italy Goebbels raised the temperature in the press, later hesitating because it suddenly occurred to him that his campaign might need to be toned down for fear of war. It is both curious and interesting to note that in his diaries the sense of 'war panic'

* This was again primarily an area of ethnic German speakers and specifically along the borders of Bohemia, Moravia and parts of Czech Silesia which had been part of Austria until 1918.

worried him. Goebbels was an intelligent man who realised that any war, let alone a major European conflict, could lead to death and destruction, and he only came to terms with this concern once he had no choice.

In the meantime, Goebbels with his anti-Semitism monitored the press, stirring it up with polemics against the Czech government, and at other times demanding restraint during more sensitive times as when the British Lord Runciman went to Czechoslovakia with a delegation. The pro-German party in Sudetenland, the SdP, were ordered directly by Hitler to create as much confrontation as they could. At the Nuremberg rally more rousing provocation was made in Goebbels' speeches. When the ensuing violence resulted in deaths, Goebbels announced this in the papers with grossly misleading figures and bias. He was not involved in Chamberlain's visit, but Hitler conferred with him later. Goebbels held the opinion that all the British wanted was to avoid war at any costs, and he was correct in this view at this moment in time. Goebbels ensured the whole of the German press were supporting Hitler's claim on protecting German nationals in the Sudetenland. Hitler, Goebbels and Göring went to Bad Godesberg for a meeting with Chamberlain, while Goebbels was proposing some form of plebiscite, or referendum which was his political device to gain some form of justification. Hitler simply announced the Wehrmacht would move in by 1 October. It was clear from both his diary entries and newspaper reports that Goebbels was convinced the situation would be achieved by diplomatic bullying rather than by war. He organised a massive show of support for Hitler's return to Berlin making sure that the Sportpalast was filled to the brim and the street pavements were tightly packed. Hitler promised his listeners it would be the last territorial demand he would make, and Goebbels gave the order for the press to carry out a direct attack on Edvard Beneš. France threatened to stand by Czechoslovakia and Britain stood alongside France, but Hitler appeared unconcerned. Goebbels on the other hand pointed out that from his observations of the general population indicated there was no appetite for another war. At the end of October, a four nation conference was decided upon with Germany, Italy, France and Britain. After the infamous Munich Agreement Goebbels was full of pleasure as it seemed that diplomacy had resolved the problem as he had hoped.

Generally, and as noted, Goebbels was kept out of the central discussions on foreign policy, but as soon as he gathered that Hitler was beginning to consider the likelihood of aggressive war, true to form, he became warlike. His articles started to stir affairs, but he was careful to place the blame anywhere but Germany. For Goebbels the problems were what he termed the international string pullers, which meant for him 'international Jewry'. He tried to make his articles less cynical and more statesmanlike, but they always managed to sound conceited and pompous. He even resorted to the royal 'we', assuming the Party and the nation were the same body. For a time, he was ill because of passing a kidney stone but was grateful when Magda took a long holiday in Italy. When he recovered, he discovered that Hitler was looking towards Czechoslovakia as his next target, and used Bratislava as some form of excuse, so he entered the fray at once. The Prague government had dismissed the Bratislava government to avoid Slovakia giving into German pressure. Hitler decided that the Slovakians should issue a cry for help, but Jozef Tiso at first declined.* Goebbels was ordered to increase the propaganda pressure, and Tiso arrived in Berlin and was told that Slovakia would remain an independent State protected by the Third Reich, which was a tempting offer under the circumstances. However, when he returned to his country Ribbentrop presented him with an ultimatum, so the Slovakian State almost immediately declared its independence. The Czech President Emil Hácha was ruthlessly bullied and threatened in Berlin, and German troops marched into Czechoslovakia and by the 15 March Hitler had arrived in Prague.

Goebbels carried out his usual duties by organising noisy ceremonial events to welcome Hitler's return. The taking of the whole of Czechoslovakia was the lighting of the fuse because it had broken the recently signed Munich Agreement, and it was now clear to the Western Allies that Hitler simply could not be trusted. In Britain, the Prime Minister Neville Chamberlain swore he would never trust Hitler again, and he would have nothing to do with him. Hitler was unconcerned and Goebbels started to attack the British in his articles and propaganda, calling the French and British protests mere

* Jozef Tiso (1887–executed 1947) was a Slovakian Roman Catholic priest and headed the 1939–45 First Slovak Republic as a satellite of the Third Reich.

stage thunder. Hitler had lit the fire, and his servant Goebbels fanned the flames. As is well known Hitler turned his attention toward Memelland with surprising speed because of the massive self-confidence that his own success was breeding.* Ribbentrop issued the same threats to Juozas Urbšys and another acquisition was gained.**

After Prague and Memelland Hitler turned towards Poland, and again Goebbels came into the attack by writing vitriolic defamatory attacks on the way German speakers were being treated. However, Poland was not going to be a mere diplomatic bullying-type victory, and Józef Beck would not be bullied by Ribbentrop and took himself off to London. The Polish and British pact was signed, and so Goebbels turned his full invective on Britain. It was at this stage that he found himself at war over his own propaganda because the Foreign Office and Wehrmacht were increasing their own propaganda offices, and under the circumstances of 1939 they were more dominant. It remained a constant source of irritation for him, and he took himself off on a private holiday across the Balkans to Egypt.

By May 1939, it was clear that Britain was going to hold fast to its moral but militarily useless agreement with Poland, and Goebbels immediately started a new outpouring in his propaganda, inciting distrust of the imperial British, the old enemy, and introduced the implication that the main problem revolved around what he termed as 'the encirclers'.[12] This was a reference to those countries which surrounded Germany with perceived threats in 1914. Goebbels, however, noted that there was not the same wish amongst the public for another major war as had been the case in 1914. He started to talk of Hitler's favourite theme of *Lebensraum* and of the British losing their empire, giving the distinct impression he was stoking the fires of war and by August he was stoking the anti-Polish fires to the extreme. As always, Goebbels merely responded to events, and he only learned about the decision-making process regarding the pact between Russia and Germany afterwards, and he immediately referred to it as a brilliant chess move by the Führer, although it meant he had to do something about explaining a serious U-turn by Hitler. His diaries reflected his own thinking and self-

* Memelland was predominantly German was separated after the Treaty of Versailles, under French jurisdiction, and later, in 1923, administered by Lithuania.

** Juozas Urbšys was the Minister for Foreign Affairs in Lithuania.

importance, but they occasionally showed the various machinations which were poorly recorded elsewhere. In the latter part of August 1939, Hitler ordered Goebbels to draw up proclamations for the public and the Party explaining why war with Poland was necessary and inevitable. He noted that Hitler still anticipated some form of arrangement with Britain, but he now believed this as unlikely. When Italy did not join the proposed affray Hitler was annoyed and concerned, but such was Goebbels' adoration he was convinced that Hitler would cope without the Italians.

Chapter Eight

The Second World War

Poland 1939

As is well known the attack on Poland was preceded by false alarms started by the SS using concentration camp victims as part of the malicious and carefully planned prefabricated claim that the Poles had started the attack. Goebbels was aware of these intrigues but entered them into his diary as if they were the absolute truth.* He made the same sort of entry over the sinking of the liner *Athenia* when he claimed it was a British trick. When the guilty U-boat arrived back to its base the truth was out, but Goebbels simply employed lies and entered it in his diary in such a way as if he thoroughly believed it to be true. As in many other entries it raises the question not so much about his psychological state of mind, but that he was foreseeing that one day his diaries would be the focus for the history of Europe. He once wrote that 'when you have told a lie you must stick to it'.[1] One biographer expressed this well when he wrote that Goebbels 'had attained the difficult acrobatic skill of telling himself one lie after another; to apply such skill to others involved no special effort'.[2] Goebbels grew myths which still hold some sway to this day. In one incident the Polish commander of a troop of cavalry ordered his troops not to surrender but to try and escape through a gap between the enemy tanks where they were cut down by machine guns. Goebbels made it sound as if the Polish troops were so badly equipped and poorly led that they had to attack tanks with horses. The myth found another unintended dimension when it was taken on board to illustrate the bravery of Polish soldiers.[3]

---

* The Poles did kill ethnic Germans in Poland; the estimates are dubious but 6,000 seems the most likely. Goebbels inflated this to 58,000. See Beevor, Antony, *The Second World War* (London: Weidenfeld & Nicolson, 2012), p.29.

For Goebbels it was essential keep the public mind on seeing Hitler as Germany's greatest ever hero and beyond criticism. He made some stupendous errors to the bemusement of many foreign correspondents, those who had the strength of character to risk staying in Germany. The American journalist and later historian William Shirer read in Goebbels' paper *Der Angriff* an article on Stalin and communism, and he realised that Goebbels had not been kept in the picture of the Molotov-Ribbentrop agreement. It is not difficult to imagine Goebbels' anger as he had to do a rapid 'U-turn'.

Hitler ordered Goebbels to ensure that radio broadcasts were issued in such a way as to make the German public understood the political rightness leading to the need for the Polish invasion. The alleged atrocities against Polish Germans were both emphasised and exaggerated out of all proportion. There had been some Polish violence, but Goebbels made sure that it was in the thousands which also led to some violent German retaliation. In the Nazi newspaper the *Völkischer Beobachter* with the headlines reading 'The Führer proclaims the fight for Germany's rights and security', and in another paper 'Terrible bestiality of the Poles...German fliers shot...Red Cross columns mowed down...nurses murdered'.[4] The truth is, as Goebbels would have known, is that the majority of newspaper readers tend to believe what is printed.

While Goebbels was busy trying to justify the Nazi war machine, he also had a fight on his hands at a personal level attempting in his changing world to maintain if not to increase his own power base. He was having a constant battle with the Wehrmacht propaganda and their news-broadcasts, as their reports tended to be matter of fact and neutral, and many foreign agencies used these reports.[5]

His most serious confrontations came with a serious clash with Ribbentrop who at this time, due to the Molotov-Ribbentrop Pact was prominent in Hitler's eyes. Later Hitler told Goebbels that he was wrong in his estimation of Ribbentrop claiming, 'he is one of the greatest men we have, and history will put him above Bismarck'.[6] Hitler brought the two protagonists together, but they failed to resolve the issue. 'Friction followed on friction, over all kinds of issues', and the antagonism between Goebbels and Ribbentrop, the two political men of prestige, lasted for the duration of the war.[7]

Goebbels was uncertain about the potential ramifications of the war and rarely, but once again, found himself in agreement with Göring who appeared concerned that the retrieval of Polish territory might just lead to another major world conflict. This was a misreading of Göring who was more concerned about a two-front war. It was at this time that Goebbels took a strong line on Germans listening to foreign radio broadcasts with threats of serious punishment, which became known as 'the radio crime'. This was the start of his efforts to bring the population into line with the Nazi theories and their approach to the necessity of war. He was aware that many Germans were unhappy about the prospect of war, the poor home economics resulting from the expenditure on the military, and the conscription of men had added fuel to this resentment. He was concerned that the speed of declaring or causing war could be damaging for the Party and his insights into the German public mind made him uneasy at the then current speed of events.

Goebbels heard from Hitler that his intention was to drive a wedge between Britain and France, and if possible and necessary to make a separate peace with France. Goebbels was in the outside corridors of power when it came to war, feeling left out by Hitler who only turned to him to start propaganda on his temporary wish for peace with the West. He was uncertain as to whether this could work, but he stoked up the propaganda against the British, and he was somewhat subdued about France. He was only able to reflect on these issues about Hitler's ideas because he was on the edge of foreign policy affairs or when these decisions were being made or discussed.

Goebbels believed that Ribbentrop would be incapable of dealing with the French or the British, which was a cynical but realistic view. When outside Hitler's presence he also criticised Ribbentrop for being too confident in the new relationship he had mapped out with the Soviet Union. When Hitler eventually made a peace offer to Britain and France, Goebbels had hoped that this would resolve all the problems he foresaw. When Chamberlain rejected the offer Goebbels realised that he had to adjust his thinking to a long-term war which he thought would be like the attritional trench warfare of 1914–18. He continued his attacks on Britain, especially in maritime matters where it was understood they held the upper hand. He turned his hand to commenting on as many events as possible if they involved Britain.

He entered in his diary on the 23 October 1939 with reference to the German sinking of the liner *Athenia* that 'Churchill answers our charges in the *Athenia* affair with bare-faced denial' (having accused him of boring holes in the liner's hull to encourage the Americans to join Britain and France). 'This enrages me so much that I immediately set to dictating a radio speech in reply, which summarises the entire case against him in the most biting form'.[8] It was an embarrassment for the Germans because at that stage Hitler had ordered that liners should not be sunk. The German admirals knew this, and they had organised a rapid cover up for the mistakes of a too eager U-boat commander to make his name. Raeder accused Churchill of the sinking, but postwar it was a 'hawk-eyed WRNS, however, who spotted that the logbook of the U-boat…had been forged and that of the official Naval War Diary had been falsified'.[9]

Goebbels took a trip to Poland even visiting Warsaw and looking with admiration at the damage done by German bombers. He met the new Governor Hans Frank and his deputy Arthur Seyss-Inquart, but as in other sphere of activity he was angry to see they had their own propaganda facilities.

Goebbels' Personal Life

After Hitler assumed total power and was creating war, he needed Goebbels less, and many of the senior Party henchmen anticipated it signalled the end of what they saw as the little tyrant. Rosenberg and others were hopeful to see the back of Goebbels, but Hitler knew he might just need him again. Goebbels was no fool and he started looking after himself at a personal level. He became expensive in his dress style and started to enjoy the good life of the detested bourgeoisie, but not 'shamelessly and openly like Göring and Amann'.[10] Nevertheless, Goebbels made sure he lived the life of the detested capitalist.

Although he was well off financially, he always appeared to have personal money problems. He had his official Berlin residence, he then acquired two other properties, one on an island in Wannsee (south-west Berlin) and Lanke on the Bogensee. He enjoyed waterfront views but wanted to stay close to the capital. With the second purchase he found himself short of money and even approached the Nazi fund banker Dr Winckler who suggested Göring might be able to help. This irritated him, but he followed the advice and was eventually helped by a personal gift from Hitler.* In making these purchases Goebbels had over-extended himself. He used the income from his book From the *Kaiserhof to the Reich Chancellery*, published in 1934 as well as advances kindly placed by the publishers at his disposal, but in the end his current income was hardly enough to maintain such expensive properties and his new lifestyle.

Unlike Göring he was not overly generous on party giving (apart from the infamous Olympics' party) and he was widely known for his austere dinner parties when it was rumoured that people left feeling hungry. It was perhaps not surprising that he had financial issues because he also purchased a motorboat which his driver Albert Tonak would take him out on Sundays. He was frequently seen at boat shows and purchased another boat, and he was constantly on the lookout for even better versions. Nothing gave him more joy than steering his boat with Hitler as his passenger, possibly seeing this as his role in the real world and at leisure. He often tried to pretend he lived an austere life as a man of the people, and especially when in the company of Göring, but it was all his usual clever deceitful fabrication. As one biographer put it, he lived the plutocratic living 'in many respects Goebbels came to live like a millionaire'.[11] He expected Magda to keep his homes open twenty-four hours a day and be ready for unexpected guests such the Duke and Duchess of Windsor and King Ferdinand of Bulgaria.[12]

An intriguing aspect of Goebbels' private life was his love for women and his pursuit of sexual adventure. His life with his wife Magda seemed too mundane for him. They had many children: Helga (1932), Hildegard (Hilda) (1934), Helmut (1935) Holdine (1937) Hedwig (Hedda) (1938) and Heidrun (Heide) (1940) as well as his stepson Harald. According to many sources he was a good father giving their children fatherly time and affection. However, his aide Semmler noted there was a lack of affection, and he was doing what he thought he ought to be seen doing. There was curious speculation over the choice of names since they all began with the letter 'H', and his relationship with Magda was marked by constant quarrelling and

---

* Hitler gave two packets of 50-mark bills, 'one can only speculate whether this deal represented compensation for services rendered in the Röhm affair'. Heiber, Helmut, *Goebbels* (New York: Hawthorn Books, 1972), p.226.

disputes. In 1934, he noted in his diary that there was a 'terrible thing about Magda' and raised the question for many later readers as to what she had been up to. Goebbels was aware of the possible would-be lover of Magda, namely Hitler lurking in the background. On the birth of Hilde, Goebbels noted that Hitler was always present, but on the other hand, Hitler had applied enough pressure on her first husband Quandt to stop his son leaving the Goebbels' household when aged 14. Quandt and Goebbels had long been at odds over this issue, but Quandt despite his wealth was up against a corrupt state. Goebbels and Magda quarrelled most of their life, and on one occasion Magda threatened divorce and left him until she responded to his order to return. They both loved Hitler and depended on his friendship which somehow held their marriage together.

One autumn Goebbels had the impression that Hitler was keeping a distance between himself and the family. He and Magda found this worrying, and when he suggested that Magda should go and see Hitler personally, they were deeply worried to find that Hitler did not have the time. Matters eventually healed for the agitated couple. It transpired that Hitler had become the subject of some gossip and was concerned about his reputation. Their dependency on him right down to the last day in the bunker was unbelievably intense and went beyond normal human behaviour.

During the years when grasping for power Goebbels had always played the radical part, a man of the people and wearing the same clothes. During the mid- to late 1930s there was an obvious change, as he started appearing in smart clothes and luxury accessories with a fascination for gloves.* He rarely drank alcohol but always smoked, and his attempts to appear to be leading an austere life had fooled only a few, but his love of expensive homes, boats and luxury cars revealed that he was prepared to live openly in his state of luxury.

Goebbels started to part from his old company of friends and even found his birth family boring and bourgeois, and he felt a distinct difference widening between himself and his brothers. He had always been close to his sister Maria, but when she married a person whom Goebbels had thoroughly checked by the police, even this relationship started to dissolve, and it

* He was also vain like Hitler and never liked it known he had to wear spectacles.

was understandably not helped by his brother-in-law whom he started to despise. It was only his mother with whom he remained close to as family, and he purchased her an apartment in Berlin. He even started keeping a distance from Magda and the family, became somewhat reclusive, but he also found time for his various and frequent affairs of the heart. Magda was virtually worn out by childbirths and suffered heart problems and had to spend considerable time in hospital. As a family they stayed close to Hitler who was a frequent visitor and obsessed by their daughter Helga. Goebbels wrote in his diary many times about his sweet and lovely children, but the biographer Peter Longerich suggested that such entries had the feeling of being purely necessary and an automatic style, and he was probably correct in this observation. [13]

It is easy to gain the impression that Goebbels in his own opinion was important, and so elevated in importance that he felt a distance between himself and family and old friends and was both becoming reclusive and bored. One thing was obvious and reinforced by reading his diary was that Goebbels liked to dominate, but the one constant feature of his life was his adoration of Hitler and the constant need to be his friend and appreciated by him. As one biographer noted 'people around Goebbels commented that Hitler drew him the way drink draws the alcoholic'.[14]

Despite his professed love for his children in 1936 Goebbels had started an intense sexual affair with a young Czech actress called Lida Baarova (sometimes mistakenly spelt Barova) whom he always called Liduschka. The biographer Heiber described this affair as a 'human and rather sympathetic episode in the life of this "Judas Iscariot", for it was the one instance when something was more important to him than his career'.[15] This was not his first case of adultery, but the biographer Heiber, despite Goebbels' various liaisons being innumerable, implies this one seemed to be more about love as well as sex. He was a physically unattractive man, but his political power made him alluring to some women, his intellectual charm worked for others, and those beautiful film industry women who refused him could anticipate 'an end to their film careers'.[16] His wife Magda had apparently been prepared for him to have the occasional 'fling', but it soon became clear to Magda that her husband had become obsessed with this actress, so she started legal proceedings for a divorce. Goebbels' reputation for having affairs was almost phenomenal. Karl Hanke (who worked for Goebbels at this time) secretly kept a list of some thirty-six women which he knew about, and Goebbels had the nickname of *Bock von Babelsberg* (the ram or billy-goat of Babelsberg), Babelsberg being the centre of the film industry.[17] He had the almost obscene power-relationship with women that so many Hollywood moguls have exploited as well as other senior dominant men in many workplaces.

The ups and downs of his relationship with Magda could make a bestselling book with the complexity of the sordid details, for those who like that sort of literature. One early German writer goes into immense detail and even wrote a book about Magda.[18] Another was Magda's biographer Hans-Otto Meissner. At one time it was claimed that Magda and Goebbels had tried to convince Lida to be part of a *ménage à trois*, which Magda decided against. Other accounts have Lida and Goebbels trying to convince Magda which seems more likely. Despite these speculations, and more to the point, Hitler was aware of the situation and started to intervene. Goebbels had always obeyed Hitler, because his obedience to the Führer was the one factor that kept him close to the total power exercised by his demi-god. There was for a time some kind of truce but it did not last long. Goebbels turned to other people to discuss the nature of his problem. He started with his State Secretary Karl Hanke only to discover later that this had prompted Magda and Hanke into their own liaison of protest at his behaviour. According to Magda's biographer, that before 'marrying Magda, Goebbels had exacted a promise from her that he should have the right to indulge in extra-marital affaires, undertaking at the same time to love only her, always to return to his beloved wife and frankly to admit to his misdemeanours. In his cunning way he succeeded in convincing her that such behaviour was necessary for a man of his virility now and again and could not in any way impair his close relationship with his wife, and Magda, it has been claimed, agreed to this. When passing this on to Ello Quandt, to whom she confided everything, she added, "Such a brilliant man, who lives three times as intensively as others, cannot be judged by the usual yardstick of the middle-class moral code". Ello was quite beside herself with indignation when she was told.'[19] Magda must have known his sexual habits, having been suspicious every now and then of locked doors in their homes, and all too aware of attractive female film stars frequently visiting him.

It is not difficult to imagine his attitude towards Hanke and at the start of the war Goebbels had ensured Hanke joined the army.* He turned to Funk who advised him to talk to Göring whom Goebbels found reassuring and pleasant, and even the Police Chief Helldorf became involved and tried to help.** Her biographer claimed that Magda was one of the last to learn of her husband's love affair, and she still believed in his fundamental loyalty. An escapade here and there would be brought to her notice, but this did not worry her. She had after all according to some sources, sanctioned this before their marriage. She also received many anonymous letters revealing her husband's infidelity, and she overheard some remarks of his adjutants which pointed in the same direction, and she too received certain clear indications, she broached the matter openly with him. 'Harmless little flirtations' he replied, brushing aside her misgivings.[20] However, it reached a peak with the circulating gossip about Lida Baarova. This love affair between Goebbels and the actress was widely known and it was a subject which was relished and often inflated in the usual social gossip chatter circles. The public saw it as typical of a man abusing his office as a major minister of government. It was all so typical of Goebbels' frequent behaviour seeking women for his personal gratification. Although this affair may possibly have had the ingredients of a more genuinely love affair, although in normal moral circles any affair cannot be acceptable. The Baarova scandal had become so well-known that it was gathering political complications of which many people were aware and some undoubtedly thrilled that it would cause Goebbels problems.

Goebbels was aware of the gossip, and by his various means of gathering information he appeared to know that Magda who had raised the issue with him in some domestic clashes, soon gathered his wife intended to see the Führer and to speak with him in private. The Führer would never permit his Propaganda Minister to be divorced, as he was adamant the regime should not be besmirched with social scandal, at times he was known for his puritanical outlook. Hitler was furious when he first heard the news

* Hanke, Karl August (1903–1945) later served as Gauleiter of Lower Silesia from 1941–45 and as the final Reichsführer for a few days. He was killed by Czech partisans.

** Later to Goebbels' shock Helldorf would be hanged because of being involved in the 20 July plot.

of this relationship problem from Göring.* Goebbels was summoned to the Berchtesgaden where he failed to convince Hitler that it was a matter of love. Hitler 'ordered him not to see Lida Baarova again. This, he said, was a *Führerbefehl*, a command that could not be disobeyed'.[21] There are other accounts which do not involve a *Führerbefehl*, in which Hitler made agreements for a one year's trial. Most biographies carry different nuances, and various shades of information, but it is of little importance, but Goebbels' life and even his family life was obviously dictated by Hitler.

It has also been noted that Hitler was also taken aback by Goebbels' apparent lack of attention to his work at this time.[22] Goebbels was both politically and emotionally fixated on Hitler and knew that if he stepped out of line it could well be the end of his personal rise to power. It also appears that Hitler was dependent on the Goebbels' family, with a special attraction towards Magda, Hitler did not want to lose this situation of personal warmth over the question of mere sex, but it was a time when some of the Party leading men like Rosenberg were hoping for Goebbels' downfall. Goebbels was not well liked by his Nazi colleagues and others, who behind his back he was 'known even by faithful National Socialists, as *Schrumpf-Germane*' (wizened old German).[23] The problems between Magda and Goebbels were becoming constant and leading to unhappiness for both sides. His pursuit of other women appeared to calm down once war started, not because he was too busy, but he obviously became more discreet. Magda had discovered one affair with his secretary climbing in through his window, and there were many others as well. Hitler for his part remained angry for a time, as he could do without the furore because he was busy planning a war against Russia.

At the end of 1938 Goebbels appeared to be falling ill and was taken to hospital for an operation which he decided against. He was suffering from depression, a feeling of rejection not only by Magda, but probably because he no longer felt the intimate relationship he had still needed with Hitler. There were several remedies he tried, one being the production of Hitler's biography, but Hitler decided the time was not right, which Goebbels would have found difficult to handle. He purchased another more expensive property

* There are other versions as to how this was drawn to Hitler's attention, one being that Magda had approached Hitler. The truth once again remains evasive.

without having the necessary money, and against the rules and regulations for the Party. He spent far too much money and was obliged to seek help, and in his need to contest some building environmental regulations he again successfully sought the help of Göring. At one time he even considered purchasing his own house in Munich. If the family were in one house, he frequently took refuge in another. Given that a few years before he had projected the image of austerity this was now impossible to pretend, because he filled his houses with treasures from all around Europe. His debts were simply phenomenal. He used his home as a place to entertain and watch all sorts of people, among the more curious was the well-known or infamous Unity Mitford the daughter of Lord Redesdale, and a visit by the Duke of Windsor.* Goebbels was always intrigued by the British aristocracy, but like some British aristocrats such as Unity Mitford, his personal life was chaotic and brought about by sex addiction.

Early War Years

During 1942, Goebbels would meet Hitler about once a month, and although he believed that Hitler agreed with his ideas of taking control of the corporate German mind, Hitler had little to contribute because he was more concerned about the conduct of the war. As far as Goebbels was concerned even the administration for legal justice had to be the servant of the State, and he had no time for the bourgeoisie whom he had always despised. He was especially critical of Göring's well-known luxurious way of life, which was somewhat hypocritical given his own behaviour in buying properties and boats. Goebbels' feelings became even more intense as the war years increased and especially when the outcome appeared bleak. He was frustrated by his lack of wider executive powers, as he was like Hitler believing in himself so much, he saw himself as the only viable solution.

Goebbels was full of aggression with huge moments of hatred in his speeches, but it has often been suggested he would have preferred there to have been no war. One biographer noting that 'Goebbels had never wanted

* Unity Mitford was a strong Nazi, fell in love with Hitler, but felt a personal conflict when war broke out against Britain. She was purported to have attempted suicide and during the early war years was enabled to return to England via Switzerland. She died just after the war finished.

war. By far the most realistic of the Nazi elite, he knew very well what war might mean'.[24] This early biographical account held some truth, but Goebbels simply believed in what Hitler wanted. On the other hand, he had never appreciated the superior role of the military as he understood that war would increase their importance and sense of power.[25] His thinking was self-seeking and egotistical, and his intelligence (which few doubted), and his reasoning foresaw that the sense of power emanating from the Führer would deviate from its traditional antennae, namely Goebbels and his growing Ministry, and move more into the military influence of military commanders. He had seen himself as the assistant driver on the national bus, but war made him feel more like an assistant bus-conductor. He had established a national power base and a major war he knew would send seismic shocks even through his and every other establishment. He went to see Hitler to point out that war would risk everything they had achieved but his efforts made no impression, which causes one to believe whether Goebbels had really read *Mein Kampf*. However, Goebbels also understood that a major war would not be popular with the German public. As far as he was concerned Hitler had achieved all that was required by either legitimate means or by diplomatic bullying. As with Hitler's anti-Semitism he simply fell in line with Hitler as soon as he knew what his master was thinking. During the political international wrangling during the years 1935–1939 Goebbels was of little importance except for elections and plebiscites. He virtually lived with Hitler who believed he had arrived at his position because of his own power, whereas Goebbels believed Hitler had succeeded because of his propaganda. Goebbels believed in himself so much and his methods which had worked for Germany, and he thought they would work overseas.

He watched, as did millions of others the initial successes. As with the rest of the world he was stunned by the rapidity of events. On the Nazi regime was the supposed credit of the *Anschluss* (annexation) of Austria, Czechoslovakia and Memel, and then rapid victory with the defeat and occupation of Poland, Denmark Norway, the Low Countries and France. Goebbels had been called in for propaganda assistance only, raging against the democracies, articles in favour of Franco, warning of the 'Red' (communist) menace in Czechoslovakia, organising plebiscites, advertising and exaggerating the behaviour of the Polish people against Germans, and in the meantime continuing his attacks on Jewish people and the Catholic Church.

He understood his new tasks at once, knowing he had the opportunity not only to push his propaganda into the minds of the occupied populations, but monitoring what they were thinking and their reactions. In doing this he always ensured he supported Hitler both in his moments of jubilation, and through to those times which became dangerously bleak. He saw Hitler almost in the same light as Hitler perceived himself, the gifted leader of the new Germany guided by providence. It was Goebbels who turned Hitler into his perception of Nietzsche's superhero, but not in the way Nietzsche had understood.

Goebbels also needed more national heroes which were not always easy to find. Günther Prien the U-boat commander who entered Scapa Flow to sink the HMS *Royal Oak* was himself killed not long after this action, and the Luftwaffe ace Adolf Galland rose quickly through the ranks to be of any propaganda use. He did, however, manage to make considerable propaganda use of Rommel not least because he 'did not come from the self-satisfied caste of monocle wearers and he was not a *von* Rommel'.[26] Later, when Rommel was implicated in the 20 July 1944 against Hitler it would have been a devastating blow for Goebbels who had built up the Rommel myth so much so even the enemy seemed to appreciate him. He even noted the 'English seem to admire Rommel', which was true, and the British often used Rommel's 'greatness' as an answer for their own failure.

Goebbels called the early war time as the 'Years of Triumph' and Hitler needed a man like Goebbels to bolster him as the months became more dismal for Nazi hopes. These earlier periods when matters did not seem so bright occurred over Hitler's relationship with his generals, their failure to crush Britain, problems with Mussolini (who contrary to popular thinking did not always agree with Hitler) and his concerns about the Balkans along with his paranoid distrust of the Soviet Union. Hitler had used Stalin and the communists in 1939, but his hatred for Stalin and the communist system was intense. Both Hitler and Stalin were tyrants, but it was not fashionable to say this for many years because 'Stalin was somehow less of a tyrant because he had fought the tyrant Hitler'.[27] Naturally, the Western Powers appeared to appreciate Stalin, addressing him as Uncle Joe in their press (which Stalin hated), but they remained suspicious of their ally which later blossomed into the Cold War.

The Operation *Barbarossa* against Russia and having to support Mussolini in the Balkans and North Africa would stretch German resources too far. Hitler's eventual declaration of war on the USA was, while joyful for the British, for Germany was a total disaster. Hitler's quarrel with his generals was becoming deep rooted. He had always regarded them with suspicion, and after his initial gambles that had paid off so well in Poland and the West, he had failed to conceive that he could ever be wrong, and assumed he knew better than his highly professional military commanders. In this self-evident egotistical nonsense in which Hitler believed he knew better than all the experts, he always had Goebbels' full-hearted support. Goebbels could almost be analogous to a pet lap dog, as he was always cheering up his master by praising him and being loyal by offering him his support and intellectual insights on how matters were working out, always for the better.

8 November Assassination Attempt

Goebbels was always in support and alongside Hitler whenever possible. On 8 November 1939, he had travelled with Hitler to the Party ceremonies in the *Bürgerbraükeller* to celebrate with the old party comrades. He and Hitler left the meeting unusually early, and while on the return journey they heard that the *Bürgerbraükeller* had been blown up in an attempted assassination. As far as Hitler was concerned it was the hand of providence, and so Goebbels regarded this as a signal that it was God's own protection of Germany's leader. He promptly blamed it on the British, but when the instigator was eventually caught it was claimed he was associated with Otto Strasser and the communists. There was probably no truth in any of these claims, but Goebbels needed to find some form of explanation as to why someone wanted his adored Führer dead. How far Hitler was aware of this possible assassination attempt is often asked as he left the meeting unusually early, but although persuasive arguments have since been deployed, the facts remain speculative.

As the so-called Phoney War unravelled Goebbels found himself in a personally complex situation, as personally he remained uncertain about

Stalin and the Soviet agreement, not least because he had a poor opinion of Ribbentrop who had manipulated the scheme. As far as Goebbels was concerned Stalin remained the main enemy, and at this time Germany's ally Italy was also causing concern by Mussolini's apparent reluctance to join the battle. In terms of the propaganda, it was a matter of treading with caution. Goebbels had banned Russian books, but most of his energy was consumed by the continuous battle with the Foreign Office over the control of propaganda, which in his opinion, had to be focused on England. He referred to the West as 'money-bag democracies run by Jews.' Once again, he was very much on the edge of the decision making. He had no idea that Hitler was planning an attack on the West, who was delayed time and time again by his generals, with weather forecasts, and the Mechelen incident.*

Scandinavia

The propaganda at this stage was easy for Goebbels because all he had to do was boast of the victories. This would last for a period, but he soon would find himself wondering how he could climb back higher on his platform of self-importance. He was 'out of place in the tumult of uniforms, medals, epaulettes, general staff stripes, and the like; there would not be much use for such a figure [as Goebbels] in a time of battle'.[28] Goebbels probably did not feel as secure as usual, nor did he have any idea that Hitler was planning an assault on the Scandinavian countries. Prompted by British interest in these countries and especially the question of Swedish iron ore and its winter exit route through Norway, plus his normal territorial greed, Hitler had been planning this next assault for many months. Goebbels had been kept in the dark until a few days before when Hitler told him. Goebbels was concerned about the possible American reaction, which was

* At Mechelen in Belgium a significant accident occurred. A Major Erich Hoenmanns carrying laundry for his wife had given a passenger seat in his aircraft to a Major Helmuth Reinberger; they had met an area of high fog and missed the Rhine, and having inadvertently turned off the fuel supply switch were forced to crash land in Belgium. Reinberger was committing the unforgivable mistake in that he was carrying plans for *Fall Gelb*. He tried to burn the plans, but at the last moment a Belgium officer saved some of the burnt documents from completed destruction, kept it quiet and convinced Reinberger that they had been destroyed. The Belgians informed the Dutch and the French, but it was too much of a risk for the German security to believe that *Fell Gelb* had not been compromised.

of no immediate concern at that time, but he was right in his perception that there could be long-term ramifications. He had spent considerable time and money trying to bring American sympathies alongside Germany. The success against Denmark was understandably immediate, but in Norway not only did the government escape, but the Germans met fierce resistance, and the British Royal Navy destroyed a significant amount of the German maritime force, especially its destroyers. Hitler explained to Goebbels that he was seeking some form of alliance with countries which had similar Aryan backgrounds, alluding to a north German confederation. Goebbels obediently made sure that the propaganda sang this same theme tune. He published and broadcast articles on the heroism of the navy, but he was developing some doubts about the wisdom of the action. He also questioned the lack of military clarity and the way the politics of Norway were developing or rather failing to develop. As in many of his observations of new people he first took a liking to Vidkun Quisling then developed serious doubts about the man and his potential. He noted the sensitivity of the Scandinavian scenario and directed the propaganda in this light. Looking at the propaganda his efforts were clever as it made it appear as if Hitler were reuniting an old family which had drifted apart, though the Danes and Norwegians would have held different views.

France

Goebbels spent considerable time with his Italian counterpart trying to make sure that Italian propaganda was in support of Germany's intentions, but it was far from easy. Hitler had explained to him only a few days before what was about to happen, and since Goebbels had no idea of the precise timing, he had to abandon his efforts to persuade his Italian colleague in trying to give a radio broadcast which was designed to explain why Germany felt obliged to invade Belgium and the Netherlands. It was of course for Goebbels a simple explanation, namely that that these two countries had breached the neutrality rules, which was nonsense as they had taken deliberate care to remain neutral, but for Hitler and Goebbels it was a typical Nazi fabrication. It was about this time that Goebbels returned to a theme in his novel *Michael* where he had outlined some hazy ideas of a united Europe with Germany in the lead position. It was this type of activity which misled him in his own mind to believe he was responsible for 'the intellectual conduct of the war'.[29]

As the German forces occupied these new countries Goebbels arranged for special broadcast teams to arrive at the occupied country's radio stations with prepared programmes and announcements. They would frequently use the normal home broadcaster to encourage a sense of ease amongst the occupied home listeners, and 'the Dutch announcers were told they might say anything they pleased: guards with loaded revolvers in their hands sat around to discourage untoward comments'.[30] Goebbels established a policy to try and make the home listener feel at ease, and there followed an attack upon their one-time leaders, then the threats of violence if people stepped out of line, and followed by the Nazi justification propaganda.

His first major task was to gloss over a Luftwaffe error when they bombed Freiburg by mistake.* He immediately shifted the blame upon the Allies, and although his diary entries make it seem as if he believed this to be true, he knew otherwise. He made a point of studying Churchill whom he appeared to loathe and yet respect at the same time. Churchill would become one of his major targets for his pure aggression. He studied Churchill with care and used information from the South African wars and Britain's colonial history to attack both Churchill and the British.

He had organised a secret radio station called *Humanité* which purported to be organised by French communists who had been popular in France until the Molotov-Ribbentrop Pact. This was a slight change in his work because he was, having tried to influence the mind of the German public, now trying to undermine the confidence of the French soldiers who over months had been bored and deflated with the Phoney War. He sent out warnings that while they were on duty British soldiers were sleeping with their women while expecting every Frenchman to die for England. It was a clever use of radio propaganda, leaving the Allied authorities often at a loss as to how they should respond.[31]

---

* The German navigation was not always good, and during Operation *Fall Gelb* one plane had accidently bombed Freiburg in mistake for Dijon, at another time they accidently bombed Dublin which had to be followed with a rapid apology.

When Paris fell on 14 June 1940, Goebbels ensured that flags were raised, and church bells were rung and under Goebbels' direction due praise for the Führer was broadcast. Hitler wanted the armistice signed at Compiègne and Goebbels prepared the necessary theatre and drama for the occasion instructing that 'no demonstrative humiliation, but the disgrace of November 1918 must be erased'.[32] It was a gratuitous demand because the humiliation was built into the whole scenario by the choice of venue. In terms of his stage management, he managed this work effectively. It was his idea to bring the railway carriage out from its museum, the same carriage to sign the end of the Great War and place it in Compiègne. The photographs of that day with Hitler looking so self-satisfied, so much show he almost seemed to do a small jig or dance, which hit the world press. Goebbels was seen as brilliant at the dramatic stage-management he had so longed for as a young ambitious man. When the defeat of France was over, he did his own victory tour through the Netherlands, Belgium and France, and he was impressed by Paris.

Hitler informed Goebbels of his intention to occupy Britain but not to dissolve the Empire, mainly for the simple reason that other countries might enjoy the colonial pickings if Britain collapsed. He was also going to ensure that the pre-1918 German colonies would be returned. Goebbels' main task was to organise a victory parade for his Führer which he choreographed, which transpired to be a major event that was naturally widely broadcast. He used his power and propaganda to make sure there was no doubt in the eyes of the world that the German nation stood as a single body behind their beloved leader. As Hitler travelled through Berlin his car and cavalcade rode over a sea of flowers all laid out by the Hitler Youth and their female opposite the BDM (*Bund Deutscher Mädel*). Goebbels ensured the whole ceremony was well organised, and no one could refuse to participate in this act of adoration for Hitler. Because of the rapid defeat of France many people, thanks to Goebbels, started to see Hitler as something of a military genius, including some of his military commanders which was a terrible mistake.

Probably for the same reason Goebbels was convinced that when Hitler offered peace to Britain it would be accepted, but when rejected Goebbels was astounded. As such he followed Hitler's instructions and concentrated his propaganda on the air war being waged to prepare for Operation *Sea*

Lion the invasion of Britain. What he never realised was that Hitler also was beginning to plan for an invasion of the Soviet Union.

Goebbels' propaganda, his stage management, pageantry, films and broadcasts were now working full out for the demands of the German war machine. As in the early 1930s he realised that the spoken word was still the most effective form of communication, and he established training facilities for would be public speakers. The loud-speaker systems were enhanced in many local places, most especially in factories where the broadcast voice could not be avoided. The response of much of the German public having to listen to his endless broadcasts and vitriol, may have been effective at times, but it is known that it was not that welcome having blaring propaganda thrust down the ears while at work or relaxing over a drink.

As far as the British were concerned, he tried to undermine their confidence by the dropping of huge hints that the invasion was on its way, but it caught him by surprise when the British attacked with retaliatory bombing raids. Heavy anti-aircraft batteries were set around Berlin, and Goebbels was concerned at the public outcry when the evacuation of children was considered. He had always been convinced that large cities such as London could never resist major bombing raids, but later in the war when he visited bombsites in Germany, he gained a better understanding.* As with most propagandists he informed the public that the British bombs were deliberately aimed at schools and hospitals. Berlin was not well organised, and this caused Goebbels some problems as he was the Gauleiter. He had appointed Julius Lippert as his State Commissioner and quickly placed the blame and responsibility on him, and he was careful not to mention Göring's well known promise that bombs on Germany would not happen. While there may have been some justification for blaming Lippert and for safety not attacking Göring, it was still no excuse for a man ultimately responsible for the German capital, simply because he was involved in his own pursuit of ambition and the life of luxury to which he had taken a fondness.

* Later in the war as retaliation 'Goebbels favoured bombing the parts of British cities where the plutocrats live', which given the Luftwaffe status at the time was too difficult. See Evans, Richard J., *The Third Reich at War* (London: Allen Lane, 2008), p.659

Russia

Part of his self-aggrandisement was his belief that he was Hitler's constant companion and friend. However, in the summer of 1940, Hitler's while military were aware of his intention to invade Russia, Goebbels was never informed. Later when he heard of German troop movements towards the east he still failed, like Stalin, to understand the obvious implications. As one German biographer noted, 'it is 'difficult to assess exactly when Hitler informed Goebbels of his Russian war-plans', but it probably left Goebbels feeling more on the outside of the power clique than he had been.[33] At first Goebbels was in awe of the military leaders and was silent on military matters, but when later Hitler began to distrust his generals, Goebbels assumed his own military ability or skills had suddenly developed and regained his normal self-confidence even in military matters of which he had absolutely no experience. Goebbels always enjoyed Hitler's attack on the generals agreeing with Clemenceau 'who thought that war was much too serious a matter to be left entirely in the hands of generals'.[34] However, Clemenceau was making the valid democratic point that a country goes to war because this is their right of decision, it was not about politicians instructing their military commanders how to conduct in detail a war situation which was Hitler's personal obsession, and led to his undoing.

Goebbels was astute enough to know when the tide started to turn, he was the first to understand that the Germans might not win, but he did not have to be a military expert to see this was happening. Nevertheless, he continued for a long time to believe that in military matters, Hitler knew what he was doing, probably based like others on the rapid victory over France. Hitler's ideas were so 'grandiose and monstrous...Goebbels was to paraphrase them by brandishing the slogans crusade and total mobilisation of Europe against Asian Bolshevism'.[35] He was equally aware that many Germans were shocked by the sudden news of Operation *Barbarossa* and wrote 'we must win and win quickly. The public mood is one of slight depression'.[36] Being a realist he also recorded in the minister's diary 'right or wrong we must win...and once we have won, who is going to question our methods? In any case, we have so much to answer for already that we must win'.[37] In this opinion he revealed his realism, his cynicism and his dismissal of any sense of morality.

Hitler was still considering some form of major European alliance against Britain and once again Goebbels remained in the dark. When he did not comprehend the possible alliances with Spain and France, he still misjudged the likely outcome, and as usual he just speculated. All he could do was comment on events after they had happened. In this fashion he was cynical about Mussolini's unexpected invasion of Greece, noting, as with Hitler, that it was a highly delicate situation in the Balkans. Overall, it is apparent that he was very much in the dark, but he still laboured away to bolster public support for everything Hitler demanded.

He had what he viewed as his personal competitors in his work area, which as always, he objected to as he was a man who needed to be at the top of his part of the political system. Hitler had allowed Max Amann to remain in charge of the Party's publications, while Otto Dietrich held control of the Party's newspapers. The general inference was that they should always liaise with Goebbels who constantly claimed that they deliberately did not defer to him. Eventually he had brought them into line as he enlarged his ministry departments from seven to fifteen, so Dietrich became one of his Undersecretaries of State. As far as he was concerned his power play was important for his own self-importance and growing sense of grandeur. To impress the Foreign Office and Wehrmacht he established a new department called the Radio Command Centre. He also ensured a single programme for all the radio stations and insisted on more light entertainment and light music, preferably dance music.

As already noted, Hitler considered himself something of a film expert and criticised Goebbels for the films lacking the latest up-to-date propaganda with mobilisation becoming urgent. It had not taken long, even in times of victory, to note that sheer manpower was essential. Germany was a large country but even with its occupied lands was not the size of Russia with its vast potential manpower.

Goebbels worked to ensure he was always in Hitler's favour, but the results were not good by any standard even for Goebbels. There was a small degree of success in the anti-Semitic film *Jud Süss* but in Germany it was only watched by hardened Party members. There were war films, often produced by the Wehrmacht but they proved to be thoroughly boring. Goebbels was too aware that the appeal of such films missed what he saw as the German intelligentsia, and he took to writing the editorial in the journal *Das Reich* (controlled by Max Amann) giving himself the opportunity to explain why Germany was at war, mainly because he had detected a degree of war wariness if not nervousness, and took the opportunity to remind the nation he was very important. His battle with the Foreign Office propaganda continued and he was pleased every time Hitler was derogatory about Ribbentrop. He managed to retrieve some of his Führer's affection as during this period as Hitler once again became a frequent guest at his home. When Magda produced another daughter called Heide, Hitler was there to share the joy.

By March 1941, it appeared that Goebbels was in the picture regarding Hitler's plans against Russia. He used 'R' in his diary as his reference to the Soviet Union, and he started his well-known diatribes against Bolshevism always linking them with the Jewish problem. Given that up to the end of the previous year of 1940 he thought the Soviet Union Pact was working well he had to do a complete *volte face*, as the American journalist and later historian Shirer had noted to his own amusement. Goebbels also had to cope with the Italian situation and the war in the Balkans with more delicacy than he usually could muster.

Propaganda Dealing with Different Issues

He had to find a high degree of sensitivity and tread carefully as soon as he heard that Hess had flown to Britain on his mysterious venture, which caused considerable embarrassment in Nazi Germany and confusion and bemusement elsewhere. Precisely why Hess took this step and how much Hitler may have known or not known remains a mystery. However, it is likely that Hitler was ignorant of his deputy's ideas, because he was beside himself with one of his customary explosions of anger. There was concern amongst all the other possible issues that Hess might inform the enemy of the secret of German intentions against Russia. Goebbels was unsure how to react, and how to determine what was or should be the Party line. At first, he deployed silence on the matter, but then soon started to work on an account of Hess' inherent weaknesses. This incident brought to light Goebbels' own weakness, as he disliked being kept in the dark and not knowing what was happening. He had projected the work of propaganda to such an extent, that in his own mind he had arrived at the conclusion that propaganda should be involved in policy making. Various explanations were concocted by him and Hitler, but in the end, it was Goebbels who decided that the matter was best kept out of the limelight and played down. He was nervous about the suggestion put forward by some people that Hess had been deluded because the question might be asked as to why the Führer had chosen a deputy in such a poor mental state. Goebbels was furious with Dietrich who had first issued this excuse for Hess' behaviour.* He never understood why the British never exploited Hess' arrival as he would have done, and noted in his diary that 'the Leader is completely crushed...what a spectacle for the world: a mentally deranged second man after the leader'.[38]

Hitler abolished the post of Führer's deputy and appointed Martin Bormann as head of the Party Chancery. As always Goebbels at first appreciated Bormann because he was useful, but soon turned against him, probably prompted when Bormann became too close to Hitler invoking Goebbels' usual sense of jealousy. He appeased himself by publishing an article against Roosevelt referring to him as a 'Jewish windbag', but then he was suddenly informed that a member of his department, a Karl Bömer had been investigated by the Gestapo who in a drunken state had mentioned the preparations against Russia in a social party. Goebbels failed to defend him, and he always put this incident down to Ribbentrop's machinations which did little to help their relationship.

Goebbels worked with Hitler and used the propaganda to lead any speculation away from the imminent attack on Russia, Operation *Barbarossa*. He even implied there was going to be another pact between Germany and Russia. He also diverted attention by mentioning Crete and suggesting a likely invasion of Britain. This did not fool the British for one moment, but it appeared to fool Stalin who shut down Russian embassies in occupied countries to demonstrate his confidence in Hitler.

---

* Goebbels' battle against Dietrich on this occasion was one of many. He made many unsuccessful attempts to depose him but that only happened on 30 March when the Russian were on the Oder heading towards Berlin.

The situation was so critical that Goebbels felt it necessary to have an old communist antagonist called Torgler released from prison to advise him on anti-communist propaganda.[39] He produced pamphlets under the greatest secrecy to be given to the soldiers about to go to war. The onslaught was kept a tight secret and for once Goebbels knew what was happening. He had kept vital staff up all night ready for his return so the various broadcasts giving reasons for the attack could be given first thing in the morning. He had sent his children to safety because he was convinced that the British would then bomb Berlin, which did not happen. The propaganda material fell under three headings. The first was that Britain could not be conquered if Russia remained undefeated because they were a potential ally. Secondly and quite cynically given that it was broadcast, it was mentioned that raw materials and food would be available, and thirdly it had to happen to maintain a long-term peace, because National Socialism and communism could not settle together as neighbours.

The secrecy appeared excellent, and Stalin and his military were caught by surprise, but so was the German population, and some military minded men who were concerned about a war on two fronts which was a justified fear. Their reaction was not one Goebbels had hoped for, and despite continuous news of military victories he still found himself having to write articles explaining why the war had to be fought. As he had done in Western Europe, he established secret radios purporting to be separatist, or nationalist, and even Trotsky-based. In his own broadcasts he became more aggressive on his theme of Jewish Bolshevism, and he also started to indicate that the war was necessary because they knew that Germany was about to be attacked by the Soviet Union. Despite the early success of the Wehrmacht, he was informed that there was still a mood of pessimism amongst the public. This fear he was told, was not helped by the Church.

Later Goebbels took a visit to see for himself the thousands of Russian PoWs kept in the most appalling and degrading situation. In his diary he noted that not all the Russians looked as animalistic as he thought, and he looked at the dreadful conditions writing that such a visit 'can give one very odd ideas about human dignity in war'.[40] This was apparently an eye-opener for him, and it is tempting to wonder whether he may have changed his mind about war had he spent time on the front line, not just visiting a prison camp, as ghastly as it was.

Back in Germany he remained concerned about public feeling, and as he had earlier disliked seeing queues for coffee, now he now detested seeing people lining up for any available tobacco. He ensured that there were wardens everywhere to monitor the public situation, even conversations. It was a crime to listen to any radio station from overseas, including their supposed allies such as Denmark (which retained control of its broadcasts for a time) and even Italy. Goebbels' analysis experts listened into the BBC but had their time limits, and too much listening could result in being sent to a concentration camp.* He was busy establishing total power and control over the German mind.

He varied his style according to the war news. The main broadcasting remained propaganda with political talks, doctored or monitored news items, and serious classical music. The Director of the Home Press Hans Fritzsche became, along with Goebbels, one of the most frequently heard voices on German radio.** Goebbels had understood that more was needed in that area which he frequently referred to as distraction. This was today commonly known as light entertainment, and he even allowed modern music to be heard so long as it was not like African-American jazz. He also introduced a special programme for the forces and appointed Hans Heinkel as the Reich Cultural Warden in charge of popular music. It was Goebbels and Hans Fritzsche who were mainly heard by the listeners, from homes to the factories, and sometimes even at the frontlines.

There was much to be heard from Hitler in the early years, but he disappeared from public sound and viewing as the Russian war looked less likely to be successful. Goebbels for his part ensured for propaganda reasons there was a German Foreign Service division which coped with nearly thirty languages. Their transmission ability gave them almost global access. As far as the British were concerned, was that Goebbels was making full use of the

* 'The fact that Goebbels' broadcasters trumpeted only Axis victories paradoxically meant that the BBC's factual statements and prognoses were plausible, even though the Germans had much more to be triumphalist about'. Burleigh, Michael, *Moral Combat: A History of World War II* (London: Harper Press, 2010), p.191

** Hans Fritzsche was tried postwar and acquitted.

infamous Lord Haw-Haw, William Joyce, the onetime cohort of Oswald Mosley the British fascist leader.* William Joyce was to pay for his avid support of fascism while in Germany by being hanged after a British trial. When active in Britain during the pre-war years he had been derided but not criminalised, but working for the Nazi regime had made him a traitor.

In many ways Goebbels had a formidable task all of which was self-inflicted in his desire for power. He was forever conscious of the public mood and had it relayed to him (apart from his observations from his mother) by his experts. He had to appease Hitler with his propaganda even down to the nature of the films, knowing when to hold information back and when to release it, and to inform the rest of the world only what he thought they needed to hear, on the grounds it might be beneficial for the Nazi regime.

There was a change of emphasis as the Eastern Front, which opened a phenomenon that was to be a characteristic for the rest of the war years, namely the emergence of the partisan and resistance fighters. Goebbels' response was one of aggressive reaction, which he termed the 'iron fist'. He supported the shooting of hostages sometimes to the ratio of fifty for one German death. It can never be entirely certain as to whether these barbaric retaliatory measures emanated from the mind of Hitler or Goebbels' suggestions. He always supported Heydrich who was being totally ruthless in Prague and saw these barbaric retaliations against the innocent as necessary.

For a time, he battled to win the 'V' sign battle against Churchill. There is some substance in the claim that it originated in Germany, but it did not work for Goebbels in the same way as it did for Churchill who turned it into an international symbol still used today. A great effort was put into the propaganda when military victories were recorded. Such victories occurred immediately after the initial offensive and were many in number. However, Goebbels was astute and less certain than others who kept claiming the war

---

* William Joyce tried to convince the British public that German radio was telling the truth. Joyce, Lord Haw-Haw, was a matter of much discussion within the public arenas. Joyce had been a fascist alongside Mosley and was in fact American born, though he was raised in Ireland. Joyce was influential within the British Union of Fascists, but he was dismissed from that organisation in 1937 when he formed a more strident pro-Nazi league called the 'British Nationalist Socialist League'. He also had a British passport which was the final excuse for the British to hang him after the war. He and his wife Margaret had fled to Germany in 1939 when he had been warned that he was likely to be arrested by the British.

against Russia had been won. He tended to be more cautious and ensured the propaganda reflected his view of realism and that the war could go on for some length of time.

By the winter of 1941, it was becoming clear that the claim that the war was almost won was embarrassingly wrong, and some careful re-treading of the propaganda had to be reviewed. Goebbels took himself off by plane to Vilnius but was caught in the wintery weather and had to be driven home. The cold weather was something of an eye-opener for him, and this writer would have liked to have read his diary had he spent a few days on the front-line with the intense cold and the imminent fear of death. However, Goebbels was concerned about the morale at home especially because he was responsible for it through his propaganda policies. He had always wanted to be in charge, but now he faced a population feeling uncertain, hungry and in fear for their future. He recognised that from the propaganda point of view, care was needed not to be too effusive about one battle, but to prepare the population for a long war. He blocked reports that seemed to him overly optimistic, and openly criticised Dietrich for doing just this with his claim the war was won. He also varied the means and ways in which he could measure the general public's temperature, though he frequently wrote that a talk with his mother (now living in Berlin) would tell him all he needed to know. He wrote several articles in which he made it abundantly clear that the war was not a matter of 'when the victory would occur', but always 'working hard towards that victory' trying to prepare the people for a long war.

He decided a sensible way to bring the public on board and to a sense of reality was to start collecting winter clothes and skis for the troops in the eastern European winter. He found the Wehrmacht uncooperative because they claimed they had the right gear, and it was a matter of transporting the material to where it was needed. Von Rundstedt was particularly unhappy stating 'it is not entirely true that preparation for a winter campaign was not made', but it failed to arrive because of difficulties with the trains.[41] Although Goebbels ran into problems he had Hitler's authority and soon millions of items were collected, including thousands of skis which were either useless for cross-country work or for the thousands of soldiers not trained in how to use them. Apparently, Hitler insisted the ones not used should be returned to their original donors. Such a moral twist is almost unbelievable.

Chapter Nine

War Turns Against Germany

Turning Points

When the USA was attacked at Pearl Harbor and Hitler declared war on America, Goebbels appeared happy, but he was no fool, realising that it was the same combination which had won in 1918. The propaganda lies which were broadcast, was that America was the aggressor. Goebbels had hoped that the USA would be too busy fighting in the Far East to be of any help to Britain or Russia. If he had had known about Churchill's joyful reaction he may have thought twice about his first response. Churchill was more in tune with America, and unlike Goebbels he had a better perspective of their industrial might. Goebbels proclaimed 'they're fighting the war with figures of fantasy. Who can take it seriously when they say they will launch fifteen new merchant ships in a month-or is it a day?'[1] Had Hitler allowed Goebbels to visit America as he had once planned, it may have helped if only because he would have had a better understanding of the American's potential industrial strength. Goebbels was delighted with the initial Japanese successes, but he was concerned about British propaganda which was rising to the occasion by questioning why the superior master German race was forming an alliance with the yellow people, then known as 'the yellow peril'. For years he had fed the German public with ideas of racial superiority, and he took the opportunity of America's involvement to increase his attack on Jewish people. He had whipped up anti-American feeling by somehow managing to obtain a 'little-known and self-published American tract, *Germany Must perish!*' in which the writer called for 20,000 doctors to carry out sterilisation on the German population. The writer was one Theodore Newman Kaufman, but Goebbels renamed him with the more Jewish Theodore Nathan Kaufman, making for excellent propaganda material as far as he was concerned.[2] There is no doubt that the propaganda war was becoming viciously immoral.

After Christmas Goebbels was becoming deeply concerned about reports emanating from the Russian front and was even more surprised when the British captured Benghazi. The question of public morale was beginning to occupy him and would aggravate him throughout the war years. He decided on tougher policies, but he also made changes in the radio broadcasts insisting on more entertaining light music, and some entertainment films. They could not be box-breaking epic films because they cost too much and took too long. He took a special interest in the film *Der große König* based on Frederick the Great, which was about the heroic German king who took the blows of attack before finally reaching victory. This was to become an important method in trying to make the German population regard Hitler with some esteem as the war unfolded. Like many others Goebbels would have known that Hitler was fixated on Frederick the Great as one of his heroes.

He then turned his attention to the black market which proliferated in most countries at war. He demonstrated an almost simplistic mind on this issue, and it took some considerable time for it to dawn on him that in his projected attack on this problem he would be putting at risk some junior and very senior Party members. When he published his articles on the subject he was irritated to find the British had taken hold of the information and had suggested that the regime was totally corrupt.

Goebbels was both clever and crafty with all propaganda opportunities. When Stalin's pilot son Yakov Dzhugashvili was captured, Goebbels had him photographed between two smiling German officers and dropped copies of the photo behind enemy lines.[3] He used any occasion to exploit the slightest information or incident to ridicule, to sow doubt, or bolster confidence, and he was often successful. He managed to manipulate Subhas Chandra Bose an Indian nationalist leader to broadcast India's demand for freedom, simply because he knew it would annoy London.[4, *] When Mussolini had been rescued by Otto Skorzeny from his mountain prison Goebbels was delighted with the propaganda element noting that 'even upon the enemy the effect of his melodramatic deliverance is enormous'.[5] When later, he heard of the tensions between the British and Americans

* Subhas Chandra Bose eventually realised the Nazis could not help his cause so in 1943 he went by U-boat to Japan. He died in 1945.

and Montgomery's behaviour he 'cleverly seized upon the incident…and through Radio Arnhem…he broadcast anti-American statements which were attributed to Montgomery and which the Americans thought came from the BBC'.[6] Not a single incident took place without Goebbels making much propaganda for some advantage.

As 1942 opened, the war appeared to improve for the Nazi regime, especially on the Eastern front in the Crimea. It was at this stage that Goebbels informed the German public to look towards a better future, promising a happy postwar life. This line of positive propaganda was challenged for him when he heard of Heydrich's assassination in Prague, not least when he discovered it had been executed by British trained Czech fighters. He wrote in his diaries that some hundreds of Berlin's Jewish citizens were arrested as if he organised this when in fact it had been carried out on Gestapo orders. He could never resist self-boasting and self-importance. When the barbaric retaliation in Lidice was reported in the foreign press Goebbels made a point of noting that the regime would always do what was best in the interests of the German people, but he kept the retaliatory measures at a low profile at public level. Many ordinary Germans did not want to hear about the barbaric behaviour of some of their troops, especially the SS which would have come as a serious shock.

By mid-1942, it was difficult for him to gauge accurately how the public was responding to news coming in from all over the globe. The First Battle of El Alamein had not been the anticipated overall success, and on the Eastern Front the Germans had reached the Rover Don and Army Group B soldiers were heading towards Stalingrad. Events dictated where Goebbels placed the emphasis in the news. He was irritated if not angry when he heard a radio broadcast by a Colonel von Choltitz who had fought at Sebastopol and who had praised the Russian soldier for his fighting spirit. This was for him a contradiction of his propaganda in which he was denigrating the Russians not praising them. Given his only early attitudes towards Russia and communism, and as more recent biographer wrote that it could 'also be seen as an obsessive attempt to kill off the last germ of this dangerous sickness in himself'.[7]

He had been informed and could see for himself that the urgency of the Eastern war was demanding more and more material including more aircraft to defend the western skies from the increasing bombing. He continued his theme of bolstering the people's morale with propaganda by claiming they were steadfast in their commitment not to give in, which worked for some but not all, as many were becoming understandably somewhat sceptical.

As always and throughout his life Goebbels continued his in-house battles with his senior staff and Nazi colleagues to assert his own personal standing. They were often deeply personal feuds where he felt his authority was being challenged or undermined. His debate with the foreign office appeared unstoppable despite Hitler's previous intervention, and Goebbels always took every opportunity to make sure that Hitler heard his viewpoint first. He remained continuously involved in a personal war with Dietrich and had never forgiven him for having announced the Russian war would be won by the end of 1941.* He was rightly concerned that some of what would be called today sound bites tended to be poor, and consisted of too many jargon type statements and clichés, and he was even more irritated and angry when he read that the enemy were referring to them as boring. He was mainly concerned about the propaganda concerning the Eastern zone, but he continued his in-house fighting with Rosenberg leading him to demand he established his own mechanisms in the East. In addition to all this acrimony he had a head-on battle with Baldur von Schirach (more well known as the head of the Hitler Youth) the Gauleiter in Vienna. Goebbels was always tactically clever in keeping Hitler in his confidence and always trying to gain his support. In this incident it was fortunate because it transpired that Hitler was not overly fond of Vienna, the city that had once dismissed him and other great artists.

Half-way through 1942 there was a degree of optimism and Hitler was thinking of pressing on to take control of the Middle Eastern oilfields. Hitler suggested to Goebbels that the necessary propaganda should be one of optimism. This created a degree of concern for Goebbels who tended to be more realistic in military and all matters because of his inbuilt cynical thinking. By September, it was appearing as if Stalingrad would be a German victory, and Dietrich had not learned his lesson, and announced that victory

* According to Reimann, Dietrich did this on the direct orders of Hitler, see Reimann, Viktor, *Joseph Goebbels: The Man Who Created Hitler* (London: Sphere Books Ltd, 1979), p.309

would be soon. Goebbels as always kept to his policy and warned people to be more cautious about public proclamations, and he told Dietrich exactly what he thought.

For his part, Hitler appeared to be fading from the public scene, only speaking to the assembled gatherings for special purposes, but less so and for two known reasons. First his health was beginning to show signs of degenerating, and secondly, the demands of his decision making with the military were time consuming, not least because there was not always agreement. This becoming a concern for Goebbels, because from the public perspective Hitler was appearing too reclusive and hidden from his adoring public which Goebbels had influenced so much. This isolation and Hitler's growing frailty was a problem because Goebbels was accustomed to portraying Hitler as the great Führer of the people, which had all been part of the Hitler myth he had so long created.

As the summer gave way to the autumn in 1942 the military news was not as promising as anticipated. The British had launched a counter offensive against Rommel's forces and Stalingrad had yet to eliminate the growing Russian resistance. Goebbels came up with a new propaganda idea he thought would appeal by looking for past parallels, pointing out that the NSDAP had taken setbacks in the past and always succeeded by keeping their nerve. This time the NSDAP and the country were facing a global conflict and soon news came through of an Anglo-American landing in North Africa, and it became clear that Vichy France could or would not help. This led Hitler to complete the total invasion of France on 11 November of all days, and he gave a rare speech in which it seemed he managed to convince the Party that he was still certain of ultimate victory.

Stalingrad

Goebbels was soon hearing the rumours that Stalingrad was beginning to look more like a potential disaster than a stunning victory. News was percolating through from the Russian front, and he garnered much of his information from his aide Rudolf Semmler who had served for a time on that front, including the dreadful wintery conditions of Stalingrad to which he had returned as a reporter. This reality of the Eastern Front was slowly percolating through with news that the temperature was minus 40 degrees centigrade, and that the Germans had lost over 200,000 killed, 700,000 wounded and 40,000 missing.

The RAF had started their thousand-bomber raids and with the British bombing by night and the Americans by day, and consequently there were many in the German population who wondered where the war was taking them as individuals and as nation. For the average civilian hearing the news from the frontline was bad enough, but after all the promises of victory to land up night after night in a bomb shelter only to find one's house a heap of rubble made many not only cynical but quietly turning against the regime. They could not voice this loudly out of sheer fear, but it is known that jokes about Goebbels, Göring and Himmler abounded. It was a problem that Goebbels met with his usual intense drive, and his propaganda tried to ensure the better news stories were sent out or broadcast while barely mentioning the defeats, and all the time he knew he now had to be cautious. He even made the death of German soldiers sound heroic and romantic, even as news of the horrors of Stalingrad inevitably seeped through by word of mouth. He wrote that 'at the moment when they gave up their lives, life itself surrounded them with a heroic rhythm…our dead are standing on the other side of life with its light shining upon them'.[8] It sounded romantic but not to those suffering and the parents of the dead.

He turned his mind to Total War and returned to his theme of a tough home policy, which included a form of labour conscription for women and closing businesses which had nothing to do with the war effort. This was really Göring's responsibility but as always Goebbels treated it as if it were his sole initiative. It was at this stage that he entered what the biographer Reimann called his Frederician period, it had to be all or nothing.[9]

Total War for Goebbels was common sense in such a major war, where for the sake of survival it was to use a common expression, 'every hand to the pump' indicating that as a community if we pull together, we can survive, and much of this type of policy had been committed to in Britain. Many women worked in Britain and toy manufacturers produced Sten machine-guns and the births of young teenagers was barely looked at so long as they looked fit. Goebbels also wanted to close expensive restaurants and believed this would release half a million people to sustain the Total War effort. Even the academic German-Jewish Professor Klemperer hiding in Dresden picked up Goebbels' efforts in his secret diary writing 'whoever resists the necessity of *total war* will lose his head…closure of luxury hotels and bars, ban on riding in the Tiergarten, no rights to holidays'.[10] The difference between Goebbels' view point and a democratic one was the lack of choice, being the nature of the Nazi choice it was not a matter hoping for volunteers but insisting to the point of coercion.

One of the most effective tools Goebbels used to rally public support was this concept of Total War, which he frequently used, especially when the war started to look less promising. He recognised that the war effort would necessitate not only military mobilisation but also the full participation of all German citizens. The Nazis used propaganda to offer the feeling of unity and promising Germany's survival, not least because by 1943 the war news was not good, and for the more astute defeat looked all too likely. This factor became a keynote for Goebbels, always stating from every form of propaganda, especially is speeches, that the nation's survival was essential and that every German, man, woman and child had a serious role to play in achieving victory.

Later in the war, he gave and broadcast a famous Total War speech which was widely thought as one of his most powerful propaganda speeches he had ever produced. It reflected his ability to use language and emotions to shape the public's perception of reality. It was the time when the war was turning in favour of the enemy against Nazi Germany, Goebbels projected in this speech the sense of necessary unity and personal sacrifice to gain victory. His speeches and propaganda efforts were all aimed to instil a sense of national unity when facing defeat, as well as to justify the Nazi regime.

Goebbels claimed that this radical policy would bring victory, and then in his usual fashion attacked those he perceived as idlers, and anyone else not overly keen to sacrifice themselves. He talked to Hitler about his views and consequently Hitler established a Committee of Three which did not include Goebbels. It was to consist of Keitel, Bormann and Lammers, which Goebbels sarcastically referred to as 'The Three Kings'. However, Hitler allowed Goebbels some input, so he called it the Committee of Four. He was concerned that his often more radical ideas would be diluted, and he was becoming more allergic to the sense that other people were also appreciated by his idol Hitler. He had been especially upset by the menacing rise of Martin Bormann within the power structure.

Goebbels had many different ideas on how to project the Russian campaign, but found he was always regarded as more of a mere observer, even though he saw himself as the second most important figure on the national scene. It was at moments of this type of disillusionment when he often thought and talked about looking forward to private retirement in which he would complete his diaries, write a German history, and become famous because of his intellectual ability.

There were times when he felt hard done by during the war years. In his own mind he believed that it was primarily he who had helped found National Socialism across the whole of Germany and had introduced the mass of working people as supporters. He felt he had been behind the necessary success in Berlin, had stage managed the pomp and ceremony for the major demonstrations, and thereby it was him alone who had presented Hitler to the people by creating the figurehead of the Führer. This had some grain of truth, but it was dangerously close to heresy because Hitler would not have agreed, and so he kept such talk to his trusted associates. The Committee of Three often failed to include him, which was always bad news for him, but he always manipulated his way back in.

The public were becoming more worried about the war news, but Goebbels cleverly decided to use the problem of Stalingrad as a means of uniting the public in the direction he wanted them to take. As the Eastern Front news grew more desperate, he managed to influence Hitler more with his concept to Total War, which involved everyone bar those in prams. There were still objections to his efforts, even Hitler insisted on lowering the age for conscripting women, dropping the minimal age from 50 to 45. If the circumstance had been less bizarre it would be amusing to know that Göring wanted some gourmet restaurants in Berlin to be allowed to evade the new restrictions and regulations. It has been noted that Goebbels was so irritated with Göring's effort to keep his favourite restaurant *Horcher* open that he gave secret orders for some outraged citizens to smash the windows.[11] After the incident Goebbels placed policemen outside to protect the premises, informing Göring it was a waste of time for the police. Göring still managed to find a way round by turning the place into an exclusive club for Luftwaffe generals and their guests.[12] There were quarrels over which businesses should be closed because this could make more men ready for war duties, which Goebbels constantly argued was essential, but it never worked as well as he had hoped.

On 30 January 1943, to celebrate the tenth anniversary of taking power, a meeting was held at the Sportpalast where Goebbels spoke instead of Hitler, who, it was often noted, was now keeping a low profile and making no public appearances. Naturally Goebbels used this occasion to push his own policies, but Hitler listened on the radio and congratulated him. The Führer State needed a Führer as Goebbels frequently said, but it must have crossed his mind that he was the major spokesman because of Hitler's reluctance to appear in public gatherings. He reacted in characteristic style and his broadcasts which announced the defeat of Stalingrad and other losses often started with the sound of muffled drums, and the printed articles had black borders. Meanwhile, as Hitler attacked his highly professional generals for causing the disaster he continued to hide himself from public sight.* Goebbels on the other hand was out and about, writing and broadcasting. Hitler disappeared into his own world where some alienated military leaders plotted and planned his downfall, and men like Göring discreetly kept a lower profile. Göring attended to his eating and hunting, and only a few were left who could bring any influence on the Führer. Goebbels and Himmler stayed close, but so did a new group of men of whom Goebbels was highly jealous because of their continued proximity to Hitler. The man most despised by Goebbels was Bormann, but Speer, Dönitz and others were too close to Hitler often making Goebbels feel at a loss, but he felt convinced he could help win the lost war.

The eventual defeat at Stalingrad under the recently last-minute promoted Field Marshal Paulus, brought about by a mixture of Soviet Russia's greater manpower and Hitler's military guidance, along with the disasters in North Africa was for many a signal of the turning of the war against Nazi Germany. It was a time when it became essential to admit and announce it, as rumours were already spreading the news, and it had to be dealt with carefully. For Goebbels he portrayed it as a matter of 'heroic resistance', and both he and

* After Stalingrad Hitler only made two public speeches and five broadcasts.

Hitler were unhappy that Paulus had not taken the hint that suddenly being promoted to a Field Marshal was the signal to kill himself and not surrender. Being made prisoner of the Soviets and the surrender did not help Goebbels' heroic resistance theme. Hitler's continuous theme of fighting to the last man was understandably ignored. In line with his own policy Goebbels managed to convince Hitler to reduce the period of national mourning from seven to three days. Hitler spoke to the party faithful and using the worn-out theme that when the Party in the old days had survived the initial defeats it won through in the end, which was obviously reflecting Goebbels' projected theme tune. How this could be drawn as a possible parallel with a serious military conflict is tenuous, but it appealed to Hitler who talked endlessly about the betrayal and weakness of their allies, and the danger of the invidious Jew.

It was Goebbels however who gave yet another major speech at the Sportpalast instead of Hitler. Here, on 18 February before an organised packed auditorium he outlined in excruciating details his theory of Total War, pointing out that only the Wehrmacht and the German people pulling together could stop the Bolshevik attack, and if they worked together in his concept of Total War it could become a short war. It was no surprise, given his main themes, that he continued to blame the Jewish people, and he used the full swing of his rhetoric demanding from the audience their full support for their great Führer. It was met with a standing ovation which he thoroughly enjoyed, and he received congratulations from Hitler. The crowd who cheered were mainly party members brought in by order, and undoubtedly there were many outside who saw this as just propaganda rhetoric, but fear of the regime would have suppressed such views from being heard too widely. The speech was filmed and carefully rehearsed and 'was designed to re-elevate Goebbels to a major role in domestic affairs and to reinvigorate flagging morale. Within limits it did both...but it could not reverse the disastrous defeat suffered at the front'.[13]

Goebbels considered changing the nature and name of the Committee of Three to the Ministerial Committee for the Defence of the Realm. Speer and others were in favour of the idea, and it was proposed that Göring should be the chairman but using Goebbels as his what would be probably his perpetual stand-in, given Göring's well-known laziness. It was therefore somewhat concerning for Goebbels when he discovered that the Führer was even contemplating sacking Göring. For a time, the projected plan had to be kept on hold. Goebbels was irritated and angry that the committee were not agreeing with all his plans for Total War. He had given the key speech at the Sportpalast, and it now appeared to him that he had become the focus of criticism because his plans were held back by others and were not happening as he had anticipated.

Part way through 1943 there was a glimmer of hope as the situation almost seemed to be improving with news of the recapture of Kharkov, but to Goebbels' irritation the SD reports on the mood of the people still seemed to be downcast. He blamed the SD, and their Reich Reports which were blocked in June 1943, and any new information was always related by reports on domestic issues. Equally annoying for Goebbels was that his effort for Total War was being calmed down even by Hitler. Horse racing, casinos and entertainment magazines still flourished, and Hitler kept worrying about expecting women to work. Nor would Hitler allow the prosecution of leading figures who were breaking the rules, especially in terms of the black market and their eating habits.

Just when Goebbels thought he might encourage Göring in his effort for Total war his own health held him back. He was once again suffering from skin problems and kidney pains and had to take to his sick bed. He started to play down parts of his Total War propaganda in the same way as he had felt obliged to do with the Katyń massacre which had for a time provided him with a new propaganda motif. His demands were seen by many people as too demanding, and Goebbels realised that some people were becoming tired and bored with his constant anti-Semitic haranguing. It was also clear that others were quietly becoming worried that because of the way the Nazi regime had treated Jewish people that their outrageous behaviour would seriously reflect against them all. Some had even heard the rumour that the devastating attacks by the British and American bombers was a retaliation for the persecution of Jews. This was a real fear, and Goebbels' emphasis on this subject had proved counter-productive, not only in stimulating more barbaric behaviour but the fear of further consequences.

Stalingrad at the start of the year proved to be a crisis moment for the regime, but now they faced the news of the defeat at Tunis where even more Germans were made PoWs. Goebbels spoke and wrote of 'the struggle to the bitter end', but he could not cover the fact that Germany was not as victorious as they had long kept proclaiming. In the same way that Field Marshal Paulus had surrendered as a prisoner, the Nazis also had the embarrassment that Rommel was safe at home during the North African catastrophe. This time they covered the moment by placing more glory on Rommel and claimed he would soon be ready for other duties, as Goebbels had made something of a military idol out of Rommel.* All this disturbing news flooded in at the same time as the government had to announce serious meat rations, not that there had been much available meat hitherto except for the rich and senior Party members. It was not surprising that his messengers warned Goebbels that people were downhearted and depressed. He was equally concerned about a growing lethargy which he detected in Göring and even Hitler, and so he directed his propaganda more to the bolstering of public morale by stating that the past victories were sufficient to claim the eventual victory.

In the summer of 1943, the regime's hopes felt bolstered when they heard of Operation *Citadel*, a plan to cut off a huge Russian military bulge before Kursk. As Goebbels visited the bomb-damaged areas such as Cologne, the first news flashes for the hope for military victory were not encouraging. In making these visits to bombed areas it was not so much as matter of showing sympathy, but by mixing with the people he claimed he enhanced his general popularity ratings higher than they had ever been before. It was supposed to have been Goebbels who organised for the *U-Bahn* (underground stations) to be used as air-raid shelters, and by doing this he was going against the advice of the administration offices. Once it had been Göring and Hitler who had been preeminent in the public view, but now Goebbels seized his chance as he often visited the bomb sites using and displaying his more charming side.

He was, however, more interested in visiting his old university of Heidelberg. Here he gave a long pompous and highly hypocritical speech in attacking what he called the intellectualism which led to much grumbling among the more educated elements in society. In July 1943, he heard of the landings in Sicily which he mistakenly regarded as the second front. It was

* Goebbels had built Rommel into something of super-hero (which was helped by the British who seemed to admire him) and when there was defeat for the Germans in North Africa Goebbels simply removed the spotlight.

later, because he remained out of the main Hitler loop, that he also heard the Kursk battle had been 'called off', in other words the military news was not good. On 17 July 1943, his diary entries made it clear that for the first time he was now beginning to doubt in a final German victory. He had many personal problems and a warped way of thinking, but he never lacked intelligence, and from July onwards he was one of the first of the prominent Nazi leaders to realise the regime had bitten off more than it could chew or digest. It dawned on him that there had to be another solution before the impending crisis became too serious, and the only one that made sense to him was to resolve the impending issues politically. His anxiety was increased as news from Italy of the encroaching Allied army made his instincts even gloomier. The invasion of Sicily had badly unsettled their Italian ally, and when Mussolini was arrested and Badoglio took charge, it then occurred to Goebbels that the future looked more black than just bleak. Hitler wanted to invade Rome and the Vatican (which Goebbels managed to persuade him against from the publicity point of view) because he blamed Rome and the Vatican for the plot against Mussolini, which, Goebbels believed was instigated by the Freemasons. It had been instigated by one-time fellow fascists, like Goebbels, gloomy about the immediate future. One of them was Mussolini's son-in-law and Foreign Minister Ciano.

It was a difficult time for him, as he had been obliged to calm down his anti-Semitic propaganda, he had no military victories in the East to boast of, and he could not offer the propaganda of retaliation for the bombing which was growing in intensity by the month. When he later heard about the bombing raid on Dresden he 'shook with rage' and 'demanded that as many Allied prisoners of war should be executed as the number of civilians killed'.[14] This appealed to Hitler but calmer voices prevailed.* Goebbels was able to use the Dresden bombing 'to engender a feeling of moral indignation in Switzerland, Sweden and other neutral countries, and he informed his department chiefs that the Geneva Convention had lost all meaning.[15] Above all Hitler was becoming more and more reclusive, and Goebbels was

* Naturally Goebbels exaggerated the deaths: 'instead of 25,000 dead, itself a vast number, Goebbels created a death toll of 250,000. From horrific reality, he created even more horrific and long-lasting myths'. Kershaw, Ian, *The End: The Defiance and Destruction of Hitler's Germany, 1944–1945* (London: Penguin Books, 2012), p.239.

worried that the German public needed to hear from their Führer to have any chance of bolstering their morale.

As the news from the East became more and more devastating and Italy seemed to be in a downward spiral, Goebbels kept returning in his diary entries for a possible political solution. Sicily had been evacuated with German success over the Messina Straits, a mini-Dunkirk, but Goebbels knew that it was a retreat. Kharkov in the East was lost, and he had no real material for an appropriate propaganda drive, especially when he heard British troops had landed on the mainland of Italy at Calabria, and later an Anglo-American force was at Salerno just south of Naples. He decided he had to approach Hitler directly about the political solution. He first asked Hitler directly about approaching Stalin, but Hitler believed that it would be the English who would be most likely to respond. This was to be one of many conversations which Goebbels managed with Hitler on this subject. In the meantime, Goebbels cheered up when he learned of Mussolini's rescue and then he heard that the Salerno invasion was being crushed.

Goebbels read a telegram that General Vietinghoff had sent to Field Marshal Kesselring and OKW:

> AFTER DEFENSIVE BATTLE LASTING FOUR DAYS ENEMY RESISTANCE COLLAPSING + TENTH ARMY PURSUING ENEMY ON WIDE FRONT + HEAVY FIGHTING STILL IN PROGRESS NEAR SALERNO AND ALTAVILLA + MANOEUVRE IN PROCESS TO CUT OFF PAESTUM FROM RETREATING ENEMY.[16]

Goebbels proclaimed it a victory and 'Lord Haw-Haw taunted the Allied troops and wished them *bon voyage*'.* However, the Allied naval gunfire was accurate, and the Allied air-superiority prevented Salerno from becoming another Gallipoli. The logistics at Salerno illustrated the near disaster for the Allies, because the Germans had inflicted 8,659 casualties whilst suffering 3,472 and the Germans took 3,000 prisoners whilst losing 630 themselves, mainly on D-Day from the beach.[17] However, close the battle was the

* Goebbels was furious with Kesselring blaming him for the misleading telegram, Goebbels, Joseph and Lochner, Louis P. (ed.), *The Goebbels Diaries, 1942–1943* (New York: Doubleday and Company, 1948), p.368 and Porch, Douglas, *Hitler's Mediterranean Gamble* (London: Weidenfeld & Nicolson, 2004), p.501.

Germans lost, and Goebbels' propaganda had to do another *volte face* and this left him next to no room for his usual manoeuvres. As with Stalingrad and El Alamein, so now in Italy, and he was appalled by the army's own efforts at propaganda.

For a brief time, the anti-Semitic approach re-appeared when it was rumoured that the Italian Foreign Minister Ciano's wife (Edda) was not the daughter of Mussolini, but one of his mistresses who was a Jewess, which was a silly and mistaken rumour put around by sheer hatred. However, Goebbels was more interested in the overall approaching disaster, and he took the next opportunity of raising his political solution again with Hitler suggesting Churchill might listen, but Hitler disagreed claiming that Churchill was too full of hate, and it now seemed to Hitler that Stalin was the more likely candidate. It did not seem to occur to Goebbels or Hitler that their regime had gone too far down the road to find any form of appeasement or political agreement.

The future looked bleak, and Goebbels worked with Bormann to lift public morale by organising discussion squads, and air raid shelter discussions. It does not take much imagination to see the disagreeable atmosphere of being confined to an air raid shelter, probably nervous if not terrified, and obliged to listen to some Party functionary praising the value of the NSDAP. Once again, Goebbels dared raise the question of a peace, arguing that Britain was probably the better potential partner in such an arrangement. It was not until the next year of 1944 that Goebbels could raise the issue again, and it occurred to both Goebbels and Himmler that German foreign policy was non-existent. For Hitler, France and Britain were small capitalistic countries, America was a racially mixed breeding ground, and the East was full of inferior Slavs. When foreign affairs went wrong, both Hitler and Goebbels, undoubtedly with some pleasure from Goebbels, blamed Ribbentrop.

Some considerable insight into Goebbels was gained during this period by his aide Rudolf Semmler who, unlike many other close servants of Goebbels, survived within his service for some time. Semmler later wrote that there were occasions when Goebbels relaxed, and he could be talkative and was often critical about fellow Party members. Semmler noticed that Goebbels would become agitated and unsettled if he felt he were not in the centre of national life, not called for by Hitler and brought in to discuss issues. 'His state of mind in this respect seems to have been almost pathological; his restless nature needed the preoccupation of incessant activity', and that had to be near the seat of power.[18]

Goebbels continued working on his long and tedious diaries dictating them at speed to Otte, his reportedly fastest short-hand writer. They were often repetitive, and it was clear that he never checked his work with the appalling flow of his language, and the repetition of the same facts and figures almost the next day. In his diaries he always portrayed himself as having a more important place in history than was the reality. In places it could be construed that he and Hitler were conducting the war and running the country between them. This self-importance he assumed is easy to detect, once Goebbels' narcissism and his perception of his important propaganda meant to him is understood. For Goebbels propaganda was a form of control over the life of all Germans, and he believed that if he could be given control of their socio-political life most of the country's problems could be resolved. It was clear that although he may have been occasionally critical of Hitler, he continued to adore the man in such a way it came close to a personality fetish. He could not help himself, but he always felt elated whenever he had a private meeting with Hitler. He made sure everyone knew about his closeness to the Führer, and he blamed any failures upon the inept generals and the bourgeoisie who failed to carry their weight in the national struggle. He really seemed to believe that Hitler was saving Germany and the rest of the world from Russian communism, and that it was not Hitler who was making the blunders and mistakes.

Goebbels always considered himself as popular, but curiously an attempt was made on his life to which he barely mentions, probably because it ran counter to his narcissistic feelings, which he believed had made him popular. The information was gleaned from Semmler concerning a man called Kumerow who tried to blow up a bridge while Goebbels was travelling over to his home on Wannsee.* Goebbels only mentions the incident when referring to the man's trial before the People's Court where, as usual in this court, he was condemned to death. Goebbels would have been happy with

* Dr Kumerow was a department chief of a radio factory.

Hitler's subsequent gift of a heavily armoured plated Mercedes with the instruction that he was not to use any other car.

Bombing Raids

Goebbels was more fearful of the British bombers than British propaganda. There were major raids on Lübeck and later Rostock. These raids burned down the old parts of the city and caused hundreds of deaths. Goebbels' main concern was the public morale, and he set about sending relief to Lübeck, only to find that from this relief effort that corrupt Party officials had enjoyed the proceeds, confirming the British accusation of Party corruption by members enriching themselves. There was an immediate investigation followed by three executions.

In terms of the bombing, it was decided to hit back in what became known as the Baedeker raids when places such as Bath and Norwich were hit to break British morale, but it was more likely from sheer revenge. As a result of these raids Hitler supposedly, as no details can be found, put Goebbels in charge of going to the assistance of bombed localities. This type of intervention was, as the British already knew, essential because it was evidently clear that it was having a marked effect on public morale. When Canterbury was bombed in response to Cologne it was given full propaganda coverage. To bolster people's reaction Goebbels informed the public it was a matter of a war of nerves, and the Germans would not be beaten by this aerial warfare.

The bombing raids were to be a consistent problem and when in May 1942 the first so-called thousand-bomber raid hit Cologne, Goebbels followed Göring and claimed that such a huge number of aircraft could not be feasible (which it was) and such information was not to be believed. Goebbels and Hitler agreed not to try a cover up the amount of damage done by such attacks if only to justify the need for similar retaliation, for which they lacked the resources.

In January 1943, the Air Raid Damage Committee met for the first time. By now the first significant bomber raids by the RAF were beginning to hit Berlin. Goebbels complained about the air defence system, and this was not without foundation given that as early as March 1943, 250 bombers managed to kill some 700 civilians. In line with his propaganda themes, he visited the damaged areas and reported that the people had the 'right bearing' (*haltung)* in the war of nerves. As the raids continued, he felt that Hitler's aura of power and leadership was in decline, and 'Hitler himself declined ever to visit any bombed-out city, it was a duty which seemed simply too painful for him to endure', and which constantly worried Goebbels.[19]

The bombing far from lessening was increasing, and Goebbels turned his mind towards possible evacuation, and was disappointed when Luftwaffe Field Marshal Milch told him that retaliation raids would have to wait, and more so when Speer pointed out that it was simply impossible to remove industry from the highly vulnerable Rhineland area. The propaganda Goebbels needed was the hope of retaliation, but it was clear from Milch that this would not happen in the immediate future. The only good thing for Goebbels was his belief in his own popularity as he visited the bomb-damaged sites, as other prominent figures tended to keep a low profile in this area of destruction.

During 1943, the bombing became not just an unpleasant problem for some areas, but it was emerging as a national crisis. At the end of July and beginning of August as the news from Russia and Italy signalled yet more serious problems of a coming defeat, the city of Hamburg suffered what is often regarded as the most serious bombing raid of the war. This raid continued for days and for the first time the British were joined by an American bombing fleet. Over 40,000 people were killed, and 40 per cent of the housing stock was destroyed. Goebbels believed that if Berlin became a target for such destruction the ramifications would be dangerously catastrophic. He busied himself with the Reich Air Defence League for the defence of the capital. Once again, he raised the question of evacuation and placed his own treasures, then his family and mother in his Bogensee residence which he considered to be safer. Bogensee was a small glacial lake near Wanditz in Brandenburg, now part of a nature park and still known as an area where Goebbels once lived and his villa still stands to this day.

Different pictures of Goebbels and his conduct regarding the bombing of Berlin emerge. The historian Lucas wrote that 'Goebbels had shown a naivety when considering the city of which he was Gauleiter, a naivety which was out of keeping with his acknowledged flair and brilliance. He refused to allow the evacuation of women and children, some had left because of Allied air raids, but the majority had stayed…Goebbels intended to carry out his dire threat that if the Nazis went down, they would drag with them the rest of the world in flames. It may be that he intended that the civilians of Berlin should suffer and perish in a *Götterdämmerung*, for such an end was very much in his nihilist nature'.[20]

Goebbels worked on moving parts of his own Ministry departments to the outskirts and beyond Berlin. There was still no hope in 1943 of a major act of retaliation, and it was anticipated that rocket development would balance the issue the following year. This time it was word by mouth propaganda as the talk of 'wonder weapons' became part of everyday chatter hoping for a miracle.*

Goebbels was very conscious that amongst the public in their small groups who huddled in air raid shelters were those elements who not only grumbled, but were critical of the regime which they knew had brought this suffering upon Germany.[21] He threatened to use the police against them, making it a crime, but he also acted in bringing together party activists who were known as public speakers, and sent them out as the regime's messengers to control the mood. It was a reversion to the Party's tactics in the early 1930s when Party thugs made sure that people towed the line. 'After more than ten years of Nazi rule the public image of the Third Reich was under control to such an extent that hardly anyone dared to criticise the regime in front of someone they did not know'.[22] It is not difficult to imagine the public fear of knowing they were watched and spied upon, with the distinct possibility of being caught in the tentacles of Himmler's terror apparatus which was generally known to be fatal.

From August on, and intensifying in November, Goebbels' fears were realised when the Anglo-British bombers turned their attention on Berlin. He was appalled at the damage and was concerned that the major Party functionaries were doing their various jobs well enough. He continued to write in his diary how the population loved him because he was at least out

* Goebbels was the one Nazi leader who showed interest in the atomic bomb. As early as 21 March 1942, he had called for the reports on the research into atomic fission. It was fortunate that the others were not interested. Even Speer lost interest when he heard that it would take at least two years of basic research.

and about sharing their misery. He was not a happy person with all that was happening, especially when he heard that his own hometown of Rheydt had been bombed. He was all too aware of the complaint that no one seemed to have heard from the Führer or even seen him, since he had disappeared from public view. As the war deteriorated from the Nazi perspective on the Eastern Front as well as the persistent bombing, Goebbels coined an expression used by Nietzsche that 'what fails to kill us, adds to our strength'.[23] It sounded the bells of courage, but it meant nothing to those suffering, for most people it was just a silly phrase for those suffering under the persistent bombing raids.

In his diary entries Goebbels made it sound as if he were entirely responsible for the air raid damage control and assistance. He was making himself sound omnipotent, but there were many agencies at work in the aftermath of a bombing attack. His visits enabled him to claim that the morale of the population was excellent, and Hitler responded by making him Inspector for Air War Damage, which was just another title for him to feel self-important. However, this new title permitted him to move into other areas and wield his needed power and advice.

The fuel shortage had become a crisis, and Goebbels was continually repeating his usual propaganda theme that the German population's morale would not be broken. He claimed bombing was murder, and he wrote an article suggesting there should be a 'pilot hunt' and announced this in a Nuremberg speech. 'In fact there were probably about 350 cases of the lynching of Allied pilots, which were usually carried out by local Party functionaries, SS members, soldiers, and police, almost all of them after the publication of this article'.[24] Even the German Jew Klemperer keeping a low profile in Dresden noted in his diary 'what will be the English reply to Goebbels' notification of murder'.[25]

By the end of 1944, the raids had increased in numbers and during the last four months of that year Germany was bombed more in that period than in the whole of 1942–43. The retaliatory propaganda of the wonder weapons, even when the V2 rockets were being deployed, did not work given the destruction of the persistent attacks by the Anglo-American bombing fleets. It did not take long before many knew that these 'miracle weapons' could win the war was sheer nonsense, but 'this bluff about the miracle weapons succeeded and remained successful to the end of the war, has rightly been described as the real miracle in the matter'.[26] Astonishingly, 'many citizens still had faith in Goebbels' promise that wonder weapons would save Germany at the last moment.'[27]

Final War Years 1944–45

It was more than apparent to the more objective observers that Nazi Germany's time was limited as the war was being won by the Allies. The Battle of Stalingrad had been a major turning point with similar losses in North Africa where the Germans were not only militarily beaten but trapped. The Russian progress, the collapse of Mussolini, the battle through Italy, the Allied bombardments, the Luftwaffe losing control of the skies and even the diminishment of the U-boat threat were all evident signs of imminent defeat. It was known that the Anglo-Americans were preparing to land in France and the Soviet armies appeared relentless in their determined and relentless advance towards Berlin. This was, as Goebbels frequently noted 'total war' and with no holds barred. It was to be a battle to be won at any cost. The Total War was one of Goebbels' main themes, and on the 28 May 1944 in the *Völkischer Beobachter* he wrote 'it is not provided in any military law that a soldier in the case of a despicable crime is exempt from punishment because he passes the responsibility to his superior, especially if orders of the latter are in evident contradiction to all human morality and every international usage of warfare'.[28] This was an astonishing statement to make given the Nazi approach, and that Göring had once said that if the police fired at anyone it was Göring's bullet. This was a theme that would dominate much of the Nuremberg trials, of obeying illegal or criminal orders.

At the beginning of 1944, Goebbels clearly recognised that the war was not going the expected way for the Nazi regime, and at this stage Hitler was 'the hidden leader'. The state of Hitler's health caused him concern because Hitler's physical frailty did not make encouraging public viewing, and Goebbels felt the Party needed the Führer's authority. Under the circumstances, he decided it was the Party, which was needed to hold the country together, and he saw himself as the main hope. Despite his distrust of Himmler, he decided he had to work with him as he was also concerned about the future, and Goebbels was even prepared to work with the detested Bormann.

None of these uneasy concerns stopped his own personal war with Rosenberg over propaganda. He had approached Hitler for support on this matter, but Hitler was overwhelmed by more serious problems than personal squabbles, and he told Goebbels that he and Rosenberg had to resolve it without his involvement. Goebbels also battled on against Dietrich continuing to criticise the Wehrmacht's propaganda. He never secured Hitler's help in any of these many disputes because Hitler had too many other more serious problems. Even in these desperate final war years Goebbels still sought power wishing to increase his control in Berlin, but it was not until April 1944 that he was appointed as the city President. Goebbels all too typically, wanted to combine this office with that of the Gauleiter, indicating that even though the future looked more than bleak he was still desperate for power in appeasing his need of self-importance.

The early months of 1944 had not shown promise for the expected future of glorious victory. The battle of Monte Cassino still raged on, the Anglo-American invasion at Anzio was underway and not that far from Rome which caught the Germans by surprise. Yet this was not as concerning for the Nazi cabal as the disasters on the Eastern Front. It was not helped by Hitler who was becoming more concerned over his allies, many of whom knew the end days were in sight, especially Finland where there were rumours of some form of agreement with Russia. This never actually happened but it was a warning to Goebbels and Hitler that their own allies were nervous. Churchill had once expressed the sentiment that Allies could be difficult, but better that than no allies at all. Goebbels could see that Italy was no longer an asset, that Finland was creaking, and they were failing to stop the Russian advances. There were problems with Horthy in Hungary, who was threatened by Hitler who was considering changing the regime, but Horthy acquiesced over the Jewish problem by persecuting them. This underlined that absurd Nazi fixation that with the Russians rolling forward the Nazi regime were concerned about their obsessive hatred of the Jews even in Hungary. For Hitler and Goebbels, the anti-Semitic attitude was almost seen as a test of reliability. This commonality of such a warped ideology was a perverted way to bind these nations together.

Goebbels, probably more than Hitler's other major cohorts, worked long hours with the occasional periods of depression. He visited the areas behind the battlefronts to offer advice and support with the usual propaganda. For some reasons he found the time to instruct his brother Hans to destroy the family papers which he failed to do, but he instructed some technicians to microfilm all his diaries, which meant working day and night. At times he talked to his aide Semmler stating that after the war he would write, and he even chatted about living in America, relying on the saying that 'dreams are free'. He was now leaning towards a new form of propaganda which was more about sacrifice, but he continued his attacks upon the encroaching Soviet Russians. He managed to create a sense of fear, perhaps justified, that Germans in the east fled west in a massive uncontrolled and risky flight as refugees even in their own country. His propaganda had become one of doom, fighting to the last man, and in this he reflected Hitler's approach from the time of Stalingrad, and as one biographer noted, 'he never ceased to goad the German people into final self-immolation'.[29] However, his usual propaganda persisted in trying to give assurance that the war could still be won, but the people 'fought on not because they believed in victory but because they saw no alternative'.[30] Goebbels changed his methods and policies the moment current circumstances changed.

Chapter Ten

The End Days

The 20 July Plot

There was a growing sense of despair and desperation across the nation, and especially among some military commanders who knew that Hitler's military plans and specific strategy were leading them to inevitable disaster. Altogether there were fifteen attempts on Hitler's life, seven of them in 1943 alone. This may in part explain Hitler's reluctance to appear in public, apart from not wanting people to see his weakening body, and his silly concept that Providence was guarding and guiding him now seemed to have lost its appeal. After the collapse of Italy Goebbels was constantly concerned by the possibility of a coup and was furious when some generals captured at Stalingrad gave their views over the radio on Hitler and National Socialism. He had decided and announced that it was not in the Prussian mentality to be traitorous.

The plot which nearly succeeded was the renowned 20 July plot and after the plot failed Hitler's revenge was ferocious. This is not the place to outline the well-known plot, but its organisation was weak given the bravery of men like Claus von Stauffenberg. Goebbels was in Berlin, and although at first, he was afraid by these developments, he quickly established that Hitler was alive if somewhat shaken. The plotters had failed to break the communication systems between Hitler's headquarters and Berlin, and after a few unsure moments Goebbels managed to assert authority over the crumbling plot. He and Himmler promptly established an enquiry which soon led to the deaths and disappearances of many people, with the precise number unknown to this day. At the start of the plot Goebbels had no idea that it was an attempted coup, only realising the situation when Major Remer became suspicious himself and contacted Goebbels, who as noted, had contacted Hitler and received instructions to crush the plot. Shaken as he was Goebbels soon followed his usual habit and portrayed himself as the saviour of the nation. The plot had allowed Goebbels to display his traditional hatred for the officer class, he 'even ridiculed their bungling' and pointed out to everyone 'the finger of divine fate', trying to echo Hitler's thoughts.[1] The plot has sometimes been derided for a variety of reasons but 'one study shows that, while slightly more than 2.8 million German soldiers and civilians died during the nearly five years between the beginning of the war and the attempt to assassinate Hitler on 20 July 1944, another 4.8 million died during the nine and half months before the war ended in early May 1945'.[2] This plot had at least demonstrated that not every German had been taken in by Goebbels' propaganda, and the myth that Hitler was loved and adored by the whole German nation.

Retaliation Propaganda

Although Goebbels believed he was the master of propaganda he was always angry when propaganda was used against the regime. The 'League of German Officers' had been formed in the Soviet Union from a group of prominent officers led by General der Artillerie Walther von Seydlitz-Kurzbach, and manipulated by the NKVD which had made Goebbels and Hitler especially nervous.[3,*] In the latter part of the war Goebbels tried every form of propaganda, but generally there were three main threads, namely the retaliatory theme, Total War, and a political solution by seeking peace on one of the two fronts.

The previous years had been frustrating for Goebbels because he had been unable to use the propaganda of retaliation because none had been available. There had been air raids on London and other British cities and ports, and although Goebbels claimed it had been extensive, he knew that they had not been that devastating on either on British morale or lifted that of the German public. The promise of the 'wonder weapons' had been postponed time and time again, and in the meantime the Luftwaffe bombing continued but resulted in its own serious fuel shortages and loss of pilots.

---

* NKVD was Stalin's secret police, 'The People's Commissariat for Internal Affairs'.

In mid-June 1944 when London had become the target of flying bombs, Goebbels was again briefly happy because he could use this as propaganda. He was cautious as was his nature, but Hitler insisted that a major propaganda exercise should be given of a retaliatory measure, portraying that this would bring England to its knees. Goebbels always claimed that he was the person for naming these weapons the V1s (vengeance weapons) whether this is true remains something of a mystery. He claimed in his propaganda that up to 90 per cent of the bombs hit their targets, when in fact it was closer to 20 per cent which brought some damage to the Greater London area. Nevertheless, with the progress of the enemy in the East and the West all Goebbels could hope for was a miracle, a prolongation of the war or a wonder weapon which would halt the enemy. His political solution of seeking peace was falling on deaf ears as far as Hitler was concerned, his efforts at Total War had met little success, and so he was obliged to continue with the theme of retaliatory propaganda. He never gave up Total War as a theme and managed with Speers to plan an effort to persuade Hitler and make him understand the need for the Total War theme. Speer organised report after report trying to show why Total War was necessary, and the manpower and armament issues which had to be resolved.

Total War

As German hopes declined it was an unexpected bonus for Goebbels in so far that Hitler extended his internal powers to ensure that every single German would contribute and fight for a German victory. However, Goebbels had wanted to be the Gauleiter of Berlin but now he was looking to the whole of Germany. As he controlled Berlin and its population so he wanted to influence Hitler so that the entire population could be brought under his control, so that everyone would agree with Hitler's line of thinking. This had long been from the early 1930s his dream, and it was still active in the final months, but it had 'passed it sell by date'.

He returned to his theme of Total War with yet greater vigour. He was later happy that at the Casablanca Conference where the Allies had agreed on total surrender, pleased mainly because he had a deep concern that the Allies would try and created a division between the Nazi Party and German population, but now it was a demand for total surrender, and it provided the reason for him to argue that the German people had no choice but to pull together.[4]

He talked for a time with Himmler, Bormann and Speer who were all concerned about the future, and this blend of different personalities amounted to what Goebbels perceived as a military dictatorship for the home front. Hitler was now more inclined to agree, but Göring remained unsure. Goebbels decided he needed Göring because he was hoping that Göring would propose him as Reich Plenipotentiary for Total War, which would have given Goebbels the opportunity to have power over the entire State mechanisms.

They were only machinations, and as they were occurring in the corridors and offices, Hitler was preoccupied with seeking revenge against the plotters, the military situation had deteriorated even further with the Russians outside Warsaw, and in the West the Germans could no longer hold the Western Allies in Normandy. When the news of the Allied invasion in Normandy had reached Goebbels his immediate response had been the claim that their success in landing was good, because now 'it would be possible to deal him [the enemy] a really devastating defeat', but Goebbels wanted to drum up from every conceivable area the maximum number of men and women for the Wehrmacht and home defence.[5] To achieve this he needed the support of the other Gauleiters who were given targets to reach, and in August 1944 he held a major meeting at Posen to make his appeal to them, or, as he would have seen it, to obey his demands. He had to impress them with the urgency of the national situation, though they would have had to have been plain stupid or extreme Nazi fanatics not to have realised the potential ramifications at this time of events.

Goebbels needed to find armament workers and fighters from every possible source and set about establishing targets he would never be able to attain, as 'Goebbels was on a manhunt'.[6] He announced details of how women aged up to 50 were to be conscripted to allow men to be released for fighting. A sixty-hour week was introduced and young teenage males, and men aged 50 to 60 and rising were ordered to serve in the *Volkssturm*.*

* A form of Home Guard.

Goebbels imposed hundreds of restrictions, travelling was virtually banned, newspapers were cut to the essentials, magazines were suspended, and he tried to initiate his opportunity to attack those he believed were not pulling their weight. There were in his opinion too many wealthy people, including Reichsleiters and Gauleiters, who were out of step by being so well-off and too privileged in a country now involved in Total War, which given his lifestyle was somewhat hypocritical. He became critical of some of the older Party members, especially Göring (when he did not need him) and believed, probably correctly, they had been promoted well beyond their competence. Göring had been in Hitler's bad books for a time because of the evident failure of the Luftwaffe, but to achieve his aims Goebbels tried to bring Göring back into the limelight as a friend against the rising new people currently surrounding Hitler. This was a renewed partnership for personal aggrandisement because both Goebbels and Göring had grown to see that Bormann, Hans Lammers and to a lesser extent Keitel now wielded the power near the throne.

Göring was of little value because Hitler had not forgiven his failures, and was aware of his personal weaknesses, and knew that consequently the general population blamed him for the devastating bombing of their homes and businesses. Goebbels on the other hand was prepared to go out to the bombsights and meet the people, whereas Göring had virtually disappeared from public view. The once loved and appreciated Göring was now deeply despised by the vast majority and there were many popular jokes about him. Goebbels called the bombing raids the 'terror attacks' (*Terrorangriff*) and used new phrases and policies such as 'Strength Through Fear'. He visited industrial sites, bombed areas and his diaries indicated that he perceived himself to be highly popular, still in a time of national disaster he was driven by personal ambition.

He even scrutinised the number of foreign women who were used as domestic help and servants making sure that they were engaged in more vital areas of war work. Hitler was in general agreement with him, but he still worried about some features of Goebbels' efforts which he considered far too radical. Goebbels managed to convince Hitler and soon theatres and orchestras were closed, but Hitler halted Goebbels from stopping the brewing of beer and making of sweets. Hitler had eventually agreed that women could be conscripted up to the age of 55 though this never actually happened.

The military news was not improving and in August the Americans landed in southern France and Goebbels realised the situation was becoming even more serious. He wanted a line drawn which could be held as an accepted end of the war boundary, but this was not realistic. Romania wanted peace, and when the Germans threatened that country it turned against Germany. The situation was evidently disastrous and even on the family front Goebbels heard that his stepson Harald had been wounded and taken prisoner. He had little choice but to press on with his Total War theory. It soon became clear that his estimated recruitment figures had not been realistic. They also led to a conflict with Speers who also needed the manpower for armaments. Goebbels threw himself into the fray with characteristic energy, blaming his staff for failure and praising himself.

As the enemy forces drew closer, Goebbels considered the possibility of extreme Total War, namely the scorched earth policy, a desperate extreme which he discussed with many, having spoken to Speer who later claimed he was not convinced. He examined with care the reports of the public mood, but such was the national depression their feelings must have been more than obvious. Somehow, he heard of Morgenthau's plan to turn postwar Germany over to agricultural use, giving him the propaganda that this Jewish banker was going to destroy Germany, and he spread this widely in the hope of stirring up greater resistance. The Morgenthau plan enabled him to paint a picture of Germany as 'the potato field' with a picture of Germans begging food at field stations.[7] This threat gave him an opportunity to instil more fear and the hoped for better and bitter resistance, it was as if he 'had been presented with a propaganda gift to help him persuade the German people that they could expect no mercy from the Western Allies, any more than from the Soviet Union'.[8]

Goebbels was obsessed with the need for Total War until the bitter end, and he was beginning to clash with Speer time and time again over armament workers in his drive to find military manpower. He was looking for any unskilled labour to help in the factories and complaining that the Wehrmacht were not processing the new recruits fast enough. This was understandable enough given the chaos the army found itself in, with no time to process and train new men. Traditionally the Wehrmacht had a long and intensive training for recruits, better than most other countries, and now Goebbels wanted them to put uniforms on weak conscripted troops, who were still civilians and expect them to perform against men who were fast becoming experienced enemy soldiers. It took Bormann and Göring to stop Goebbels conscripting women to fight. This clash was not helped by Goebbels who constantly suspected that Bormann was jealous of his position. This was an extraordinary matter of petty behaviour given the appalling circumstances their country was now facing. Göring had even given Goebbels permission to check the Luftwaffe for better conscription, but this never worked. Eventually by 1945, Goebbels gave Göring away as a spent force, but even in the closing months he still continued to fight his personal battles with Ribbentrop, Rosenberg and the Wehrmacht's propaganda units.

His quarrel with Speer eventually led to a meeting with Hitler who sought the usual compromise. It was a complex issue because they needed more soldiers, but in a modern war soldiers needed weapons. Hitler was now thinking the war would be won by the new 1928 recruits because they had been a generation totally influenced by the NSDAP. Goebbels promptly produced figures and statistics for his goals which were unrealistic, were never achieved, wrote lies, then the issue faded.

Part of his final drive for Total War was the formation of the German *Volkssturm* which conscripted all men between 16 and 60 but often the age barriers were ignored. He even formed a unit from his own household.[9] He administered their oath and believed this would raise the morale of the population, which was an unbelievably ridiculous hope. To the older more discerning men it must have seemed as if the regime had lost it sanity.

There was a moment's hope when he believed Hitler may have turned the war in Germany's favour with the Ardennes Offensive, more commonly known as the Battle of the Bulge. At first it appeared successful, and Hitler wanted as much propaganda as possible, but Goebbels was still suffering his normal bout of doubts about overdoing something that might turn in the wrong direction. He was right because eventually the Allies held the line and then counter attacked. Hitler increased Goebbels' powers by permitting him to inspect the Wehrmacht itself to find more frontline soldiers. 'However, the Wehrmacht's losses in terms of deaths amounted to 450,000 men in

January alone and in the following months to nearly 300,000 each month, not to mention soldiers who were no longer deployable because of injury or because they had been taken prisoner'.[10] It was an impossible task, and a political solution seemed to offer the only hope.

Political Solution

It was as early as 1943 that Goebbels had been suggesting to Hitler that some form of peace negotiations could be made. As mentioned above Hitler had listened and pointed out that Churchill was far too hostile and Stalin could not be trusted, with Hitler showing a greater insight into the enemy than Goebbels. He had prepared a lengthy memorandum for Hitler on the way peace negotiations could be reached and how they could work, but it never reached Hitler's desk because Bormann had decided that the Führer had too much else on his plate to worry about such fantasies, leaving Goebbels furious. By 1943, it was clear to the Allies that they could win, and by 1944 they were almost certain of victory, and by 1945 it was simply a political military race between the Allies and the Soviets.

As the hopelessness of the military situation became apparent, and despite Hitler's refusals, Goebbels returned to his theme of a political solution in 1944 with renewed vigour. He started to concoct or misread the international situation claiming that there were some in England who would welcome peace as a means of extricating themselves from the bond with communist Russia. This strange concept would not entirely disappear, but Goebbels and many others failed to realise that although the West were distrustful of the Soviets, and the feeling was mutual, their primary consideration always remained the total defeat of Germany.

There were rumours and counter rumours of Japan and Russia seeking talks to bring peace, and Goebbels completely or deliberately misread the Quebec Conference speculating that the British and American talks had been concentrating on the problem of Russia, when in fact the conference was about the nature of postwar Germany. It was increasingly obvious that Goebbels and the other leading lights of the Nazi regime were now living in their own concocted fantasy world.

On the 16 October 1944, the first major German city of Aachen was captured by American forces and the Russians were in East Prussia with news of their barbaric reprisals coming from the village of Nemmersdorf.* At first Goebbels thought it would make excellent propaganda to build up resistance, but there were criticisms that the area should have been evacuated, and Goebbels abandoned the idea on the grounds that such news would not encourage the German troops. The pictures of raped and crucified women 'caused panic and the *Ostflucht*, namely the great flight from the East began'.[11] The news of the Eastern Front's brutality with Russians raping and pillaging their way westwards was widely known, creating more fears than a bombing raid.** Goebbels was informed that 'instead of blaming all of Germany's misfortunes on the Jews, many now regretted their harsh treatment as the cause of present German woes'.[12] In some of the bombing raids there had been rumours amongst many people that it was revenge attacks because of what had been done to Jewish people. Goebbels saw this as a positive factor in 'ensuring their continued fanaticism and backing for the regime (often underpinned by belief in some ferocious Jewish revenge)'.[13] Noting the popular fear of the populace that they would be held responsible for the extermination of the Jews, Goebbels consoled himself claiming 'experience tells us that a movement and a people which has broken the bridges behind itself, fights much more unreservedly than those which still possess the possibility of retreating'.[14]

Both Goebbels and Hitler continually hoped the enemy coalition would break up. It was not entirely ridiculous to think like this because the relationship between Stalin and the West had always been strained, and it was known that the Anglo-Americans feared communism. However, the Nazi regime had completely failed to understand the hatred felt towards them and the determination of their many enemies to destroy the Nazi power at whatever the cost, even if it meant aligning with other potential enemies. This was seen with the postwar breakup of the East-

* This was first indicator of Russian brutality against the German civilians.

** The climate for revenge by the Russians was fanned by officials, and the Russian novelist Ilya Ehrenburg helped stimulate this by appalling stories of German conduct and calling for 'anything goes'. See Davies, Norman, *Europe at War 1939–1945: No Simple Victory* (London: Viking, 2006), p.340.

West coalition, but it was put on hold until Germany had been destroyed and divided. Hitler tended to vacillate between the English and Russians, while Goebbels insisted that Ribbentrop was incapable of manipulating the international scene. Ribbentrop being as ambitious as Goebbels, thought he was the only man able to achieve such a result. For a time, Goebbels liaised with Göring concerning his Swedish connections, but Göring claimed he would not operate without Hitler's permission as he knew he had to tread with care.

The propaganda was almost out of control in the final months, and Goebbels resorted to more anti-Semitic abuse, anti-Bolshevist attacks, and yet tried to tone down the Russian barbarity for the sake of the public who by now were already too aware of these issues. The people were equally conscious that the wonder weapons had apparently not solved their problems. Hitler had undergone some medical work on his throat, but Goebbels was unable to persuade him to go near a microphone.

He adored Hitler and in a quasi-religious fashion he had sacrificed himself to his work, including his family, and given his life to the Führer, yet he was in these end days somewhat critical of Hitler's failure in several matters. He simply could not understand why Hitler did not rid himself of Göring, he was worried about Hitler's leadership qualities and decision making, and he had noted that the public mood towards the Führer was changing. He was also distressed by Hitler's decline in health, particularly his shaking left hand. Nevertheless, because of his obvious intelligence and intellect it has been noted that 'Goebbels could free himself from his total psychological dependence on his Führer', but he never did.[15]

In the final weeks, Hitler had set aside any hope in the possibility of peace with the West and for a moment looked towards Stalin. This pleased Goebbels for the almost childish delight he took in knowing that Göring, Himmler, and Ribbentrop were looking to the West. At least for Goebbels, he and Hitler were of the same mind, which would be no surprise because Goebbels had followed Hitler like a lap dog for the last 14 plus years. The various peace feelers which had been extended via Sweden, Spain and Switzerland had all failed. When Roosevelt's death was announced there was a glimmer of hope which lasted for a few days only.* Goebbels even instructed his staff 'to write very objectively and noncommittally about Truman, to say nothing to irritate the new President', as if Truman would have cared what the enemy thought or pretended to think.[16] This arose in his mind because Goebbels had gained the notion that Truman 'feared communism more than Nazism'.[17]

When the Americans had crossed the Rhine at Remagen and were quickly followed by the British at Wesel the end was noticeably in sight. The scorched earth policy, known as the Nero Order, was again reviewed but opposed by Speer who somehow managed to modify the order. There was an experiment with the infamous Werewolf policy of 'behind the lines resistance' which led to the death of Franz Oppenhoff whom the Allies had appointed Oberbürgermeister of Aachen. Goebbels wanted to run this organisation in place of the SS, in this he failed but ran their propaganda for what it was worth. Nevertheless, the Werewolf threat was taken seriously by the Western Allies because of Goebbels' propaganda, but it never amounted to any great problem, apart from creating a degree of anxiety which soon evaporated.

Goebbels' Life During the End Days of Nazism

Goebbels was overworked, still driven by ambition even when the country and himself were heading towards a form of Hades, which they had brought upon themselves under Hitler's leadership backed by Goebbels. Goebbels was almost a social isolate, many steering clear of him, and even at work where he even forbade people speaking to him as he entered the building, and with his own self-importance would dress them down for the slightest infringement. When an editor questioned whether it was appropriate to broadcast classical music instead of a football match, he was threatened with the concentration camp. Such were the depths to which his coercive nature had sunk that he could make this threat on a mere mild suggestion by a staff member.

* Goebbels phoned the Führer and said 'my Führer, I congratulate you. Roosevelt is dead. It is written in the stars that the second half of April will be the turning point for us'. Beevor, Antony, *The Second World War* (London: Weidenfeld & Nicolson, 2012), p.732.

His ambition and subsequent rise to power had made him tyrannical. His home life with Magda appeared to have been more settled but the overwork had made him ill. He remained prone to kidney problems and occasionally developed some form of rash which kept him awake and which took him to hospital. As with his youth he also had moments of serious depression. He was overworked, isolated from family and friends and ill, but he still found time for his propaganda aggression. The one consolation he felt in his life was his adoration of Hitler. During this period even that closeness to the Führer was made difficult because Hitler was on the move between HQs, and although Goebbels often tracked him down, the information he needed was to become more and more by telephone. When Hitler was in Berlin, Goebbels had relished the time spent with him. First the war reports, then the home front and the necessary propaganda, and finally the cosy friendship talk when Hitler would reminisce and Goebbels would like to hear who was in Hitler's good or bad books, and direct some of his perceived enemies into the latter.

Of all the Nazi henchmen Goebbels remained the most astute and clear-sighted when looking at the imminent collapse of the regime. He had been 'cautious from the outset about the chances of a major triumph in the Ardennes', and when the Russians started moving towards Germany, he told his wife 'we've had it, bled white, finished, there's nothing to be done', and once the Allies had crossed the Rhine he was 'clear-sighted enough to see that Germany's last hope of a political settlement had collapsed'.[18] Near the end of the war and warning that it was off the record, he told a group of foreign correspondents that 'only a hair's breadth separates us from the Abyss'.[19] Even so at times such were the mixtures of hope and fear that even for Goebbels 'reality and illusion were closely interwoven'.[20]

He worked on from his bomb damaged office where his two brief cases 'had to be placed on his office desk at an exact distance from the edge, just as his secretaries had to lay out his carefully sharpened pencils in a neat parade, ready for work'.[21] Despite the circumstances of the day he continued to lavish luxuries on himself, he pretended he lived a Spartan life but in reality it was 'more baronial'.[22]

Hitler by now was seriously and noticeably dysfunctional, deluding himself and those gullible enough to believe him that the war could still be won with secret weapons. Despite his obvious physical and mental breakdown Hitler still seemed able to transfix those surrounding him with his strange charismatic hold, and he certainly held the loyalty of Goebbels and Magda to the bitter end. Bormann, whom Goebbels hated, also stayed loyal, Speer started to look to postwar Germany and claimed he worked against Hitler, and both Göring and Himmler sidled away when the dangers were clearly apparent, and Ribbentrop was now regarded as of no value. Goebbels was delighted that in the final months Hitler emerged from his hole in the ground in January to have tea with him and his family, such adoration but not surprising as he had become their demi-god.

Regarding his family, Goebbels talked of the children and Magda moving south or at least towards the Anglo-Americans where he sensibly believed they would be treated better than falling into Russian hands. However, Magda, who like her husband, was emotionally and politically attached to Hitler refused to think of this as viable, and early on contemplated suicide and the death of her own six children, and requested special phials of poison from Hitler's dubious doctor Morell.* As noted, her first son Harald was at this stage in a British PoW camp and had been wounded.** As Magda contemplated her family's dark future, Goebbels as the Berlin Gauleiter was busy preparing the people of Berlin to defend the city to the last man. Shelters and defence positions were rapidly being built, and he tried to influence Hitler to move south. As Hitler's closest friends fled to what they hoped for safer places, Goebbels still hankered after more power. On the 19 April, the eve of Hitler's birthday, he gave his last broadcast still speaking of hope, but only a bare handful if any would have believed him. The one rational matter he managed, was to reach an agreement with Speer in not destroying Berlin's bridges which would have made life even more dangerous for Berlin residents. He continued to write to the end, predicting that an 'iron curtain' would fall across Europe. It would be interesting to know whether Churchill used Goebbels' expression, or they produced it virtually simultaneously. He

* Göring dubbed Morell Reichsspritzenmeister (Reich Master of Injections), see Evans, Richard J., *The Third Reich in History and Memory* (London: Abacus, 2015), p.147.

** After the war Harald and his half-brother Herbert Quandt revived their father's fortunes and became multi-billionaires with interests in many companies including BMW. See Davies, Norman, *Europe at War 1939–1945: No Simple Victory* (London: Viking, 2006), p.394.

wrote his last article on 22 April for *Das Reich* entitled 'Resistance at all Cost'. As with much of his thinking he was now ensuring that he had a place in posterity. The same day he wrote this article on 'fighting to the last man' as he moved to the supposed safety of the bunker.

The Bunker

On Sunday 22 April 1945, Goebbels and his family left home for the underground existence of the well-known notorious Bunker. Even as he entered the disagreeable setting of this shelter it was claimed by Naumann that Goebbels remained hopeful of victory in believing the Western Allies would unite with Hitler to destroy the Russians.* It was a surreal atmosphere in the Bunker which needs no description in this study. Magda and the children had their own room, and she had brought little change of clothing for them because she had not anticipated having to hide below ground for long. In his biography of Magda, Hans-Otto Meissner refers to life in the bunker where Hanna Reitsch bravely landed her aircraft in bombed Berlin and went to the bunker where she helped to care for Magda's children. He used her own book to gather the various insights.[23] He quoted her directly from her memoirs:

> When my services as nurse to Field Marshal von Greim were not required, I devoted myself to the Goebbels' children. Shortly after I had been greeted by Hitler, Frau Goebbels took me to her room one floor up, to clean myself up after my flight. As I entered the room, the faces of six lovely children between the ages of four and thirteen greeted me with lively curiosity from their air raid shelter bunks. Their childish imaginations were fired by the fact that I could fly, and whilst I, still overwhelmed by the experiences of the last few hours, washed myself, their little mouths prattled away questioning me so insistently that, whether I would or not, I was drawn into their colourful little world. From then on, I had to join them at every mealtime, describe the various countries and people I had seen, tell them all about my flights, or recount the fairy tales they liked to hear. Each one of the children exerted charm in his or her own innately subtle and revealing way. The love of the little siblings for one another was quite touching to see.[24]

* Werner Naumann (1909–1982) was Goebbels' State Secretary and entered the Bunker with him.

This personal insight into the children in the bunker indicating a happy family group even under the strained conditions of underground life makes their end painful to read about demonstrates the extreme fanaticism of both Goebbels and Magda.

Goebbels also had his adjutant Günther Schwaegermann with him. Göring had travelled south to safety, and Himmler moved north looking to the Swedish Count Bernadotte seeking to negotiate for Germany, but basically for his own survival. When news of these actions reached the Bunker, Hitler was beside himself with fury as he saw it as betrayals, not helped by news that Ribbentrop had fled north. Speer confessed to Hitler that he had not carried out all his demolition plans which apparently Hitler surprisingly appeared to accept. Hitler was almost psychologically damaged by Himmler and Göring's actions and promptly had Eva Braun's brother-in-law Hermann Fegelein shot, because he had been Himmler's aide and had left the Bunker with the intention of seeking safety. The Russians were heading towards the Bunker and life outside was dangerous, but with Hitler's temperament, it was also dangerous for those living inside the underground rooms. On Sunday, 29 April, the bizarre marriage of Hitler Eva Braun took place with Goebbels and Bormann acting as the witnesses, as Hitler had once done for Goebbels and Magda. Before he died, Hitler carried through his final organisational changes. Dönitz was made Reich President and Supreme Commander of the Armed Forces and Hitler organised his so-called Cabinet. Bormann was made Party Chancellor and Goebbels created the Reich Chancellor, 'at least on paper and in a few thousand feet of air-raid shelter under the Chancellery'.[25] Goebbels was no fool and knew his appointment was of no importance but probably hoped it would boost his name in history and posterity.

Hitler left his last will and testament with Goebbels and Bormann as signatories. Goebbels was later to do the same thing, but the remaining survivors were not prepared to risk their lives by trying to save this material. Goebbels also added an attachment to Hitler's testament in which he stated that he would not follow the Führer's order to escape, writing that 'my wife and my children associate themselves with this refusal. First, for humanitarian grounds and out of personal loyalty, we would never be able to desert the Führer in his darkest hour: secondly it would always seem to me to be a dishonourable act...I would lose my self-respect and the respect of the people'.[26] He was seeking a place in posterity as usual, adding to his valedictory statement, 'if I were to do otherwise, for the rest of my life I would regard myself as a dishonourable traitor with a vile blackguard and would lose my self-respect as well as the self-respect of my fellow citizens. (Signed) Dr Goebbels Given in Berlin, 29 April 1945 at 5.30 p.m.'[27] This all said much about the man, he was simply morally bankrupt involving his children and remaining self-centred and egotistical to the end.

As is well known Hitler and his wife committed suicide, and Goebbels and Bormann gave the Nazi salute as the only two mourners. Dönitz was informed but Goebbels made two more efforts to call a truce with the Russians. This action alone demonstrated his incredible naivety about the nature of the conflict, which he had called Total War without understanding the ramifications. The Russian commander Zhukov had consistently made it clear that unconditional surrender was meant. When Goebbels heard that General Krebs' delegation to the Russians had been informed and that only unconditional surrender was possible, he refused and demanded the return of Krebs.[28,*]

Goebbels and his wife committed suicide, and it will always remain an enigma as to how their sheer fanaticism drove them to kill their children who were innocent of any guilt, as well as at their age ignorant of their mother's insane dedication to a corrupt cause. It is unlikely to be known for sure whether it was Magda's decision alone, but Goebbels was the man who took his family into the fatal setting of the Bunker. There are various accounts of how the poison and deaths were administered and the truth will never be known.[**] The biographer Heiber reminds us that the youngest child was just over 4 years of age, the eldest 13 and claims it was Goebbels' decision.[29] Heiber also insists it was Goebbels' decision based on the grounds that their children would not survive, which was another miscalculation as

* Apparently when Krebs met the Russian General Chuikov he stated that the day of the meeting (1 May) was a 'great holiday for our two nations' upon which Chuikov replied, 'We have a great holiday today, how things are with you over there is hard to say'. Shirer, William L., *The Rise and Fall of the Third Reich* (London: Mandarin, 1960), p.1135.

** According to Toland, Dr Stumpfegger would not have it on his conscience and so Goebbels had to seek another doctor, see Toland, John, *The Last 100 Days* (New York: The Modern Library, 1996), p.545.

proved by the children of Himmler, Göring and Bormann who survived. Goebbels could have stopped his wife but he was looking to posterity, creating a uniquely tragic death legend, it 'was his last act of propaganda'.[30] The commonly held account is that Magda took cyanide and Goebbels shot himself, but curiously the historian Martin Gilbert claims Goebbels had himself shot by an SS orderly and William Shirer supports this side note as does Toland, not that it matters.* His misconceived principles aside it may simply be that being an intelligent man he foresaw the way the Allies would treat him for promulgating Nazi evil.

When Goebbels had been created Reich Chancellor by Hitler in the final hours this must have been like a pleasant sedative for his life long's ambition and ego. He had reached the level of power he had craved for all his life. From his earliest days he had sought recognition and admiration from those surrounding him, and as he grew in status with those surrounding him expanded rapidly, first from attaching themselves to a perceived rising star, and later many others out of fear. His need to be seen as important can be read in his diaries which revealed his various characteristics such his love of himself and his self-adulation. Cleverly described by one biographer with the words, 'His character fulfilled all the essential criteria recognised in current psychoanalytic practice as defining a narcissistically disturbed personality'.[31] Goebbels shared with Hitler the same megalomaniac fantasies about raising himself in power, whatever the cost. For his part Goebbels had attached his life and his future to Hitler by trying and often succeeding to bring the German population out in support of Hitler. The fact that Hitler and the Nazis were popular amongst many Germans for a long period of time is undeniable, and much of this was because of Goebbels driving force in propaganda. As he had risen as the central star with the Führer's inner circles, his self-conceit had increased, often revealing as many psychoanalysts have observed, a basic insecurity which can undoubtedly be traced to his youth. His remains were discovered by the Russians, checked by many and then disappeared. They were 'identified by the Russians from the special boot he wore for the club foot'.[32] In our current understanding of the man

---

* Gilbert, Martin, *Second World War* (London: Phoenix, 1997), p.682 and Shirer, William L., *The Rise and Fall of the Third Reich* (London: Mandarin, 1960), p.1136 and Toland, John, *The Last 100 Days* (New York: The Modern Library, 1996), p.548.

Stalin they are probably somewhere in Russia, but 'no Red Army officer, including Zhukov, was allowed to know of its discovery'.[33] According to the historian Andrew Roberts many of the remains were dumped at Magdeburg in a Russian counter-intelligence site, but years later Yuri Andropov ordered them to be dug up, burnt and thrown in the river to stop them being a site for neo-Nazis.[34] The current author while travelling in the Soviet Union in the 1970s heard the rumour that Stalin had kept Goebbels' or Hitler's jawbone in his desk, but this was only hearsay within hearsay. Hitler's remains disappeared as well 'with the ensuing stream of macabre kitsch for several decades'.[35]

Even after his death Goebbels' propaganda and lies were still proving effective. When in Italy the Supreme Commander Alexander reported to the Russians that the Germans had made peace overtures he was taken aback by the Russian response of querulous suspicion, because 'Goebbels and his agents had spread thoroughly, continuously and convincingly the lie that the Western Allies would, sooner or later join forces with the Germans and march against the Russians'.[36] This played into Stalin's paranoid mind, but it seemed that Goebbels' ability in crafty propaganda outlived him.

Chapter Eleven

Final Observations

From the moment that Goebbels as a young man turned his personal ambitions to the politics of the NSDAP and became fixated with the figure of Hitler, he became a major pillar of support in Hitler's quest for power. In the early stages of Nazi growth it was 'under Goebbels' guiding hand Hitler appeared for the first time as the central figure in the Party's propaganda' and later the crowds would appear in thousands to worship their new saviour, often orchestrated by Goebbels' clever propaganda.[1] Right up to 1941–2 Goebbels succeeded in creating this political divinity and Himmler's terror-structure ensured no one questioned his creation. Goebbels had changed all his previous early life's ambitions and directions, and the historian Longerich gives the date 1923 as the start of his vicious anti-Semitism, and it also appeared to increase year by year.[2] Goebbels had modelled himself on Hitler, turned him into his personal deity with all the necessary sense of adoration and total obedience. His hopes for being 'someone' in the Roman Catholic Church or a respected literary figure were simply binned once he turned towards the political scene.

Goebbels soon became an essential figure in Hitler's meteoric rise to power which had such appalling ramifications for Germany, Europe, and the world at large. His propaganda not only helped bring Hitler to power, but somehow managed to retain his popularity even during some of the most desperate times. Ed Murrow the famous wartime broadcaster and journalist noted in terms of prevailing propaganda 'this is the age when nation hurled invective into nation', and Goebbels was the undoubted master of this form of mass communication.[3] However, he never gained the total power of the propaganda machine which he had always wanted, Otto Dietrich retained many powers, Amman stayed in charge of the publishing side, but undoubtedly Goebbels was recognised as the propaganda wizard.[4] There is no question that 'Goebbels' propaganda technique was supreme.

No political propagandist before him had been so fertile in inventing such catch phrases and slogans'.[5] The nature of propaganda in the early twentieth century was changing, and 'out of next to nothing, Goebbels was to create the Third Reich, by sheer force of his propaganda'.[6] Goebbels had appealed to the masses, and although he had the greatest contempt for them he never revealed this publicly, and captured their hearts and minds, later holding their support through sheer fear.

He had always demanded the control of the way people thought, and he believed he could control the German public mind. It is known from a wide variety of sources that as life in Germany became more difficult Goebbels' speeches, declarations, and overall propaganda were treated with growing cynicism. By this stage it was too dangerous to be seen mocking him and his messages, and by 1942–3 it was too late anyway. Nevertheless, the major point of importance is that he was a critical factor in providing Hitler's popularity and supporting him when the tide turned against him. He was able to do this because he had taken propaganda to new heights (or depths) and for many years had persuaded many people to see Hitler as their Führer. He continued this work of persuasive propaganda even when most Germans had accepted that the war which Hitler had started was now being lost and defeat had become clearly imminent to most objective Germans. The German-Jewish academic Victor Klemperer who bravely kept diaries of nearly everyday life in Dresden, protected from concentration camps because he had married a so-called Aryan, noted how Goebbels used the same words to defend what was happening, with the same phrases about certain victory, of 'time working for us, of the new weapons still to come, are hammered into people'.[7] Klemperer cynically wrote it was 'Dr Goebbels (always Dr, their famous university man, always the worn-out fanatical) claiming Berlin can hold out for months!'[8] Klemperer was rightly cynical, but for many people Goebbels' rantings actually worked probably because under the developing circumstances some hope was needed.

One of the major tools he deployed was his continuous attacks upon Jews, which he deployed with unbelievable venom. There is little doubt that he was aware of the Jewish suffering, from *Kristallnacht* to the extermination camps, and had he not committed suicide this would have been a major element in the Nuremberg prosecution case and unquestionably would have led him directly to the gallows. He was so deeply involved in this activity the clever and bright Dr Goebbels could be legitimately described as a psychopath. Many experts agree that psychopaths 'lack remorse and empathy and feel emotion only shallowly. In extreme cases, they might not care whether you live or die. These people are called psychopaths. Some of them are violent criminals and murderers. But by no means all'.[9] Like Himmler, Goebbels never, as far as is known, personally killed no one except himself, but he sowed so much vitriolic hatred he was probably more guilty than Julius Streicher the infamous 'Jew-baiter'. He may not have pulled the trigger, but he organised and encouraged others. Often people only associate Goebbels with propaganda, but he was a prime example of a war criminal for stirring up so much racial hatred and was a major factor in this persecution of the Jews. It is only necessary to read his diaries or propaganda speeches to feel his personal dedication towards who was Jewish or even distantly tainted by Jewish blood. From a youngster who appeared to have few qualms about race, a member of the Church where the central figurehead of his faith, Jesus Christ was Jewish, he had become a fanatical racist.

Although his attack on the Church was less violent because he was aware of some of the public's sensitivities in this matter, it was still a serious attack on the German public mind, as Germany had been known as a sound Christian country, with both Roman Catholic and Protestant supporters, a country with a history of good theologians and famous missionaries. He was aware that men and officers in the multitudinous combat zones still had their personal religious faith, but his derisive attitude towards the Church and its clergy meant many landed up in concentration camps. His contempt for Jews and Christianity knew no bounds, and his whole life was driven by these hostile or evil actions.

The question must be asked, as to why this would-be young academic who as a young man showed no signs of anti-Semitism, had been an involved Christian within the Roman Catholic denomination with hopes of becoming a literary figure, should change so dramatically. He was like so many other members of humanity he was driven by ambition to be seen as important, and many of his biographers have felt that his early life was influenced by being born with a crippled foot. This writer is not going to disagree with this reasoning, except to point out that that many people with early disabilities do not take the same road, and many others born perfectly well are also driven by ambition. It is perhaps good to have ambition, but when it becomes driven it can be excessive, defined as 'doing whatever it takes to achieve the goal'. A person driven by financial greed, if it becomes excessive will often commit fraud, robbery, and even murder. Goebbels sought power and started by jettisoning his known early values of 'loving God and one's neighbour' and to achieve his ambition threw these fundamental values into the dustbin. If he had become accustomed to worshipping a figurehead, it took only a brief time to exchange the Christian God and Jesus Christ for Adolf Hitler, a man whose name has gone down in history as almost an aberration of a human being.

He had promptly understood that blind obedience to Hitler was the necessary pathway, and to ensure this he turned Hitler into his personal idol. It has been suggested by one biographer that 'while it is true that Goebbels never became an anti-Semitic in the sense Hitler was, he had nevertheless adopted an enmity towards Jews when he joined the party, and from the autumn of 1925 had used that enmity to further his ends.'[10] This writer thinks this comment too kind, while it was true that Goebbels may have become staunchly anti-Semitic to emulate Hitler, his efforts with his condemnation of the Jews easily reached the same depths as Hitler.

If Hitler changed his mind, so did Goebbels, so when Hitler turned against the SA, which Goebbels had used and personally befriended Röhm and some of that man's senior officers, he joined Hitler on the Night of the Long Knives to show his idol where he stood. When Hitler killed himself, Goebbels with his wife and children in tow did the same thing, his suicide may have been the easy way out, but by taking his children with him in this final act, was indicative that his driven ambition was excessive. He was a psychologically warped personality obsessed with self-importance, and nobody else mattered, and should never stand in his way because he always believed he was right in his decisions. His ambition was to grasp as much power as he could, which led him into intense quarrels and squabbles with Hitler's other similar minded henchmen, and even with his own staff serving him. It proved impossible to find any genuine reference from anyone who spoke well of him, or in a kind way. Even in the mid-1930s the visiting Australian Professor Roberts had not the slightest praise for him, and like most people recognised he was intelligent and clever but saw in him a man who despised everyone else apart from himself. Driven ruthless ambition are the best words to describe Goebbels' life.

In his private life he was just as excessive, in his youth he had many girlfriends, but he was throughout his existence what could be called a sex addict, which was widely known at the time. This habit continued when married to Magda, which caused a few eruptions, and as mentioned in the main text, when he was responsible for the film world, many women knew they might become stars if they fulfilled his wishes. Hitler once interfered to keep Goebbels' marriage as stable as possible.

Goebbels always made it known that unlike Göring he lived an austere life, but even his diary revealed that he had purchased several expensive properties and was in and out of boat exhibitions because he loved boating on Berlin lakes. Compared to Göring he was austere but in matters of lifestyle and wealth Göring would have been at the very top of the rich list. In 1932, Goebbels' income as the Berlin Gauleiter was a modest RM 619. A year later, he was receiving an annual ministerial salary of RM 38,000 and supplemented by other incomes'.[11] When it came to all Hitler's henchmen, they were all personally corrupt to one degree or another, a factor they held in common, but Goebbels kept to the pretence that he lived an austere life, but those who watched him knew he led the life of one of the well-off Junker's class. He probably pretended that he was not well-off for the same reason that he made a point of visiting bombed areas, because like his master he hoped the people liked him.

Life for Goebbels always revolved around him, be it his personal or professional life, other people were irrelevant except for his idol Hitler. His self-importance had started to show itself as a young man and blossomed during the Nazi regime. He could be cruel, vindictive, filled with hate, spitting out venom like a dangerous snake, and from whatever angle he is viewed he was an unpleasant specimen of humanity. His personal life was only raised in this study, because it confirms for us the type of person he was, but he becomes of historical interest because he used his intelligence to support and maintain Hitler in power who brought death and destruction to the world.

He has left a warped legacy by using his undoubted skills in propaganda as he provided a major tool for public persuasion and soon took total control of all information while removing any signs of dissent. He was able to do this because of his intellectual ability he had found a way in terms of human psychology to penetrate the minds of the public, appealing to them through their emotions. He had undoubtedly developed these skills as developing academic and his observations of human behaviour and reactions. He had recognised, like many others, the post First World War humiliation Germany had suffered, and projecting Hitler as the saviour had promised a restoration of national pride and a better future. He managed to create a major personality cult around the figure of Hitler to mythic proportions of near divinity, which made a powerful tool for the NSDAP by fostering the public sense on national unity, all based on indoctrination.

Goebbels and his persuasive propaganda are a stark reminder and warning that when the propaganda is used for the wrong purpose it can still happen, despite these lessons from the past. His historical influence cannot be ignored as he is a reminder of the power of propaganda which can be used in a dangerous destructive way. In today's world with the social networking, digital media of all types which are becoming a prominent feature of our daily lives, the need to ensure ethical standards remain important, as misinformation and lies can lead to serious disaster.

Goebbels is a life which reminds us of unchecked political power, the ease with which the public mind can be influenced and the danger of some political ideologies with a stark warning of any form of autocracy.

Notes

Foreword

1. Baird, J.W., *The Mythical World of Nazi War Propaganda, 1939–1945* (University of Minnesota Press, 1975)

Introduction to Goebbels and Propaganda

1. Reimann, Viktor, *Joseph Goebbels: The Man Who Created Hitler* (London: Sphere Books Ltd, 1979), p.x
2. Ebermayer, Erich and Meissner, Hans-Otto, *Evil Genius: The Story of Joseph Goebbels* (London: Allan Wingate, 1953), p.77
3. See Reimann, Viktor, *Joseph Goebbels: The Man Who Created Hitler* (London: Sphere Books Ltd, 1979), p.xi
4. Boyd, Douglas, *Voices from the Dark Years, The Truth About Occupied France* (Stroud: The History Press, 2015), p.119
5. Burleigh, Michael, *The Third Reich: A New History* (London: Pan Books, 2000), p.16
6. Heiber, Helmut, *Goebbels* (New York: Hawthorn Books, 1972), p.76
7. Guderian, Heinz, *Panzer Leader* (London: Penguin Books, 2009), p.293
8. Ibid., p.448
9. Luck, Hans von, *Panzer Commander: The Memoirs of Colonel Hans von Luck* (London: Cassell, 1989), pp.224–5
10. Neitzel, Sönke & Welzer, Harald, *Soldaten – On Fighting, Killing and Dying: The Secret Second World War Tapes of German POWs* (London: Simon & Schuster, 2012), p.213
11. Ibid., p.212
12. Evans, Richard J., *The Third Reich in History and Memory* (London: Abacus, 2015), p.148
13. Roberts, Stephen, *The House that Hitler Built* (London: Methuen, 1938), p.27
14. Ibid., p.28
15. Ibid., p.29
16. Ibid., p.13
17. Ibid., pp.121–2
18. Ibid., p.27

Chapter One

1. See Reimann, Viktor, *Joseph Goebbels: The Man Who Created Hitler* (London: Sphere Books Ltd, 1979), p.2
2. Heiber, Helmut, *Goebbels* (New York: Hawthorn Books, 1972), p.3
3. See Reimann, Viktor, *Joseph Goebbels: The Man Who Created Hitler* (London: Sphere Books Ltd, 1979), p.2
4. Manvell, Roger and Fraenkel, Heinrich, *Doctor Goebbels: His Life and Death* (Barnsley: Frontline Books, 2010), p.3

5. Reimann, Viktor, *Joseph Goebbels: The Man Who Created Hitler* (London: Sphere Books Ltd, 1979), p.3
6. Ebermayer, Erich and Meissner, Hans-Otto, *Evil Genius: The Story of Joseph Goebbels* (London: Allan Wingate, 1953), p.11
7. Heiber, Helmut, *Goebbels* (New York: Hawthorn Books, 1972), p.5
8. Longerich, Peter, *Goebbels* (London: Penguin Vintage, 2016), pp.689–90
9. Ebermayer, Erich and Meissner, Hans-Otto, *Evil Genius: The Story of Joseph Goebbels* (London: Allan Wingate, 1953), p.19
10. Reimann, Viktor, *Joseph Goebbels: The Man Who Created Hitler* (London: Sphere Books Ltd, 1979), p.4
11. Longerich, Peter, *Goebbels* (London: Penguin Vintage, 2016), p.11
12. Manvell, Roger and Fraenkel, Heinrich, *Doctor Goebbels: His Life and Death* (Barnsley: Frontline Books, 2010), p.5
13. Heiber, Helmut, *Goebbels* (New York: Hawthorn Books, 1972), p.7
14. Ebermayer, Erich and Meissner, Hans-Otto, *Evil Genius: The Story of Joseph Goebbels* (London: Allan Wingate, 1953), p.18
15. Reimann, Viktor, *Joseph Goebbels: The Man Who Created Hitler* (London: Sphere Books Ltd, 1979), p.5
16. Henderson, Sir Nevile, *Failure of a Mission* (London: Hodder and Stoughton, 1940), p.76
17. Reimann, Viktor, *Joseph Goebbels: The Man Who Created Hitler* (London: Sphere Books Ltd, 1979), p.13
18. Longerich, Peter, *Goebbels* (London: Penguin Vintage, 2016), p.23
19. Reimann, Viktor, *Joseph Goebbels: The Man Who Created Hitler* (London: Sphere Books Ltd, 1979), pp.6–7
20. Longerich, Peter, *Goebbels* (London: Penguin Vintage, 2016), p.4
21. Manvell, Roger and Fraenkel, Heinrich, *Doctor Goebbels: His Life and Death* (Barnsley: Frontline Books, 2010), p.33
22. Ebermayer, Erich and Meissner, Hans-Otto, *Evil Genius: The Story of Joseph Goebbels* (London: Allan Wingate, 1953), p.39
23. See Longerich, Peter, *Goebbels* (London: Penguin Vintage, 2016), p.14
24. See Reimann, Viktor, *Joseph Goebbels: The Man Who Created Hitler* (London: Sphere Books Ltd, 1979), p.18
25. See Heiber, Helmut, *Goebbels* (New York: Hawthorn Books, 1972), p.23
26. Ibid., p.33
27. Quoted in Longerich, Peter, *Goebbels* (London: Penguin Vintage, 2016), p.36
28. Ebermayer, Erich and Meissner, Hans-Otto, *Evil Genius: The Story of Joseph Goebbels* (London: Allan Wingate, 1953), p.41
29. Toland, John, *Hitler* (London: Wordsworth Editions, 1997), p.214
30. See Heiber, Helmut, *Goebbels* (New York: Hawthorn Books, 1972), p.38
31. Longerich, Peter, *Goebbels* (London: Penguin Vintage, 2016), p.54

Chapter Two

1. This entry for 14 June in 1926, Goebbels, Joseph and Lochner, Louis P. (Ed.), *The Goebbels Diaries, 1942–1943* (New York: Doubleday and Company, 1948), p.7
2. Evans, Richard J., *The Third Reich in History and Memory* (London: Abacus, 2015), p.54

3. Reimann, Viktor, *Joseph Goebbels: The Man Who Created Hitler* (London: Sphere Books Ltd, 1979), p.31. It is also stated in Ebermayer, Erich and Meissner, Hans-Otto, *Evil Genius: The Story of Joseph Goebbels* (London: Allan Wingate, 1953), p.44
4. Reimann, Viktor, *Joseph Goebbels: The Man Who Created Hitler* (London: Sphere Books Ltd, 1979), p.38
5. See Heiber, Helmut, *Goebbels* (New York: Hawthorn Books, 1972), p.45
6. Orlow, Dietrich, *The History of the Nazi Party* Vol. 1 (Newton Abbott: David and Charles, 1969), p.72
7. Manvell, Roger and Fraenkel, Heinrich, *Doctor Goebbels: His Life and Death* (Barnsley: Frontline Books, 2010), p.54
8. Reimann, Viktor, *Joseph Goebbels: The Man Who Created Hitler* (London: Sphere Books Ltd, 1979), p.36
9. Quoted in Reimann, *Joseph Goebbels,* p.42
10. Heiber, Helmut, *Goebbels* (New York: Hawthorn Books, 1972), p.41
11. Orlow, Dietrich, *The History of the Nazi Party* Vol. 1 (Newton Abbott: David and Charles, 1969), p.93
12. Heiber, Helmut, *Goebbels* (New York: Hawthorn Books, 1972), p.62
13. Trevor-Roper, H.R. (Ed.), *Hitler's Table Talk* (London: Weidenfeld and Nicolson, 1953), p.532
14. Heiber, Helmut, *Goebbels* (New York: Hawthorn Books, 1972), p.49
15. Reimann, Viktor, *Joseph Goebbels: The Man Who Created Hitler* (London: Sphere Books Ltd, 1979), p.73
16. Longerich, Peter, *Goebbels* (London: Penguin Vintage, 2016), p.75
17. Ebermayer, Erich and Meissner, Hans-Otto, *Evil Genius: The Story of Joseph Goebbels* (London: Allan Wingate, 1953), p.67
18. Quoting A. Bullock in Manvell, Roger and Fraenkel, Heinrich, *Doctor Goebbels: His Life and Death* (Barnsley: Frontline Books, 2010), p.71
19. Reimann, Viktor, *Joseph Goebbels: The Man Who Created Hitler* (London: Sphere Books Ltd, 1979), p.90
20. See Heiber, Helmut, *Goebbels* (New York: Hawthorn Books, 1972), p.74
21. See Reimann, Viktor, *Joseph Goebbels: The Man Who Created Hitler* (London: Sphere Books Ltd, 1979), p.100
22. See Heiber, Helmut, *Goebbels* (New York: Hawthorn Books, 1972), p.91
23. Ibid., p.104
24. Longerich, Peter, *Goebbels* (London: Penguin Vintage, 2016), p.94
25. See Heiber, Helmut, *Goebbels* (New York: Hawthorn Books, 1972), p.55
26. Reimann, Viktor, *Joseph Goebbels: The Man Who Created Hitler* (London: Sphere Books Ltd, 1979), p.114
27. Finney, Patrick (Ed.), Taylor, A.J.P., *The Origins of the Second World War* (London: Arnold, 1997), p.352
28. See Heiber, Helmut, *Goebbels* (New York: Hawthorn Books, 1972), pp.183–4

Chapter Three

1. Ibid., p.72
2. Ibid., p.63

3. See Manvell, Roger and Fraenkel, Heinrich, *Doctor Goebbels: His Life and Death* (Barnsley: Frontline Books, 2010), p.88. Also Ebermayer, Erich and Meissner, Hans-Otto, *Evil Genius: The Story of Joseph Goebbels* (London: Allan Wingate, 1953), p.65
4. See Longerich, Peter, *Goebbels* (London: Penguin Vintage, 2016), p.123
5. Heiber, Helmut, *Goebbels* (New York: Hawthorn Books, 1972), p.69
6. Ibid., p.97
7. Ibid., p.188
8. Toland, John, *Hitler* (London: Wordsworth Editions, 1997), p.238
9. Reimann, Viktor, *Joseph Goebbels: The Man Who Created Hitler* (London: Sphere Books Ltd, 1979), p.152
10. Ibid., p.137
11. See Longerich, Peter, *Goebbels* (London: Penguin Vintage, 2016), p.121
12. Ibid., pp.140–1
13. See Reimann, Viktor, *Joseph Goebbels: The Man Who Created Hitler* (London: Sphere Books Ltd, 1979), p.146
14. Ebermayer, Erich and Meissner, Hans-Otto, *Evil Genius: The Story of Joseph Goebbels* (London: Allan Wingate, 1953), p.78
15. Meissner, Hans-Otto, translated from German by Gwendolen Mary Keeble, *Magda Goebbels: The First Day of the Third Reich* (New York: The Dial Press, 1980)
16. Ibid., p.4
17. Ibid., p.100
18. Ibid., p.38
19. Ibid., p.79
20. Ibid., p.80
21. Ibid., p.84
22. Ibid., p.90
23. See Reimann, Viktor, *Joseph Goebbels: The Man Who Created Hitler* (London: Sphere Books Ltd, 1979), pp.142–5
24. Meissner, Hans-Otto, translated from German by Gwendolen Mary Keeble, *Magda Goebbels: The First Day of the Third Reich* (New York: The Dial Press, 1980), pp.95–6
25. Ibid., p.125
26. Manvell, Roger and Fraenkel, Heinrich, *Doctor Goebbels: His Life and Death* (Barnsley: Frontline Books, 2010), p.95
27. Reimann, Viktor, *Joseph Goebbels: The Man Who Created Hitler* (London: Sphere Books Ltd, 1979), p.165
28. Ibid., p.168
29. Ibid., p.148
30. See Heiber, Helmut, *Goebbels* (New York: Hawthorn Books, 1972), p.96
31. Quoted in Reimann, Viktor, *Joseph Goebbels: The Man Who Created Hitler* (London: Sphere Books Ltd, 1979), p.179
32. See Longerich, Peter, *Goebbels* (London: Penguin Vintage, 2016), pp.194–5
33. Helmut Heiber quoted in Reimann, Viktor, *Joseph Goebbels: The Man Who Created Hitler* (London: Sphere Books Ltd, 1979), p.182
34. Reimann, Viktor, *Joseph Goebbels: The Man Who Created Hitler* (London: Sphere Books Ltd, 1979), p.182
35. Longerich, Peter, *Goebbels* (London: Penguin Vintage, 2016), p.199

36. Goebbels, Joseph, *Vom Kaiserhof zur Reichskanzlei* (Eher, 1934) and the English translation *My Part in Germany's Fight* (Paternoster Library, 1938) and the original edition by Hurst and Blackett 1935; all quoted extensively in Manvell, Roger and Fraenkel, Heinrich, *Doctor Goebbels: His Life and Death* (Barnsley: Frontline Books, 2010), p.98 ff.
37. Manvell, Roger and Fraenkel, Heinrich, *Doctor Goebbels: His Life and Death* (Barnsley: Frontline Books, 2010), p.103
38. Heiber, Helmut, *Goebbels* (New York: Hawthorn Books, 1972), p.195
39. Manvell, Roger and Fraenkel, Heinrich, *Doctor Goebbels: His Life and Death* (Barnsley: Frontline Books, 2010), p.116

Chapter Four

1. See Reimann, Viktor, *Joseph Goebbels: The Man Who Created Hitler* (London: Sphere Books Ltd, 1979), p.188
2. Manvell, Roger and Fraenkel, Heinrich, *Doctor Goebbels: His Life and Death* (Barnsley: Frontline Books, 2010), p.120
3. Padfield, Peter, *Himmler Reichsführer-SS* (London: Macmillan, 1990), p.105
4. Ebermayer, Erich and Meissner, Hans-Otto, *Evil Genius: The Story of Joseph Goebbels* (London: Allan Wingate, 1953), p.96
5. Ibid.
6. Heiber, Helmut, *Goebbels* (New York: Hawthorn Books, 1972), p.218
7. Reimann, Viktor, *Joseph Goebbels: The Man Who Created Hitler* (London: Sphere Books Ltd, 1979), p.257
8. Ibid., p.190
9. Ibid., p.243
10. Burleigh, Michael, *The Third Reich: A New History* (London: Pan Books, 2000), p.223
11. Heiber, Helmut, *Goebbels* (New York: Hawthorn Books, 1972), p.186
12. Ebermayer, Erich and Meissner, Hans-Otto, *Evil Genius: The Story of Joseph Goebbels* (London: Allan Wingate, 1953), p.102
13. Ibid.
14. Heiber, Helmut, *Goebbels* (New York: Hawthorn Books, 1972), p.127
15. Ibid., p.120
16. Ibid., p.131

Chapter Five

1. Welch, David (Ed.), *Nazi Propaganda: The Power and the Limitations* (London: Routledge, 2015), p.134
2. Longerich, Peter, *Goebbels* (London: Penguin Vintage, 2016), p.215
3. Ebermayer, Erich and Meissner, Hans-Otto, *Evil Genius: The Story of Joseph Goebbels* (London: Allan Wingate, 1953), p.97
4. See Heiber, Helmut, *Goebbels* (New York: Hawthorn Books, 1972), p.146
5. Ibid., p.151
6. See Longerich, Peter, *Goebbels* (London: Penguin Vintage, 2016), p.223
7. Reimann, Viktor, *Joseph Goebbels: The Man Who Created Hitler* (London: Sphere Books Ltd, 1979), p.227
8. Heiber, Helmut, *Goebbels* (New York: Hawthorn Books, 1972), p.160
9. Ibid., p.161
10. See Longerich, Peter, *Goebbels* (London: Penguin Vintage, 2016), p.409

11. Welch, David (Ed.), *Nazi Propaganda: The Power and the Limitations* (London: Routledge, 2015), p.73
12. Reimann, Viktor, *Joseph Goebbels: The Man Who Created Hitler* (London: Sphere Books Ltd, 1979), p.221
13. Quoted in Longerich, Peter, *Goebbels* (London: Penguin Vintage, 2016), p.223
14. See Rother, Rainer (translated by Rainer Rother), *Leni Riefenstahl: The Seduction of Genius* (London: Continuum, 2002), p.168
15. See Longerich, Peter, *Goebbels* (London: Penguin Vintage, 2016), p.252
16. Shirer, William L., *The Rise and Fall of the Third Reich* (London: Mandarin, 1960), p.241
17. Reimann, Viktor, *Joseph Goebbels: The Man Who Created Hitler* (London: Sphere Books Ltd, 1979), p.217
18. Heiber, Helmut, *Goebbels* (New York: Hawthorn Books, 1972), p.136
19. Reimann, Viktor, *Joseph Goebbels: The Man Who Created Hitler* (London: Sphere Books Ltd, 1979), p.249
20. Heiber, Helmut, *Goebbels* (New York: Hawthorn Books, 1972), p.143
21. Reimann, Viktor, *Joseph Goebbels: The Man Who Created Hitler* (London: Sphere Books Ltd, 1979), p.197
22. Heiber, Helmut, *Goebbels* (New York: Hawthorn Books, 1972), p.128
23. Ibid., p.165
24. Reimann, Viktor, *Joseph Goebbels: The Man Who Created Hitler* (London: Sphere Books Ltd, 1979), p.207
25. Heiber, Helmut, *Goebbels* (New York: Hawthorn Books, 1972), p.182
26. Ibid., p.221
27. Ebermayer, Erich and Meissner, Hans-Otto, *Evil Genius: The Story of Joseph Goebbels* (London: Allan Wingate, 1953), p.110
28. Manvell, Roger and Fraenkel, Heinrich, *Doctor Goebbels: His Life and Death* (Barnsley: Frontline Books, 2010), p.153
29. Reimann, Viktor, *Joseph Goebbels: The Man Who Created Hitler* (London: Sphere Books Ltd, 1979), p.229
30. See Heiber, Helmut, *Goebbels* (New York: Hawthorn Books, 1972), p.126

Chapter Six

1. Röhm in the early days had been a constant visitor at Goebbels' house but he was never liked by Magda. See Ebermayer, Erich and Meissner, Hans-Otto, *Evil Genius: The Story of Joseph Goebbels* (London: Allan Wingate, 1953), p.104
2. See Manvell, Roger and Fraenkel, Heinrich, *Doctor Goebbels: His Life and Death* (Barnsley: Frontline Books, 2010)
3. Longerich, Peter, *Goebbels* (London: Penguin Vintage, 2016), p.266
4. Reimann, Viktor, *Joseph Goebbels: The Man Who Created Hitler* (London: Sphere Books Ltd, 1979), p.262
5. See Heiber, Helmut, *Goebbels* (New York: Hawthorn Books, 1972), p.222
6. Ibid., p.224
7. Bullock, Alan, *Hitler: A Study in Tyranny* (London: Penguin Books, 1990), p.306
8. Reimann, Viktor, *Joseph Goebbels: The Man Who Created Hitler* (London: Sphere Books Ltd, 1979), p.269
9. Meissner, Hans-Otto, translated from German by Gwendolen Mary Keeble, *Magda Goebbels: The First Day of the Third Reich* (New York: The Dial Press, 1980), p.73

10. Reimann, Viktor, *Joseph Goebbels: The Man Who Created Hitler* (London: Sphere Books Ltd, 1979), p.45
11. Ibid., p.108
12. Ebermayer, Erich and Meissner, Hans-Otto, *Evil Genius: The Story of Joseph Goebbels* (London: Allan Wingate, 1953), p.111
13. Longerich, Peter, *Goebbels* (London: Penguin Vintage, 2016), p.302
14. See Ibid., p.357
15. Reimann, Viktor, *Joseph Goebbels: The Man Who Created Hitler* (London: Sphere Books Ltd, 1979), p.285
16. Heiber, Helmut, *Goebbels* (New York: Hawthorn Books, 1972), p.247
17. Ibid., p.247
18. Longerich, Peter, *Goebbels* (London: Penguin Vintage, 2016), p.464
19. Quoted in Longerich, Peter, *Goebbels* (London: Penguin Vintage, 2016), p.502
20. Quoted in Ibid., p.514
21. Quoted in Gilbert, Martin, *Second World War* (London: Phoenix, 1997), p.24
22. Quoted in Ibid., p.312
23. Göbbels Diary quoted in Manvell, Roger and Fraenkel, Heinrich, *Doctor Goebbels: His Life and Death* (Barnsley: Frontline Books, 2010), p.207
24. Ibid., p.208
25. Longerich, Peter, *Goebbels* (London: Penguin Vintage, 2016), p.548
26. Quoted in Ibid., p.567
27. Heiber, Helmut, *Goebbels* (New York: Hawthorn Books, 1972), p.276
28. Davies, Norman, *Europe at War 1939–1945: No Simple Victory* (London: Viking, 2006), pp.13–14
29. Burleigh, Michael, *Moral Combat: A History of World War II* (London: Harper Press, 2010), p.532
30. See Davies, Norman, *Europe at War 1939–1945: No Simple Victory* (London: Viking, 2006), p.182
31. Sangster, Andrew, *The Unfolding Agony of Oppression* (Ethics International Press, 2023), p.46
32. Reimann, Viktor, *Joseph Goebbels: The Man Who Created Hitler* (London: Sphere Books Ltd, 1979), p.264
33. Quoted in Longerich, Peter, *Goebbels* (London: Penguin Vintage, 2016), p.331
34. Reimann, Viktor, *Joseph Goebbels: The Man Who Created Hitler* (London: Sphere Books Ltd, 1979), p.267
35. Stargardt, Nicholas, *The German War: A Nation Under Arms, 1939–45* (London: Vintage, 2015), p.145
36. See Evans, Richard J., *The Third Reich at War* (London: Allen Lane, 2008), p.99
37. Stargardt, Nicholas, *Witnesses of War: Children's Lives Under the Nazis* (London: Jonathan Cape, 2005), p.87
38. Evans, Richard J., *The Third Reich at War* (London: Allen Lane, 2008), p.93

Chapter Seven

1. Heiber, Helmut, *Goebbels* (New York: Hawthorn Books, 1972), p.220
2. See Ebermayer, Erich and Meissner, Hans-Otto, *Evil Genius: The Story of Joseph Goebbels* (London: Allan Wingate, 1953), p.108

3. Reimann, Viktor, *Joseph Goebbels: The Man Who Created Hitler* (London: Sphere Books Ltd, 1979), p.258
4. Longerich, Peter, *Goebbels* (London: Penguin Vintage, 2016), p.245
5. Ibid., p.416
6. Heiber, Helmut, *Goebbels* (New York: Hawthorn Books, 1972), p.221
7. Ibid., p.189
8. Ebermayer, Erich and Meissner, Hans-Otto, *Evil Genius: The Story of Joseph Goebbels* (London: Allan Wingate, 1953), p.123
9. CBS World Roundup Broadcast, 13 March 1938, Columbia Broadcasting System retrieved from: http://otr.com/ra/news/CBS_Roundup_3-13-1938.mp3
10. See Longerich, Peter, *Goebbels* (London: Penguin Vintage, 2016), p.379
11. Evans, Richard J., *The Third Reich in History and Memory* (London: Abacus, 2015), p.106
12. See Longerich, Peter, *Goebbels* (London: Penguin Vintage, 2016), p.419

Chapter Eight

1. See Ebermayer, Erich and Meissner, Hans-Otto, *Evil Genius: The Story of Joseph Goebbels* (London: Allan Wingate, 1953), p.155
2. Heiber, Helmut, *Goebbels* (New York: Hawthorn Books, 1972), p.76
3. See Davies, Norman, *Europe at War 1939–1945: No Simple Victory* (London: Viking, 2006), p.78
4. Hastings, Max, *All Hell Let Loose* (London: Harper Press, 2011), p.14
5. See Reimann, Viktor, *Joseph Goebbels: The Man Who Created Hitler* (London: Sphere Books Ltd, 1979), p.295
6. Quoted in Reimann, Viktor, *Joseph Goebbels: The Man Who Created Hitler* (London: Sphere Books Ltd, 1979), p.346
7. Heiber, Helmut, *Goebbels* (New York: Hawthorn Books, 1972), p.280
8. Gobbels, Joseph (Translated by Taylor, Fred), *The Goebbels Diaries, 1939–41* (London: Hamish Hamilton, 1982), p.28
9. Tusa, Ann and Tusa, John, *The Nuremberg Trial* (London: BBC Books, 1995), p.185
10. Reimann, Viktor, *Joseph Goebbels: The Man Who Created Hitler* (London: Sphere Books Ltd, 1979), p.269
11. Heiber, Helmut, *Goebbels* (New York: Hawthorn Books, 1972), p.231
12. See Ebermayer, Erich and Meissner, Hans-Otto, *Evil Genius: The Story of Joseph Goebbels* (London: Allan Wingate, 1953), p.121
13. See Longerich, Peter, *Goebbels* (London: Penguin Vintage, 2016), p.362
14. Heiber, Helmut, *Goebbels* (New York: Hawthorn Books, 1972), p.238
15. Ibid., p.240
16. Ebermayer, Erich and Meissner, Hans-Otto, *Evil Genius: The Story of Joseph Goebbels* (London: Allan Wingate, 1953), p.127
17. Reimann, Viktor, *Joseph Goebbels: The Man Who Created Hitler* (London: Sphere Books Ltd, 1979), p.274
18. Ebermayer, Erich and Meissner, Hans-Otto, *Evil Genius: The Story of Joseph Goebbels* (London: Allan Wingate, 1953), pp.125–146
19. Meissner, Hans-Otto, translated from German by Gwendolen Mary Keeble, *Magda Goebbels: The First Day of the Third Reich* (New York: The Dial Press, 1980), p.129
20. See Ibid., p.171

21. Manvell, Roger and Fraenkel, Heinrich, *Doctor Goebbels: His Life and Death* (Barnsley: Frontline Books, 2010), p.170
22. Ebermayer, Erich and Meissner, Hans-Otto, *Evil Genius: The Story of Joseph Goebbels* (London: Allan Wingate, 1953), p.138
23. Meissner, Hans-Otto, translated from German by Gwendolen Mary Keeble, *Magda Goebbels: The First Day of the Third Reich* (New York: The Dial Press, 1980), p.90
24. Ebermayer, Erich and Meissner, Hans-Otto, *Evil Genius: The Story of Joseph Goebbels* (London: Allan Wingate, 1953), p.147
25. See Heiber, Helmut, *Goebbels* (New York: Hawthorn Books, 1972), p.251
26. Ibid., p.262
27. Davies, Norman, *Europe at War 1939–1945: No Simple Victory* (London: Viking, 2006), p.464
28. Heiber, Helmut, *Goebbels* (New York: Hawthorn Books, 1972), p.256
29. Ebermayer, Erich and Meissner, Hans-Otto, *Evil Genius: The Story of Joseph Goebbels* (London: Allan Wingate, 1953), p.174
30. Manvell, Roger and Fraenkel, Heinrich, *Doctor Goebbels: His Life and Death* (Barnsley: Frontline Books, 2010), p.186
31. Reimann, Viktor, *Joseph Goebbels: The Man Who Created Hitler* (London: Sphere Books Ltd, 1979), p.296
32. Quoted in Longerich, Peter, *Goebbels* (London: Penguin Vintage, 2016), p.452
33. Reimann, Viktor, *Joseph Goebbels: The Man Who Created Hitler* (London: Sphere Books Ltd, 1979), p.306
34. Ebermayer, Erich and Meissner, Hans-Otto, *Evil Genius: The Story of Joseph Goebbels* (London: Allan Wingate, 1953), p.199
35. Michel, Henri, *The Second World War* (London: Deutsch, 1975), p.211
36. Quoted in Hastings, Max, *All Hell Let Loose* (London: Harper Press, 2011), p.144
37. Overy, Richard, *Why the Allies Won* (London: Pimlico, 2006), p.372
38. Quoted in Evans, Richard J., *The Third Reich at War* (London: Allen Lane, 2008), p.169
39. Ebermayer, Erich and Meissner, Hans-Otto, *Evil Genius: The Story of Joseph Goebbels* (London: Allan Wingate, 1953), p.178
40. Quoted in Longerich, Peter, *Goebbels* (London: Penguin Vintage, 2016), p.485
41. Messenger, Charles, *The Last Prussian: A Biography of Field Marshal Gerd von Rundstedt* (Barnsley: Pen & Sword, 2012), p.154

Chapter Nine

1. Quoted in Ebermayer, Erich and Meissner, Hans-Otto, *Evil Genius: The Story of Joseph Goebbels* (London: Allan Wingate, 1953), p.182
2. Stargardt, Nicholas, *The German War: A Nation Under Arms, 1939–45* (London: Vintage, 2015), p.237
3. See Beevor, Antony, *The Second World War* (London: Weidenfeld & Nicolson, 2012), p.204
4. See Gilbert, Martin, *Second World War* (London: Phoenix, 1997), p.304
5. Roberts, Andrew, *The Storm of War* (London: Allen Lane, 2009), p.405
6. Michel, Henri, *The Second World War* (London: Deutsch, 1975), p.667
7. Longerich, Peter, *Goebbels* (London: Penguin Vintage, 2016), p.533
8. Quoted in Longerich, Peter, *Goebbels* (London: Penguin Vintage, 2016), p.549
9. Reimann, Viktor, *Joseph Goebbels: The Man Who Created Hitler* (London: Sphere Books Ltd, 1979), p.311

10. Klemperer, Victor, *To the Bitter End: The Diaries of Victor Klemperer 1942–45* (London: Weidenfeld & Nicolson, 1999), p.194
11. Reimann, Viktor, *Joseph Goebbels: The Man Who Created Hitler* (London: Sphere Books Ltd, 1979), p.330
12. See Ebermayer, Erich and Meissner, Hans-Otto, *Evil Genius: The Story of Joseph Goebbels* (London: Allan Wingate, 1953), p.206
13. Weinberg, Gerhard L., *A World at Arms: A Global History of World War II* (Cambridge: CUP, 1994), p.460
14. Beevor, Antony, *The Second World War* (London: Weidenfeld & Nicolson, 2012), p.718
15. Toland, John, *The Last 100 Days* (New York: The Modern Library, 1996), p.157
16. Quoted in Hickey, Des and Smith, Gus, *Operation Avalanche, The Salerno Landings, 1943* (London: Heinemann, 1983), p.226
17. Graham, Dominick and Bidwell, Shelford, *Tug of War: The Battle for Italy, 1943–45* (Yorkshire: Pen & Sword, 2004), p.91.
18. Manvell, Roger and Fraenkel, Heinrich, *Doctor Goebbels: His Life and Death* (Barnsley: Frontline Books, 2010), p.196
19. Shirer, William L., *The Rise and Fall of the Third Reich* (London: Mandarin, 1960), p.1008
20. Lucas, James, *Last Days of the Reich: The Collapse of Nazi Germany, May 1945* (London: Arms and Armour Press, 1986), p.37
21. Goebbels built his own personal air-raid shelters which were luxurious. See Heiber, Helmut, *Goebbels* (New York: Hawthorn Books, 1972), p.297
22. Longerich, Peter, *Goebbels* (London: Penguin Vintage, 2016), p.599
23. See Ebermayer, Erich and Meissner, Hans-Otto, *Evil Genius: The Story of Joseph Goebbels* (London: Allan Wingate, 1953), p.187
24. Longerich, Peter, *Goebbels* (London: Penguin Vintage, 2016), p.629
25. Klemperer, Victor, *To the Bitter End: The Diaries of Victor Klemperer 1942–45* (London: Weidenfeld & Nicolson, 1999), p.307
26. Heiber, Helmut, *Goebbels* (New York: Hawthorn Books, 1972), p.310
27. Toland, John, *The Last 100 Days* (New York: The Modern Library, 1996), p.10
28. Quoted in Hébert, Valerie Geneviève, *Hitler's Generals on Trial: The Last War Crimes Tribunal at Nuremberg* (Kansas: University of Kansas, 2010), p.142
29. Manvell, Roger and Fraenkel, Heinrich, *Doctor Goebbels: His Life and Death* (Barnsley: Frontline Books, 2010), p.267
30. Evans, Richard J., *The Third Reich in History and Memory* (London: Abacus, 2015), p.129

Chapter Ten

1. Heiber, Helmut, *Goebbels* (New York: Hawthorn Books, 1972), pp.303–304
2. Fest, Joachim E., *Plotting Hitler's Death: The German Resistance to Hitler, 1933–1945* (London: Phoenix, 1997), pp.3–4
3. See Beevor, Antony, *The Second World War* (London: Weidenfeld & Nicolson, 2012), p.549
4. Ebermayer, Erich and Meissner, Hans-Otto, *Evil Genius: The Story of Joseph Goebbels* (London: Allan Wingate, 1953), p.200
5. Heiber, Helmut, *Goebbels* (New York: Hawthorn Books, 1972), p.302
6. Ibid., p.308
7. Ibid., p.320
8. Beevor, Antony, *The Second World War* (London: Weidenfeld & Nicolson, 2012), p.638
9. Heiber, Helmut, *Goebbels* (New York: Hawthorn Books, 1972), p.331

10. Longerich, Peter, *Goebbels* (London: Penguin Vintage, 2016), p.667
11. Davies, Norman, *Europe at War 1939–1945: No Simple Victory* (London: Viking, 2006), p.121
12. Stargardt, Nicholas, *Witnesses of War: Children's Lives Under the Nazis* (London: Jonathan Cape, 2005), p.268
13. Kershaw, Ian, *The End: The Defiance and Destruction of Hitler's Germany, 1944–1945* (London: Penguin Books, 2012), p.391
14. Stargardt, Nicholas, *The German War: A Nation Under Arms, 1939–45* (London: Vintage, 2015), p.378
15. Longerich, Peter, *Goebbels* (London: Penguin Vintage, 2016), p.676
16. Toland, John, *The Last 100 Days* (New York: The Modern Library, 1996), p.378
17. Overy, Richard, *Why the Allies Won* (London: Pimlico, 2006), p.344
18. Kershaw, Ian, *The End: The Defiance and Destruction of Hitler's Germany, 1944–1945* (London: Penguin Books, 2012), pp.164, 243 & 281
19. Overy, Richard, *Why the Allies Won* (London: Pimlico, 2006), p.376
20. Kershaw, Ian, *The End: The Defiance and Destruction of Hitler's Germany, 1944–1945* (London: Penguin Books, 2012), p.244
21. Manvell, Roger and Fraenkel, Heinrich, *Doctor Goebbels: His Life and Death* (Barnsley: Frontline Books, 2010), p.241
22. Heiber, Helmut, *Goebbels* (New York: Hawthorn Books, 1972), p.310
23. See Reitsch, Hanna (translated by Lawrence Wilson), *The Sky My Kingdom: Memoirs of the Famous German World War II Test Pilot* (London: Greenhill Books 1955)
24. Meissner, Hans-Otto, translated from German by Gwendolen Mary Keeble, *Magda Goebbels: The First Day of the Third Reich* (New York: The Dial Press, 1980), p.256
25. Heiber, Helmut, *Goebbels* (New York: Hawthorn Books, 1972), p.353
26. Quoted in Lüdde-Neurath, Walter, *Unconditional Surrender* (London: Frontline, 2010), p.131 Appendices.
27. Meissner, Hans-Otto, translated from German by Gwendolen Mary Keeble, *Magda Goebbels: The First Day of the Third Reich* (New York: The Dial Press, 1980), p.260
28. See Lucas, James, *Last Days of the Reich: The Collapse of Nazi Germany, May 1945* (London: Arms and Armour Press, 1986), p.56
29. Heiber, Helmut, *Goebbels* (New York: Hawthorn Books, 1972), p.356
30. Ebermayer, Erich and Meissner, Hans-Otto, *Evil Genius: The Story of Joseph Goebbels* (London: Allan Wingate, 1953), p.236
31. Longerich, Peter, *Goebbels* (London: Penguin Vintage, 2016), p.xii
32. Roberts, Andrew, *The Storm of War* (London: Allen Lane, 2009), p.560
33. Beevor, Antony, *The Second World War* (London: Weidenfeld & Nicolson, 2012), p.756
34. See Roberts, Andrew, *The Storm of War* (London: Allen Lane, 2009), p.563
35. Burleigh, Michael, *The Third Reich: A New History* (London: Pan Books, 2000), p.792
36. Lucas, James, *Last Days of the Reich: The Collapse of Nazi Germany, May 1945* (London: Arms and Armour Press, 1986), p.151

Chapter Eleven

1. Longerich, Peter, *Goebbels* (London: Penguin Vintage, 2016), p.691
2. See Longerich, Peter, *Goebbels* (London: Penguin Vintage, 2016), p.701
3. Burleigh, Michael, *Moral Combat: A History of World War II* (London: Harper Press, 2010), p.58

4. See Longerich, Peter, *Goebbels* (London: Penguin Vintage, 2016), p.693
5. Reimann, Viktor, *Joseph Goebbels: The Man Who Created Hitler* (London: Sphere Books Ltd, 1979), p.242
6. Ebermayer, Erich and Meissner, Hans-Otto, *Evil Genius: The Story of Joseph Goebbels* (London: Allan Wingate, 1953), p.59
7. Klemperer, Victor, *To the Bitter End: The Diaries of Victor Klemperer 1942–45* (London: Weidenfeld & Nicolson, 1999), p.343
8. Ibid., pp.345 and 439
9. Chivers, Tom, *Daily Telegraph*, 19 August 2017
10. Heiber, Helmut, *Goebbels* (New York: Hawthorn Books, 1972), p.62
11. Burleigh, Michael, *Moral Combat: A History of World War II* (London: Harper Press, 2010), p.99

Bibliography

Baird, J.W., *The Mythical World of Nazi War Propaganda, 1939–1945* (Minnesota University Press: 1975)

Beevor, Antony, *The Second World War* (London: Weidenfeld & Nicolson, 2012)

Boyd, Douglas, *Voices from the Dark Years, The Truth About Occupied France* (Stroud: The History Press, 2015)

Bullock, Alan, *Hitler: A Study in Tyranny* (London: Penguin Books, 1990)

Burleigh, Michael, *The Third Reich: A New History* (London: Pan Books, 2000)

——, *Moral Combat: A History of World War II* (London: Harper Press, 2010)

CBS World Roundup Broadcast 13 March 1938, Columbia Broadcasting System retrieved from http://otr.com/ra/news/CBS_Roundup_3-13-1938.mp3

Chivers, Tom, *Daily Telegraph*, 19 August 2017

Davies, Norman, *Europe at War 1939–1945: No Simple Victory* (London: Viking, 2006)

Ebermayer, Erich and Meissner, Hans-Otto, *Evil Genius: The Story of Joseph Goebbels* (London: Allan Wingate, 1953)

Evans, Richard J., *The Third Reich in History and Memory* (London: Abacus, 2015)

——, *The Third Reich at War* (London: Allen Lane, 2008)

Fest, Joachim E., *Plotting Hitler's Death: The German Resistance to Hitler, 1933–1945* (London: Phoenix, 1997)

Finney, Patrick (Ed.), Taylor, A.J.P., *The Origins of the Second World War* (London: Arnold, 1997)

Gilbert, Martin, *Second World War* (London: Phoenix, 1997)

Goebbels, Joseph, *Vom Kaiserhof zur Reichskanzlei* (Eher, 1934)

Goebbels, Joseph and Lochner, Louis P. (Ed.), *The Goebbels Diaries, 1942–1943* (New York: Doubleday and Company, 1948)

Graham, Dominick and Bidwell, Shelford, *Tug of War: The Battle for Italy, 1943–45* (Barnsley: Pen & Sword, 2004)

Guderian, Heinz, *Panzer Leader* (London: Penguin Books, 2009)

Hastings, Max, *All Hell Let Loose* (London: Harper Press, 2011)

Heiber, Helmut, *Goebbels* (New York: Hawthorn Books, 1972)

Henderson, Sir Nevile, *Failure of a Mission* (London: Hodder and Stoughton, 1940)

Hébert, Valerie Geneviève, *Hitler's Generals on Trial: The Last War Crimes Tribunal at Nuremberg* (Kansas: University of Kansas, 2010)

Hickey, Des and Smith, Gus, *Operation Avalanche, The Salerno Landings, 1943* (London: Heinemann, 1983)

Kershaw, Ian, *The End: The Defiance and Destruction of Hitler's Germany, 1944–1945* (London: Penguin Books, 2012)

Klemperer, Victor, *To the Bitter End: The Diaries of Victor Klemperer 1942–45* (London: Weidenfeld & Nicolson, 1999)

Longerich, Peter, *Goebbels* (London: Penguin Vintage, 2016)
Lucas, James, *Last Days of the Reich: The Collapse of Nazi Germany, May 1945* (London: Arms and Armour Press, 1986)
Luck, Hans von, *Panzer Commander: The Memoirs of Colonel Hans von Luck* (London: Cassell, 1989)
Lüdde-Neurath, Walter, *Unconditional Surrender* (London: Frontline, 2010)
Manvell, Roger and Fraenkel, Heinrich, *Doctor Goebbels: His Life and Death* (Barnsley: Frontline Books, 2010)
Meissner, Hans-Otto, translated from German by Gwendolen Mary Keeble, *Magda Goebbels: The First Day of the Third Reich* (New York: The Dial Press, 1980)
Messenger, Charles, *The Last Prussian: A Biography of Field Marshal Gerd von Rundstedt* (Barnsley: Pen & Sword, 2012)
Michel, Henri, *The Second World War* (London: Deutsch, 1975)
Neitzel, Sönke & Welzer, Harald, *Soldaten – On Fighting, Killing and Dying: The Secret Second World War Tapes of German POWs* (London: Simon & Schuster, 2012)
Orlow, Dietrich, *The History of the Nazi Party* Vol. 1 (Newton Abbott: David and Charles, 1969)
Overy, Richard, *Why the Allies Won* (London: Pimlico, 2006)
Padfield, Peter, *Himmler Reichsführer-SS* (London: Macmillan, 1990)
Porch, Douglas, *Hitler's Mediterranean Gamble: The North African and the Mediterranean Campaigns in World War II* (London: Weidenfeld & Nicolson, 2004)
Reimann, Viktor, *Joseph Goebbels: The Man Who Created Hitler* (London: Sphere Books Ltd, 1979)
Reitsch, Hanna (translated by Lawrence Wilson), *The Sky My Kingdom: Memoirs of the Famous German World War II Test Pilot* (London: Greenhill Books 1955)
Roberts, Andrew, *The Storm of War* (London: Allen Lane, 2009)
Roberts, Stephen, *The House that Hitler Built* (London: Methuen, 1938)
Rother, Rainer (translated by Rainer Rother), *Leni Riefenstahl: The Seduction of Genius* (London: Continuum, 2002)
Sangster, Andrew, *The Unfolding Agony of Oppression* (Ethics International Press, 2023)
Shirer, William L., *The Rise and Fall of the Third Reich* (London: Mandarin, 1960)
Stargardt, Nicholas, *The German War: A Nation Under Arms, 1939–45* (London: Vintage, 2015)
——, *Witnesses of War: Children's Lives Under the Nazis* (London: Jonathan Cape, 2005)
Toland, John, *Hitler* (London: Wordsworth Editions, 1997)
——, *The Last 100 Days* (New York: The Modern Library, 1996)
Trevor-Roper, H.R. (Ed.), *Hitler's Table Talk* (London: Weidenfeld and Nicolson, 1953)
Tusa, Ann and Tusa, John, *The Nuremberg Trial* (London: BBC Books, 1995)
Weinberg, Gerhard L., *A World at Arms: A Global History of World War II* (Cambridge: CUP, 1994)
Welch, David (Ed.), *Nazi Propaganda: The Power and the Limitations* (London: Routledge, 2015)

Index